ECONOMICS
FOR
CANADIAN
TRADE UNIONISTS
(Second Edition)

SIDNEY H. INGERMAN

D0830171

LABOUR COLLEGE OF CANADA
Ottawa

ISBN 0-9690345-1-2

Legal deposit first quarter 1985
Bibliothèque nationale du Québec

Cover design by Janet Jorgensen
Public Service Alliance of Canada

Edited by Heather Lang-Runtz

Printed in Canada by Mutual Press Limited

Published by the Labour College of Canada
545 King Edward Avenue
Ottawa, Ontario K1N 7N5

This book was published with financial assistance from Labour Canada.

Dedicated

to the graduates and staff

of the

Labour College of Canada

TABLE OF CONTENTS

vii

Preface To The Second Edition

The first edition of *Economics For Canadian Trade Unionists* was published in 1980. It has been used as a textbook by the Labour College of Canada for both the eight-week residential program and the correspondence course and by labour educators throughout the country. The book has been read widely by union members, elected leaders, and union staff members who have been concerned with economic questions.

The positive response and continuing demand for the first edition confirmed the need for a revised book on economics written especially for the labour movement.

The basic structure of the first edition has been maintained, but the content in this revised edition reflects the many comments, suggestions, and criticisms that have come from students, teachers, and trade unionists who have used the book. The revision also has taken into account the dramatic changes that have occurred in the Canadian economy since the research and writing of the first edition was completed in 1980.

Wherever possible, statistical data has been updated and new data, previously not available, has been added to the text. It also has been possible to cite new research in both the text and the footnotes.

Changes in economic policies since 1980 and possible future changes are discussed in a number of chapters. Chapter 2 includes new information on immigration and current immigration policy. Chapter 7 contains additional discussion of corporate tax and subsidy policies. Chapter 8 provides a fuller discussion of government deficits and the argument that the debt associated with these deficits is "crowding-out" private investment. Chapter 10 includes a detailed discussion of the economic theory underlying the 1982-1983 federal government's "6 & 5" incomes policy, as well as an appraisal of Reaganomics as practised in the United States. Chapter 11 gives additional coverage to the debate between those who advocate free trade and those who advocate protectionism in international trading arrangements. Chapter 12, in its discussion of short- and long-run solutions to Canada's economic problems, includes a discussion of the demands for shorter working time being made by the Canadian Labour Congress and by many labour organizations in Western Europe.

I am confident that the changes in the second edition of *Economics For Canadian Trade Unionists* will ensure that the book will continue to serve the labour movement in the collective bargaining and political arenas.

Acknowledgements

Comments and criticisms from students attending the residential programs of the Labour College of Canada from 1980 to 1983 who worked with the first edition have been invaluable in preparing the second edition. The Labour College Class of '84 patiently worked with draft copies of the second edition and helped to "de-bug" it. Steven Langdon, Ronald Meng, and Daniel Hara, who have taught Economics at the Labour College, provided valuable comments that have influenced the process of revision. Louis Ascah, a member of the Economics Department at the University of Sherbrooke, made detailed analytic comments on various sections of the first edition and made useful suggestions for improvements that were taken into account in the second edition. Pierre Chapleau updated statistical data and suggested many improvements in the presentation of the data.

I am grateful to the students and my colleagues for their generous assistance. However, it should be understood clearly that the author bears full responsibility for both the "point of view" and any errors contained in this second edition.

As was the case in publishing the first edition of *Economics For Canadian Trade Unionists*, Jean Bezusky, Associate Registrar of the Labour College of Canada, has been the driving force behind the second edition.

Heather Lang-Runtz edited the manuscript. The office staff of the Labour College, especially Inge Woltemade who typed the manuscript, conscientiously performed the many tasks associated with publishing this edition. To all of them, I extend my appreciation and thanks.

Sidney H. Ingerman
February 1985

Preface To The First Edition

The Labour College of Canada annually holds an eight-week residential program providing highly motivated, experienced trade unionists with the opportunity to study five academic subjects, one of which is economics.

Trade unionists are a very special kind of clientele. Standard economic textbooks that would meet their needs could not be found. *Economics For Canadian Trade Unionists* has been written to fill the vacuum.

The book has five parts. Labour educators and others who use this book will find that each part can be used independently. However, Parts Three, Four, and Five require that students have some previous knowledge of economics.

Part One, **ECONOMICS AND POLITICS**, is concerned with the formulation of national economic goals for Canada. It maintains that different views of appropriate economic goals and the means to achieve them are in large measure related to the political and ideological views of the economists and policy makers who formulate the goals. The discussion of national economic goals is used to begin the development of a vocabulary of economic terms.

Part Two, **FULL EMPLOYMENT AND ECONOMIC GROWTH**, examines the goal of full employment and how it is related to the rate of growth of output (production) in the total economy. Chapter 2 presents a definition of full employment, which is used again in Chapters 3 to 5 to study labour force growth, concepts, and statistics, as well as alternative views of full employment. Chapters 6, 7, and 8 look at measures of total output and the growth of total output. Theories of the determination of total output and the economic policies that governments use to influence output and employment also are discussed.

In Part Three, **INCOME DISTRIBUTION AND INFLATION**, the division of output among groups or classes is examined. Particular attention is given to the effects of income distribution on output and the relationship between income distribution and inflation. Chapter 9, Income Distribution and Corporate Power, begins with a discussion of the concepts of the **functional** and **size** distribution of income and the statistics associated with these concepts, followed by an examination of the relationship between wealth and income. Finally, this chapter presents a brief historical view of theories of income distribution with special attention being given to the relevance of industrial organization and corporate power to a modern theory of income distribution. Chapter 10, Inflation, explores the impact of inflation and the relationship between inflation and employment. A number of measures of inflation are presented with emphasis being placed on the importance of the Consumer Price Index (CPI). This chapter also reviews standard explanations for inflation and presents a theory that links inflation to economic changes and disturbances that affect income distribution. Also, a number of the remedies advocated to reduce inflation are analyzed.

Part Four, **FOREIGN TRADE**, explains the importance of foreign trade to Canadian employment and output. The method of recording foreign trade transactions in the national income accounts, exchange rates of national currencies in international trade, and the relationship between changes in the balance of payments and government economic policy also are explained.

Part Five, **THE WAY AHEAD**, analyzes alternative solutions to Canada's economic problems. It maintains that policies that mainly rely on the private sector to provide full employment are doomed to failure. The main thesis of this chapter is that full employment and a more equitable distribution of income are possible in Canada through national economic planning and democratic socialism. The book concludes with the observation that the achievement of the solution is as much a problem of practical politics as it is a problem requiring economic expertise.

The preparation and publication of this book would not have been possible without the assistance and encouragement of many individuals through the years. Joe Morris, President Emeritus of the Canadian Labour Congress, and Bert Hepworth, former Registrar of the Labour College of Canada, initially agreed to publish this book. Larry Wagg, the present Registrar, carried the project through to fulfillment. They have steadfastly supported the idea that the Labour College of Canada should enter into the field of publishing labour-oriented academic books. Jean Bezusky, Associate Registrar of the Labour College, has been the driving force, providing the author with encouragement, reading and improving endless drafts, and finally arranging for the physical production of the text. She has made this book possible.

A number of persons read the manuscript and offered valuable comments. Many of these comments have been incorporated into the text. The author is especially grateful to Ronald Lang, Steven Langdon, Michel Lizée, Ruth Rose-Lizée, Marie Mullally, Alex Vicas, and Allen Zeesman for their assistance. In addition, over the years, students attending the Labour College have contributed ideas and observations from their vast store of practical knowledge. It should be made clear, however, that the author bears full responsibility for both the "point-of-view" and any errors that the book contains.

Perry Shearwood edited the book. The office staff of the Labour College — Brenda Cosentino, Lise Francoeur, and Lynn Sauvé — conscientiously typed, proofread, and did many other related tasks. My thanks to them.

I also wish to record my appreciation to the United Steelworkers of America for their generous donation to the Labour College to help defray the printing costs.

Effectiveness in collective bargaining and in the political arena requires that general economic education is made available to the leadership and the membership of unions. *Economics For Canadian Trade Unionists* is intended as a contribution to this task.

Sidney H. Ingerman

PART ONE

ECONOMICS AND POLITICS

CHAPTER 1

ECONOMIC GOALS FOR CANADA

To evaluate and influence the performance of the Canadian economy, it is necessary to have some idea about what we want our lives to be like. Once we are clear about our goals, we have to decide if current economic policies are helping us to achieve them.If they are not, then we have to determine whether a revision of these policies or the development of new policies will be more successful in attaining these goals. Therefore, the first question to be considered is: what are our goals? The nature of national goals seldom is obvious. Individuals and groups with different interests living in different parts of the country have different ideas about what is good for them and what is good for the country. It is here that politics enter into the consideration of economic objectives.

Political parties present programs at the local, provincial, and federal levels that are designed to satisfy the needs and aspirations of a sufficiently large portion of the population to allow them to govern. Thus, the policies of elected governments are considered to be a reflection of the population's will as expressed through the political process.

The political process reflects the nation's history, legal structures, power relations among various groups, and the continual contest between new and old ideas. These factors interact in complex ways to produce economic goals that are defined often vaguely and economic programs at the local, provincial, and federal levels that may be related imperfectly to these goals.

SIX IMPORTANT GOALS

Economists during the last three decades have discussed Canadian economic policy in terms of six important national economic goals. These are:

1. full **employment;**

> **Employment** refers to the number of persons who receive pay or other material compensation for work performed.[1]

2. adequate **economic growth;**

> **Economic growth** is the rate at which the output of all goods and services produced in the economy is increasing. It is measured by observing changes in Gross National Product (GNP) or Real Domestic Product (RDP).

3. reasonable **price stability;**

> **Price stability** describes a situation in which the level of prices of goods and services sold in the economy is changing slowly and predictably. Statistics Canada produces a number of measures or indexes of prices, of which the most well known and frequently used is the Consumer Price Index (CPI).

4. a viable **balance of payments position;**

> The relationship between a country's expenditures and receipts in international transactions is reflected in its **balance of payments position**. Should the value of these expenditures and receipts differ markedly and persistently, patterns of international trade will be altered. One common effect of such an imbalance is a change in the value of the country's currency relative to that of other countries with which it trades.

5. equitable **distribution of income;**

> **Distribution of income** refers to the manner in which the value of the production of the economy is divided among individuals and groups.

---

[1] "Work includes any work for pay or profit, that is, paid work in the context of an employer-employee relationship, or self-employment. It also includes unpaid family work where unpaid family work is defined as unpaid work which contributed directly to the operation of a farm, business, or professional practice owned or operated by a related member of the household." Statistics Canada, "Notes-Scope of Labour Force Survey," in any current issue of *The Labour Force* (Catalogue No. 71-001, monthly).

6. and, balanced **regional development.**

> **Regional development** involves the standard of living and economic
> growth of particular parts of the country.

THE NATURE OF THE GOALS AND THE APPROPRIATE MEANS TO ACHIEVE THEM

These six goals will seldom excite controversy, but judgements about their nature and the appropriate means of achieving them underlie most debates about economic policy.

Differences in judgement about the nature of these goals often reflect the fact that different segments of Canadian society are concerned to a greater or lesser degree with different goals at different times. Economists and government policy makers who are involved in these debates tend to reflect the interests of particular groups or a specific economic and political ideology. Differences in outlook revolve around what is meant by "full" in full **employment**, "adequate" in adequate **economic growth**, "reasonable" in reasonable **price stability**, etc. For example, a Canadian Labour Congress economist would define the goal of full employment as a situation in which national employment is high enough to maintain the annual average unemployment between 2.5 and 3 per cent of the labour force. Such a situation would provide steady employment for most working people and would assist workers in improving their standard of living through collective bargaining and by other means.

However, in 1978, with the average annual unemployment in Canada rising to over 8 per cent of the labour force, the governing federal Liberal party was maintaining that the situation was not that bad. The Liberals argued that the economy was not that far from full employment, which they said was consistent with a 4 or 5 per cent national unemployment rate.

At about the same time, an important American economist writing in *The Wall Street Journal* urged his readers to accept the idea that a 7 per cent unemployment rate was consistent with full employment. Among other things, he argued that a "heightened sense of national obligation to provide jobs — or, at least, a paycheck — had as its corollary a lowered sense of private responsibility to work," which contributed to a 7 per cent irreducible rate of unemployment.[2]

By 1983, economists in the Policy Formulation Branch of the Canadian Ministry of State for Economic Development were describing unemployment of 10 per cent or less as "reasonable" levels.[3]

---

[2] Herbert Stein, "Full Employment at Last?" *The Wall Street Journal*, 14 September 1977, p. 22.
[3] Canada, Ministry of State for Economic Development, Policy Formulation Branch, *The Rocky Road to 1990*, A Staff Paper on Economic Development Priorities, 26 January 1983, p. 6.

Thus, differences in values, ideology, and vested interests are expressed at the policy level by differences in the meaning given to the adjectives "full," "adequate," "reasonable," "viable," "equitable," and "balanced" that modify each concept in the traditionally accepted list of economic goals.

While particular interest groups stress the importance of one or another of these economic goals, economists recognize that attempts to achieve any one goal or combination of goals must affect the achievement of other goals. It is not possible to achieve and maintain full employment without influencing economic growth or price stability, for example. It is here that economic theory enters the picture.

To determine the **appropriate means** to achieve certain goals, it is necessary to understand how the economy works so proper policies are chosen that will lead to the achievement of desired goals. A **theory** is an attempt to describe simply the relations existing between the various economic forces at work in an economy.

However, theories in economics are not independent of politics and ideology. During the period of the Great Depression (1929-1939) most economists accepted a theory about how the economy functions that led them to advocate a policy of wage reduction as a cure for unemployment and the depression. The economic theorists of **laissez-faire** capitalism argued that if only free markets existed (and in particular labour markets without unions) wages would fall more than prices and full employment would be restored. This argument struck a sympathetic chord among the rich and powerful, who hated unions and did not understand that, while lower wages in one enterprise might increase profits or reduce losses in that enterprise, a general decrease in money wages in all enterprises would result in a lower demand for goods and services and therefore would lower total employment and profits.

This theory, which was discredited after the publication of John Maynard Keynes's *The General Theory of Employment Interest and Money* in 1936, reappears in the late 1970's and early 1980's along with a resurgence of political ultra-conservatism. In its June 1982 budget, the federal Liberal government used this theory to justify its policy of limiting income increases to 6 and 5 per cent during the following two years.[4]

Another example of the use of a theory in a partisan and political way is the contention that a trade-off exists between unemployment and inflation (rising prices). In other words, increased unemployment reduces inflation and reduced unemployment increases inflation. Using this theory as support, governments in a number of countries, including Canada, have justified their unwillingness to institute policies to lower unemployment because they claim this would increase inflation. Examination of unemployment and inflation figures in the 1970's and early 1980's shows that, on average, **both** were increasing. These observations

---

[4] For a detailed discussion of this justification see, Sidney Ingerman, *6 & 5, The Bankruptcy of Liberal Economic Policy* (Ottawa: Canadian Centre for Policy Alternatives, 1983), pp. 7-13.

have tended to discredit the theory or at least to force its advocates to recognize that factors other than unemployment are needed to explain inflation.

Therefore, meaningful discussions about the **nature** of our economic goals are almost always contentious, and decisions about the **appropriate means** to achieve these goals can be influenced by theories that have significant ideological and political biases embedded in them.

NEW CONCERNS AND OTHER ECONOMIC GOALS

Canadians also have become more concerned with the effect of uncontrolled economic activity on the environment and with the consequences of the growth of ownership of Canadian industry by United States-based firms.

Concern for the environment derives from a growing recognition that, as the economy produces more goods and services and with more highly processed and synthetic materials, great amounts of waste products in the form of air, water, and noise pollution are thrust upon the population. Enterprises that produce pollution in the course of making profits impose costs on others that often do not affect their profits. Air and noise contamination in the workplace affect workers' health. Acid rain destroys lakes, forests, and agricultural land not only in the industrialized regions where sulfur dioxide is emitted into the atmosphere but also across large land masses and even oceans as wind currents carry it all over the world. The dumping of waste materials into waterways and unregulated land-fill sites has become a matter of deep concern because of its effects on human health, and the contraction of publicly available swimming and fishing locations near to urban areas is a common observation of ordinary Canadians.

Pollution particularly affects those who are not rich and who therefore do not have the means to escape it or to substitute private goods and services for the polluted "gifts of nature."

Environmentalists and other concerned citizens insist that one of Canada's economic goals should be the maintenance of proper control levels over the production and disposal of waste products. Here, once again, economic and political judgements come into play. To what degree are political authorities willing to limit certain kinds of production that pollute the environment if, in the short run at least, profits, employment, and output will be affected?

Foreign and especially American control of Canadian resource and manufacturing industries is considered now by many Canadians to be a barrier to the proper development of the Canadian economy. Those who hold this view advocate the goal of returning ownership of these industries to Canadians. If one accepts this goal, the issues then are, what are the appropriate means for achieving it, and what will be the short- and long-run consequences of such a policy? The Foreign Investment Review Agency (FIRA) was set up under federal legislation in 1974. This act declares that:

8

... control of Canadian business enterprises may be acquired by persons other than Canadians, and new business enterprises may be established by persons other than Canadians, . . . , only if it has been assessed that the acquisition of control of those enterprises or the establishment of those new businesses . . . is or is likely to be of significant benefit to Canada.[5]

The operation of FIRA has been a source of continued debate. The American business magazine *Barron's* summed up its view of this agency's effectiveness: "It is difficult to imagine a legitimate business venture which would be impeded by the Foreign Investment Review Agency. The only U.S. business which wouldn't be cordially invited is Murder Incorporated."[6]

However, in 1982, a major Canadian mining executive George R. Albino, Chairman of Rio Algom Limited, declared that, as a result of FIRA's activities, "Canada is perceived internationally as attempting to devalue and displace foreign investments" and that this has upset our allies and trading partners.[7] The pre-September 1984 Progressive Conservative federal opposition in Parliament frequently criticized FIRA, claiming it discouraged needed foreign investment in Canada. One of the first legislative proposals of the Progressive Conservative federal government, elected with an overwhelming majority in September 1984, was the Investment Canada Act, which would replace FIRA and reduce barriers to foreign investment in Canada.

THE POLITICS OF ECONOMISTS

Many Canadian economists believe that, even though achievement of some of the goals works against the achievement of others, a politically acceptable mix is possible within the framework of existing political and economic arrangements. (By existing economic arrangements, we mean the current predominantly private control over Canadian industry.)

A large number of these economists would agree that concerns over pollution and the environment should and can be dealt with through lobbying and other accepted political pressure tactics. Few of these economists would be at ease with the idea of government intervention to end foreign control of Canadian industry. This group can be classified as small "l" liberals because they advocate the 19th century liberal philosophy of minimizing state intervention in the affairs of individuals.

Some — not many — Canadian economists believe that the six traditional goals can be achieved only if there are substantial changes in economic arrange-

5
---
[5] *Foreign Investment Review Act*, S.C. 1973-74, c. 46, s. 2 (1).
[6] *Barron's*, cited in *Weekend Magazine*, Montreal, 12 March 1977, p. 19.
[7] "Fira's opponents have lots of company," *The Financial Post*, 6 March 1982, p. S13.

ments within the existing political system. They tend to be concerned about the environment and to favour the return of control of Canadian industry to Canadians. They also advocate government intervention in production and distribution when the private sector cannot satisfy the social and cultural needs of Canadians and when private-sector investment is inadequate. A sophisticated spokesperson for this group would insist that such intervention can and must be done efficiently. This group of economists can be classified as social democrats because they favour socialism, which is to be achieved by stages through the existing electoral process.

A few Canadian economists believe that the contradictions between all the goals discussed are insurmountable in modern capitalist economies. They cite the simultaneous existence of unacceptable levels of unemployment, threats of renewed inflation, the instability of the world banking system and international money markets, and the deterioration of the environment as evidence that both the economic **and** the political systems cannot satisfy acceptable standards of performance and therefore need to be replaced by a socialist system. This group of economists can be classified as radicals. They view the state as an instrument of private capital and therefore believe that socialism can be achieved only by the replacement of an essentially repressive state apparatus.

THE AUTHOR'S VIEWS

If it is true that the goals advocated by economists and the policies they recommend to achieve those goals are affected by ideological and political considerations, readers have a right to know the author's views on what are the proper economic goals and how they can be achieved.

The **central** goal of Canadian economic policy in the 1980's must be **full employment**. The achievement of this goal in the present historical context requires the progressive elimination of major inequalities of income between individuals, groups, and regions of the country. The necessary and appropriate means for achieving this goal given the Canadian context during the last two decades of the twentieth century is efficient and democratically determined national economic planning. Economic growth, price stability, balance of international payments, regional development, environmental control, and repatriation of the ownership of Canadian industry present technical and political problems for governments, which can be dealt with in the context of achieving the central goal of full employment.

Full employment accompanied by a progressive elimination of income inequality is not part of the programs of either the Liberal or Conservative parties. The economic programs of these parties, rationalized by inappropriate theories, cannot meet satisfactorily Canada's current or future needs. In order to make this argument, these theories and policies must be examined and understood seriously. Trade unionists are faced with the same theories and policies in the political arena and in collective bargaining.

Most likely, the New Democratic Party and other political parties on the left would accept full employment as the central immediate goal of economic policy. Debate, however, would arise about appropriate means to achieve this goal. Careful consideration of the kind of theory that properly explains how the economy functions and how its performance can be influenced in the future is required.

PART TWO

EMPLOYMENT AND ECONOMIC GROWTH

CHAPTER 2

FULL EMPLOYMENT

A chievement of the full employment goal should mean that persons who want to work can find appropriate jobs during their normal life cycle.

Young people should be able to gain work experience, some financial independence, and a feeling of self-worth while they are completing their education and preparing for adult employment.

Men and women of prime working age should be assured secure patterns of employment in safe and satisfying jobs. This assurance of employment must be available to those who interrupt their employment to raise a family as well as to those who are affected by technological change and the shutdown of enterprises.

People who are approaching the end of their full-time working careers should be able to adjust their hours of work so that they can have more leisure time prior to retirement when they so desire. Productive labour should be available to the elderly.

These basic considerations underlie the full employment goal. A definition of full employment that can guide economic policy as well as provide general standards to judge the effectiveness of these policies follows.

A DEFINITION OF FULL EMPLOYMENT

Full employment as other economic goals is interpreted differently by economists sympathetic to one or another ideology or political point of view. However, the following is a reasonable definition of full employment:

Full employment exists when everyone who wants to work can find a job within a reasonable period of time, without involuntary disloca- tion, at the established wage rate for that person's skills.

To better understand the definition, it can be divided into five elements:

1. Everyone
2. who wants to work
3. can find a job within a reasonable period of time
4. without involuntary dislocation
5. at the established wage rate for that person's skills.

An examination of each of these elements also will allow us to become familiar with labour force statistics, and many of the economic concepts related to these statistics.

THE POTENTIAL LABOUR FORCE

In Canada, labour force statistics are gathered by Statistics Canada in the Labour Force Survey. This survey was started in 1945 and was conducted on a quarterly basis until 1952; since then it has been carried out monthly. The survey gathers data on employment, unemployment, and non-labour force activity of Canadians who are considered able to work.

Beginning in January 1976, substantial changes were made in the Labour Force Survey so that users of the survey statistics must be cautious in comparing pre-1976 data with data from surveys taken since January 1976.

In 1983, about 56,000 households were visited by interviewers each month.[8] The interviewers complete a questionnaire for each member of the household 15 years of age and over. The results of these surveys are published monthly and describe the labour force activity of everyone in the population 15 years of age and over except for certain excluded groups.[9] The persons included in the popu- lation that is surveyed are called the **potential labour force**.[10]

Residents of the Yukon and the Northwest Territories, native people living on reserves, inmates of institutions, and full-time members of the armed forces are excluded from the monthly household Labour Force Survey and do not appear in Canadian labour force, employment, or unemployment statistics. Persons in the excluded categories constitute approximately 2 per cent of the Canadian population 15 years of age and over. The exclusion of the Yukon, the Northwest Territories, and Indian reserves is based on:

---

[8] A selected household remains in the sample for six consecutive months. Rotation of the sample is arranged so that one-sixth of the households are new to the sample each month.
[9] This monthly publication is: Statistics Canada, *The Labour Force* (Catalogue No. 71-001).
[10] In some texts, this group is called "the working-age population," in others, "the population age 15 and over."

. . . both operational and statistical considerations, namely the difficulties involved in carrying out monthly surveys in such areas and
the general inapplicability of the survey concepts and definitions to
the measurement of labour market conditions in northern and isolated
reserve communities.[11]

When population and economic activity grow in importance in the Yukon and
the Northwest Territories, they undoubtedly will be included in the sample
survey.

Questions have been raised about the exclusion of native people on reserves
from the survey. Although they constitute a small proportion of the total Canadian population, they are an important part of the population of certain regions.[12]

The appropriate minimum age for including persons in the household survey
and therefore in the **potential labour force** also has been discussed. In 1976,
Statistics Canada raised the minimum from 14 to 15 years of age. In the United
States, the minimum is currently 16 years of age. The main reason for raising the
minimum age is the shift in population out of rural and agricultural regions into
urban areas. In urban areas most employers are legally prohibited from employing persons who are under 16 years of age.

To summarize, "everyone" is the **potential labour force**, which is defined as
all persons 15 years of age and over except in categories excluded from the
Statistics Canada monthly household Labour Force Survey.

Underlying changes in the **potential labour force** are changes in the size and
age composition of the total population. Under normal conditions population
changes are the result of **natural population growth** and **net migration**.[13] Between 1911 and 1983 the Canadian population increased by 17,641,000 from
7,206,600 to 24,847,600.[14]

NATURAL POPULATION GROWTH

Annual birth and death rates determine the natural rate of increase of population. The birth rate is the number of births per 1,000 population each year; the
death rate is the number of deaths per 1,000 population each year.

---

[11] Ian Macredi and Bruce Petrie of the Labour Force Survey Division of Statistics Canada, "The
Canadian Labour Force Survey," a paper presented at the 10th Annual Meeting of the Canadian
Economics Association, 1 June 1976, p. 1.

[12] In December 1979 there were 574 Indian bands in Canada whose registered band membership was
309,590. Of these, 195,363 Indians lived on reserves, 22,909 lived on Crown land, and 91,318 lived
off reserves and Crown land. Indian and Northern Affairs Canada, *Registered Indian population by
sex and residence 1979*, p. xvii.

[13] Abnormal conditions would include natural or man-made disasters such as wide-spread fatalities
from an epidemic or a war.

[14] Employment and Immigration Canada, *Background Paper on Future Immigration Levels: A Companion
Report to the Annual Report to Parliament on Future Immigration Levels* (Ottawa: Supply and Services
Canada), 1 November 1983, p. 53 (Catalogue No. MP22-7/1983).

The natural rate of increase of population is computed by dividing the excess of births over deaths each year by the total population and then by multiplying by 1,000. Statistics for population, births, and deaths are used in the following example to calculate the birth rate, death rate, and the natural rate of increase of population in Canada in 1982.[15]

$$
\begin{array}{lll}
\text{Population} & — & 24{,}603{,}000 \\
\text{Births} & — & 371{,}505 \\
\text{Deaths} & — & 172{,}221
\end{array}
$$

Birth rate $= \dfrac{\text{Births}}{\text{Population}} \times 1{,}000 = \dfrac{371{,}505}{24{,}603{,}000} \times 1{,}000 = 15.1$ births per thousand of population

Death rate $= \dfrac{\text{Deaths}}{\text{Population}} \times 1{,}000 = \dfrac{172{,}221}{24{,}603{,}000} \times 1{,}000 = 7.0$ deaths per thousand of population

Natural Rate of Increase of Population $= \dfrac{\text{Births - Deaths}}{\text{Population}} \times 1{,}000 = \dfrac{371{,}505 - 172{,}221}{24{,}603{,}000} \times 1{,}000 = 8.1$ population increase per thousand population

Birth rates, death rates, and the natural rate of increase of the Canadian population at five-year intervals from 1950 to 1980 are presented in *Table 1-2*.

TABLE 1-2

Birth Rates, Death Rates, and the Natural Rate of Increase of Population in Canada at Five-Year Intervals, 1950 to 1980

	Birth Rates	Death Rates	Natural Rate of Increase
1950	27.1	9.1	18.0
1955	28.2	8.2	20.0
1960	27.0	7.9	19.1
1965	21.5	7.6	13.9
1970	17.6	7.4	10.2
1975	15.9	7.4	8.5
1980	15.4	7.1	8.3

Source: Canada, Department of Finance, *Economic Review April 1983*, Reference Table 1, p. 119 (Catalogue No. F1-21/1983E).

---

[15] The source of this data is Canada, Department of Finance, *Economic Review April 1983*, Reference Table 1, p. 119 (Catalogue No. F1-21/1983E).

The dramatic fall in birth rates since the Second World War "baby boom" has been accompanied by a moderate fall in death rates. Consequently, since 1955 the natural rate of increase in the population has fallen markedly. But this data does not give a complete picture of what is happening to expected **trends** in natural population growth. By 1972, Canadian women were not giving birth to babies at a sufficient long-term rate to replace themselves, their spouses, and the few female children who die before adulthood.[16] The reason that birth rates have not fallen faster than is shown in *Table 1-2* is that there were a large number of young couples, the children of the 1945-1955 "baby boom," who were having children in the 1970's. When this group completes its child-bearing period, natural population growth will become zero or even negative if present attitudes favouring smaller families continue and as death rates rise with an increasing proportion of elderly people in the total population.

NET MIGRATION

Between 1975 and 1982 the Canadian population increased by 1,854,000 persons. Of this increase 1,374,100 or 74.1 per cent resulted from natural population increases and 479,900 or 25.9 per cent resulted from net migration, that is, by the difference between **immigration** and **emigration**.[17] If natural increases in population in the 1980's are small or possibly negative as a consequence of expected low birth rates, increases in the size of the population and therefore of the potential labour force will be governed by net migration to Canada.

Immigration is determined by the number of persons who want permanent residence in a country and the number of persons whom the government of the country allows such status. The number and characteristics of applicants for admission to Canada is governed in large part by economic and political conditions in Canada, as well as by those same conditions in other countries.

The Canadian government controls the inflow of immigrants under regulations provided by various laws and also by the way the regulations are administered in Canada and at Canadian immigration offices throughout the world.[18]

---

[16] This is measured by the **gross reproduction rate** (some writers use the term **total fertility rate**). An explanation of the method used in computing this rate can be found in "Vital Statistics Terms and Definitions," in Statistics Canada, *Vital Statistics* (Catalogue No. 84-204-6). "For almost fifty years fertility fluctuated between 2.6 and 3.9, but since 1960, it has declined to the present rate of 1.7 — well below the replacement level of 2.1." The **replacement fertility rate** is the number of children per 1,000 women aged 15-49 who must be born to ensure that the parents are merely replaced. Assuming no increase or decrease from net migration, a replacement fertility rate means that, if maintained, a non-growing (stable) population would result. See, Employment and Immigration Canada, *Background Paper on Future Immigration Levels: A Companion Report to the Annual Report to Parliament on Future Immigration Levels, op. cit.,* pp. 53 and 67.

[17] Employment and Immigration Canada, *Annual Report to Parliament on Future Immigration Levels*, 1 November 1983, p. 29 (Catalogue No. MP22-8/1983).

[18] Section 95 of the British North America Act, which is now part of the Canadian constitution, gives the federal government supreme authority over immigration. Quebec has been delegated some authority to deal with immigration to that province.

Prior to 1962, immigration legislation and the administration of the legislation encouraged immigration from Great Britain, northern Europe, and the United States and discouraged Asian, African, and other Third World immigrants.

In 1885, Chinese immigration was discouraged by a head tax of $50, which was raised to $100 in 1900 and to $500 in 1903. In 1907-1908, legislation was amended so that immigrants were required to make a "direct continuous journey from their native land to Canada." This amendment effectively barred immigration from India. The recession following the First World War, coupled with labour unrest (for example, the Winnipeg General Strike), provoked immigration prohibitions in 1918 and 1919 against Doukhobors, Mennonites, Hutterites, illiterates, alcoholics, and conspirators.[19]

In 1962, immigration practices that discriminated by national origin were outlawed and skill and employment eligibility became the main criteria for independent (not sponsored by relatives) immigration. The only remaining concession allowed to previously favoured groups was the ability to sponsor a wide range of relatives who wanted to come to Canada.[20]

Total immigration to Canada between 1946 and 1970 and a ranking of the most important countries providing immigrants are shown in *Table 2-2*.

TABLE 2-2

Immigration to Canada from the Eight Most Important Countries of Origin and from All Countries for the Period 1946-1970

Country	Immigrants	Percentage of Total
Britain	923,930	27.1
Italy	448,104	12.8
United States	311,911	9.1
West Germany	308,297	9.0
Netherlands	172,942	5.1
Poland	100,000 +	2.9 +
Greece	100,000 +	2.9 +
France	100,000 +	2.9 +
All countries	3,414,857	100.0

Source: Canada, Department of Manpower and Immigration, *Immigration Statistics 1970*, p. 21.

---

[19] For further reading on the background of these events see, Ted Ferguson, *A White Man's Country: An Exercise in Canadian Prejudice* (Toronto: Doubleday, 1975) and Donald Avery, *"Dangerous Foreigners": European Immigrant Workers and Labour Radicalism in Canada 1896-1932* (Toronto: McClelland and Stewart, 1979).

[20] Histories of Canadian immigration policy can be found in Lawrence M. Officer, "Immigration and Emigration," *Canadian Economic Problems and Policies*, L.H. Officer and L.B. Smith, eds. (Toronto: McGraw-Hill, 1970), pp. 142-156, and William L. Marr, *Labour Market and Other Implications of Immigration Policy for Ontario* (Toronto: Ontario Economic Council, November 1976), pp. 1-19.

While legislation in 1962 prohibited discrimination in immigration regulations, it was not until 1966 that the government took positive steps to end discriminatory preferences. This was done in a *White Paper on Immigration,* which stressed the positive aspects of immigration,[21] proposed regulations to end racial discrimination, and suggested a fairer and more efficient processing procedure. The ensuing legislation, enacted in 1967, introduced many new regulations, the most important of which was a point system that is not related to the immigrants' country of origin. Points are based on age, employment prospects, education, relatives in Canada, fluency in French and English, and certain other factors.[22] A prospective independent immigrant must get at least 50 out of a possible 100 points to qualify for immigration.

Under the influence of the 1967 regulations, the proportion of immigrants arriving from the Third World countries grew from 8 per cent in 1961 to 52 per cent in 1975.[23] In terms of age, sex, and family size, Third World immigrants are similar to other immigrants. However, they are, on the average, both more educated and skilled.[24] They are also more likely to settle in cities.

Persistent and growing unemployment, coupled with urban congestion as both rural and immigrant populations moved into large cities, complicated the already difficult task of adaptation for these new immigrant groups.[25] Instead of responding to this problem within the framework of a full employment policy and by promoting improved urban planning, the federal government set up a special joint committee of Parliament that conducted hearings throughout the country on immigration policy and recommended new legislation that was adopted by Parliament in the **Immigration Act, 1976**. Article 3(a) of this Act lists as one of its objectives:

---

[21] Jean Marchand, Minister of Manpower and Immigration, *White Paper on Immigration* (Ottawa: Queen's Printer, 1966). On page 8, the economic benefits of immigration are described as follows: "A bigger population means increased domestic markets for our industries. A larger home market permits manufacturing firms to undertake longer, lower-cost production runs, and it broadens the range of industry we can undertake economically; for both these reasons, population increase in turn improves our competitive position in world markets. A bigger population also yields lower per capita costs of government, transportation and communications, and stimulates the development of more specialized services. These are the very important economic reasons why immigration tends to increase the real income per person available to all Canadians."

[22] A detailed discussion of the operation of this system can be found in "Immigration and Citizenship," Statistics Canada, *Canada Year Book 1972*, Chapter IV, pp. 219-222.

[23] Economic Council of Canada, *For A Common Future: A Study of Canada's Relations With Developing Countries* (Ottawa: Supply and Services Canada, 1978), p. 115.

[24] The previously cited Economic Council of Canada study, *For A Common Future: A Study of Canada's Relations With Developing Countries,* maintains that, using the concept of replacement cost, Canada would have had to spend $2.9 billion between 1966 and 1974 to train its own human capital in the absence of immigration from Third World countries. See p. 117.

[25] One indication of the problems many immigrant groups have in adapting to the Canadian environment is their linguistic ability. "About half of the immigrants landed in 1982 had a knowledge of the English language, 6.4 per cent had an ability in French, 4 per cent were bilingual and the remaining 39.5 per cent had a linguistic ability in languages other than French or English." Employment and Immigration Canada, *Background Paper on Future Immigration Levels: A Companion Report to the Annual Report to Parliament on Future Immigration Levels, op. cit.,* p. 22.

. . . to support the attainment of such demographic goals as may be established by the government of Canada from time to time in respect of the size, rate of growth, structure and geographic distribution of the Canadian population.

Few observers would dispute the proposition that Canada cannot have totally unrestricted immigration and that from time to time it may be necessary to reduce the flow of immigrants. Those who are concerned about the **Immigration Act, 1976** object to the possibility that restrictions will be based on race, colour, creed, or national origin, rather than the characteristics of individual persons and their ability to contribute to the well-being of Canada.[26]

CURRENT IMMIGRATION

In 1981, 3.9 million persons or 16 per cent of the total Canadian population were immigrants.[27] The geographic origin of recent immigration is presented in *Table 3-2*. Asia and the Pacific, as well as Europe, were the largest sources of immigrants in 1980, 1981, and 1982.

TABLE 3-2
Immigration by World Area, 1980-1982

	1980		1981		1982	
	Landings	%	Landings	%	Landings	%
Africa and Middle East	9,534	6.7	10,254	8.0	9,859	8.1
Asia and Pacific	68,895	48.1	45,716	35.5	38,459	31.8
Americas (excluding the U.S.A.)	13,594	9.5	15,783	12.3	17,196	14.2
U.S.A.	9,926	6.9	10,559	8.2	9,360	7.7
Europe (excluding the U.K.)	22,932	16.0	25,145	19.6	29,711	24.5
United Kingdom	18,245	12.8	21,154	16.4	16,445	13.6
Not Stated	—	—	7	—	117	0.1
Total	143,117	100.0	128,618	100.0	121,147	100.0

Source: Employment and Immigration Canada, *Background Paper on Future Immigration Levels*, 1 November 1983, Table 1, p. 19 (Catalogue No. MP22-7/1983).

---

[26] Opponents of the Act have maintained that political discrimination is likely under Article 19, which provides among other things that "persons who there are reasonable grounds to believe are likely to engage in acts of violence that would or might endanger the lives or safety of persons in Canada or are members of or are associated with an organization that is likely to engage in such acts of violence," may be denied admission to Canada or, if they are not citizens, may be expelled from the country.

[27] Employment and Immigration Canada, *Background Paper on Future Immigration Levels: A Companion Report to the Annual Report to Parliament on Future Immigration Levels, op. cit.*, p. 56.

Current immigration policy considers three main reasons for allowing permanent residence in Canada: social, humanitarian, and economic. Social considerations affect the immigration of close family members of persons who are already in Canada. Humanitarian considerations allow for immigration of refugees as well as certain other groups that the federal government chooses to assist.[28] Economic considerations are applied to immigrants who have labour market skills that are scarce in Canada and to persons who have funds to invest in Canadian business. In 1982, there were 121,147 immigrants to Canada: 49,980 or 41 per cent were family-class immigrants; 16,925 or 14 per cent were refugees; and 54,242 or 45 per cent were independent immigrants.[29]

Government policy has attempted to direct immigrants to geographic areas where labour shortages exist. This has been done by allowing entry points to a potential immigrant who intends to go to an area where there are significant employment opportunities.

Since the Second World War immigrants have tended to go to urban areas in provinces where economic activity is expanding. French-speaking immigrants tend to settle initially in Quebec. A study of Employment and Immigration Canada declares:

> The tendency of immigrants to settle in metropolitan areas reflects a general postwar trend in North America toward urbanization, although there is some evidence that the rate has moderated in the past few years. The settlement decisions of immigrants selected for the labour market are usually governed by economic considerations, with prearranged or prospective employment being the chief determinant. Members of the family class often settle near their sponsoring relatives, while refugees and members of designated classes are not characteristically guided by one motivation but instead respond to such considerations as the availability of employment, language training, and other settlement services; the presence of sponsors (in the case of those who have been sponsored by relatives or non-governmental organizations); and the presence in the community of others who share some aspects of their linguistic or cultural heritage.[30]

In 1982, 74 per cent of all immigrants chose to settle in large metropolitan areas, with 23.3 per cent in Toronto, 13.5 per cent in Montreal, and 10.3 per cent in Vancouver.[31]

Conditions in Canada and abroad affect the extent of immigration in any period. Political and economic conditions often are reflected in legislative and administrative policies.

---

[28] For a more detailed discussion of these programs see, *ibid.*, pp. 35-39.
[29] *Ibid.*, p. 20.
[30] *Ibid.*, p. 22.
[31] *Ibid.*, p. 23.

22

On May 1, 1982, with national unemployment above 12 per cent, the Minister of Immigration restricted immigration of selected workers so that only workers with arranged employment were admitted.[32] In November 1983, with national unemployment still above 11 per cent, the Minister of Immigration announced that "although the economy is improving and the rate of unemployment is down, I am continuing the restriction on selected workers from abroad to protect jobs for Canadians." He added that "under this 'Canadians first' policy citizens and permanent residents have the first opportunity to fill the jobs."[33]

Data on immigrant landings in Canada from 1972 to 1982 are presented in *Table 4-2*.

TABLE 4-2

Immigrant Landings in Canada, 1972-1982

Year	Landings
1972	122,008
1973	184,200
1974	218,465
1975	187,881
1976	149,429
1977	114,914
1978	86,313
1979	112,098
1980	143,117
1981	128,618
1982	121,147

Source: Employment and Immigration Canada, *Background Paper on Future Immigration Levels*, 1 November 1983, Figure 1, p. 18 (Catalogue No. MP22-7/1983).

ILLEGAL MIGRATION

Illegal migration to North America has attained by all estimates significant proportions during the 1970's and 1980's. Estimates of the number of illegal migrants, at best, are educated guesses by observers close to the problem. These

---

[32] **Selected workers** are immigrants in the independent categories who are selected for their labour market skills when Canadians are unavailable or cannot readily be trained. Other immigrants are referred to as "non-selected workers" if they have indicated an intention to work in Canada. These other immigrants could be members of the family class, refugees, members of designated classes, entrepreneurs, self-employed persons, or the spouses and dependents of selected workers. *Ibid.*, p. 43.

[33] Canada, Minister of Employment and Immigration, press release, 1 November 1983.

educated guesses have produced estimates that between three and six million illegal migrants are in the United States and an upper limit of 50,000 such migrants are in Canada.[34]

EMIGRATION

Emigration tends to offset the effect of immigration on population. Indeed, during the period 1851-1945 while 6,740,000 persons immigrated to Canada, 6,239,000 emigrated.[35] Emigration was 93 per cent of immigration.

Statistics on the extent and country of destination of Canadian emigrants are not accurate.[36] However, all available evidence indicates that the United States has attracted a large proportion of Canadian emigrants. One important source of emigration was the mass migration of French-Canadians to the United States between 1830 and 1930. High unemployment and a shortage of arable land in rural Quebec coupled with expanding employment opportunities in New England factories, especially in the textile industry, promoted the emigration of an estimated 800,000 French-Canadians during this period.[37]

Up until 1921 unrestricted migration existed between the United States and Canada. An immigrant to North America could migrate just as easily across national borders as between provinces or states. In 1921, the United States instituted a system of national immigration quotas. These quotas prevented unrestricted immigration to the United States of Canadian **immigrants** while allowing Canadian-born persons continued free access to reside in the United States.

United States immigration policy changed again in 1965, resulting in an imposed quota of 120,000 on North and Latin American immigration to the United States. This quota was applied, beginning in 1968.

While the quota system undoubtedly has restricted Canadian emigration to the United States, another provision of the United States immigration law had a more direct and immediate impact. Under regulations that came into effect December 1, 1965, Canadians entering the United States with the intention of

---

[34] W.G. Robinson, *Illegal Migrants in Canada* (Ottawa: Supply and Services Canada, 1983), p. 26 (Catalogue No. MP23-64/1983E).

[35] Lawrence H. Officer, "Immigration and Emigration," *Canadian Economic Problems and Policies, op. cit.*, p. 149.

[36] Three data sources are used to estimate the number of people leaving Canada each year. First, quarterly reports containing data on the number of immigrants to the United States from Canada are provided by the U.S. immigration and naturalization service. Second, quarterly estimates of the number of persons entering the United Kingdom from Canada are taken from an international passenger survey based on a stratified sample of all passengers using the main sea and air routes between the United Kingdom and other countries. Third, an assumed level of the number of emigrants moving from Canada to countries other than the United States and the United Kingdom is added to the data described above.

[37] See, John Porter, *The Vertical Mosaic: An Analysis of Social Class and Power in Canada* (Toronto: University of Toronto Press, 1965), pp. 32 and 33.

working there must obtain certification from the U.S. Department of Labor that they will not displace American workers.[38] The number of persons entering the United States with the intention of establishing permanent residence there dropped sharply after the implementation of the 1965 United States certification provision. (See *Table 5-2.*)

The reduction in Canadian emigration to the United States after 1965 is not simply a result of the United States regulation. Undoubtedly, social and political instability in the United States coupled with a tendency for Canadian wage rates to rise relative to United States wage rates also have been contributory factors.[39]

TABLE 5-2

Canadian-Born Persons Entering the United States from Canada and Elsewhere, and All Persons Entering the United States from Canada, Years Ended June 30, 1961-1970 and 1975*

Year	Entering U.S. from Canada		Canadian-Born Entering U.S. from Elsewhere
	Canadian-Born	All Persons	
1961	31,312	47,470	726
1962	29,569	44,272	808
1963	35,320	50,509	683
1964	37,351	51,114	723
1965	37,519	50,035	808
1966	27,707	37,273	651
1967	22,729	34,768	713
1968	27,189	41,716	473
1969	18,196	29,303	386
1970	13,466	26,850	338
1975	7,308	11,215	—

*Includes only persons who have declared their intention of remaining permanently in the United States when applying for a visa.

Sources: Statistics Canada, *Canada Year Book 1972*, p. 232, and *Canada Year Book 1978-79*, p. 151.

---

[38] Persons entering Canada without landed immigrant status who wish to work in Canada must obtain similar certification.

[39] When adjusted for the exchange rate between United States and Canadian dollars, in 1965, Canadian workers in manufacturing received 75 per cent of the average hourly earnings of workers in manufacturing in the United States. By 1975, there was no difference in average hourly earnings in manufacturing between the two countries. Computed from U.S. Department of Labor, Bureau of Labor Statistics, *Monthly Labor Review*, February 1980, and Statistics Canada, *Employment, earnings and hours.*

One source of concern about emigration to the United States during the 1960's was that skilled and professional workers, born and educated in Canada, were being attracted to the United States, thereby hindering Canadian economic development. This problem, which came to be known as the "brain drain," seems to have become less serious in recent years.[40]

Between 1976 and 1982 total emigration from Canada to all destinations was 375,600 persons or an average of 53,657 per year.[41] Emigration estimates for each of these years are presented in *Table 6-2*.

TABLE 6-2

Emigration, Canada 1976-1982

Year	Emigrants
1976	64,400
1977	61,400
1978	63,500
1979	54,700
1980	45,200
1981	42,000
1982	44,400

Source: Employment and Immigration Canada, *Annual Report to Parliament on Future Immigration Levels*, 1 November 1983, p. 29 (Catalogue No. MP22-8/1983).

NET MIGRATION AND THE POTENTIAL LABOUR FORCE

Since the mid-1960's the natural rate of growth of the Canadian population has been decreasing as a result of birth rates falling more rapidly than death rates. Despite the dramatic fall in the natural rate of growth of the population, net migration (immigration-emigration) has caused total population and, consequently, the potential labour force to expand markedly. During the periods 1966-1971, 1971-1976, and 1976-1982 net migration accounted respectively for 29.8 per cent, 34.4 per cent, and 25 per cent of overall population growth.[42] Should current trends in birth and death rates continue, government policies affecting net migration will continue to play a decisive role in determining the size and characteristics of the potential labour force.

---

[40] In the year ended June 30, 1975, of the 7,308 Canadian-born persons entering the United States, 947 were in professional and technical occupations; 384 were clerical and kindred workers; and 229 were craftsmen and kindred workers. Statistics Canada, *Canada Year Book 1978-79*, p. 151.

[41] Employment and Immigration Canada, *Annual Report to Parliament on Future Immigration Levels*, 1 November 1983, p. 29 (Catalogue No. MP22-8/1983).

[42] *Ibid.*, and Statistics Canada, *Canada Year Book 1978-79*, Table 4.2, p. 154.

CHAPTER 3

EMPLOYMENT, UNEMPLOYMENT, AND THE LABOUR FORCE

I n our definition of full employment "everyone" was defined by the concept of the potential labour force. This chapter discusses what is meant by "everyone **who wants to work**." It is concerned also with unemployment, employment, and labour force participation rates.

THE LABOUR FORCE

The sum of the employed plus the unemployed is defined as **the labour force**. **The labour force** is "everyone who wants to work."

Members of the potential labour force who are neither employed nor unemployed are in a category called **not in the labour force**. The answer to the puzzle about how someone can be neither employed nor unemployed can be found in Statistics Canada's definition of these terms. An examination of these terms also will show how data on **employment, unemployment**, and **the labour force** are compiled in Statistics Canada's monthly household Labour Force Survey.

In the Labour Force Survey, the employed are those persons who during the reference week surveyed:

(a) did any work at all for profit or pay;
(b) had a job but were not at work due to:
— their own illness or disability
— personal or family responsibilities

— bad weather
— a labour dispute
— vacation
— certain other reasons (for example, jury duty).

A person who works one hour during the reference week is counted as employed. This practice makes employment and unemployment statistics insensitive to changes in hours worked as the economy expands and contracts.

In the Labour Force Survey, the unemployed are those persons who during the reference week surveyed:

(a) were without work, had actively looked for work in the past four weeks, and were available for work;
(b) had not actively looked for work in the past four weeks but had been on layoff for 26 weeks or less and were available for work;
(c) had not actively looked for work in the past four weeks but had a new job to start in four weeks or less and were available for work.

A person who is without work and is not actively seeking a job is not counted as unemployed, unless that person is in category (b) or (c). This person is considered to be **not in the labour force**.

The monthly household Labour Force Survey makes possible estimates of employment and unemployment, which are then added together to determine the size of the labour force. The labour force computation reveals how many members of the potential labour force **want to work** during each survey period.

The calculation of the number of persons in the labour force and not in the labour force in Canada in March 1983 is as follows:

The Labour Force = Employed + Unemployed = 10,236,000 + 1,658,000 = 11,894,000.

Not In The Labour Force = The Potential Labour Force − The Labour Force = 18,746,000 − 11,894,000 = 6,852,000.

THE UNEMPLOYMENT RATE

The percentage of persons who want to work and cannot find jobs is an indicator of how far the economy is from full employment. **Changes** in this percentage from one period to another indicate whether job opportunities are expanding or contracting in relation to the number of people in the labour force. The statistic that is used to make these observations is the **unemployment rate**, which is the number of persons who are unemployed as a percentage of the labour force.

The calculation of the unemployment rate for a particular period of time would proceed as follows:

$$\text{The Unemployment Rate (in per cent)} = \frac{\text{Unemployed}}{\text{Labour Force}} \times 100.$$

However, it has been shown that

The Labour Force = Employed + Unemployed.

Therefore,

$$\text{The Unemployment Rate} = \frac{\text{Unemployed}}{\text{Employed} + \text{Unemployed}} \times 100.$$

The calculation of Canada's unemployment rate, using the March 1983 data for employment, unemployment, and the labour force previously cited is as follows:

$$\text{Unemployment Rate} = \frac{1,658,000}{10,236,000 + 1,658,000} \times 100$$

$$\frac{1,658,000}{11,894,000} \times 100 = 13.9\%.$$

This calculation reveals that, in March 1983, 13.9 per cent of the labour force was unemployed.

A similar computation for March 1982, one year earlier, reveals that 10.5 per cent of the labour force was unemployed. This is partial evidence that Canada's unemployment problem was more severe in March 1983 than it had been in the same month one year earlier. More complete evidence requires an examination of the **labour force participation rate**.

In addition to monthly statistics, annual average unemployment statistics are produced and published by Statistics Canada. Annual average unemployment and the annual average unemployment rate for Canada for each year from 1954 to 1983 are presented in *Table 1-3*. These annual average figures for unemployment and the unemployment rate are simply the sum of each of these statistics for the 12 months of the year divided by 12.

In 1975, Statistics Canada made changes in the Labour Force Survey that affected the estimates of employment and unemployment. To show the effects this change would have had on earlier measures of unemployment, Statistics Canada published comparable data going back to 1966, which is presented in *Table 1-3*. Notice that this change in the Labour Force Survey produced lower estimates of unemployment and the unemployment rate for the years when comparisons are available.

The marked increase in national unemployment rates between 1966 and 1983, shown in *Table 1-3*, has been the source of much discussion among economists who have devised various theories to explain it. These theories are discussed in Chapter 5.

Thus far, discussion of unemployment rates and other labour force statistics has been limited to national data. However, national averages are simply the sum of regional experiences. Annual average unemployment rates for Canada and its regions for the years 1975 through 1983 are presented in *Table 2-3*.

TABLE 1-3

Annual Average Unemployment and Unemployment Rates for Canada, 1954-1983

Year	Annual Average Unemployment (thousands)		Annual Average Unemployment Rate (per cent)	
1954	250		4.6	
1955	245		4.4	
1956	197		3.4	
1957	278		4.6	
1958	432		7.0	
1959	372		6.0	
1960	446		7.0	
1961	466		7.1	
1962	390		5.9	
1963	374		5.5	
1964	324		4.7	
1965	280		3.9	
1966	267	251*	3.6	3.4**
1967	315	296	4.1	3.8
1968	382	358	4.8	4.5
1969	382	362	4.7	4.4
1970	495	476	5.9	5.7
1971	552	535	6.4	6.2
1972	562	553	6.3	6.2
1973	520	515	5.6	5.5
1974	525	514	5.4	5.3
1975	707	690	7.1	6.9
1976		726		7.1
1977		849		8.1
1978		908		8.3
1979		836		7.4
1980		865		7.5
1981		898		7.5
1982		1,314		11.0
1983		1,448		11.9

Sources: 1954-1975: Unemployment and unemployment rates (annual averages), F.H. Leacy, ed., *Historical Statistics of Canada*, 2nd edition (Ottawa: Statistics Canada, 1983), Series D477-483 and Series D491-497 (Catalogue No. CS11-516E).

*1966-1983: Unemployment (annual averages), Statistics Canada, *Historical Labour Force Statistics — Actual Data. Seasonal Factors, Seasonally Adjusted Data, 1983* (Ottawa Supply and Services Canada, 1984), p. 139 (Catalogue No. 71-201, annual).

**1966-1983: Unemployment rates, Statistics Canada, *Historical Labour Force Statistics . . . 1983*, p. 181 (Catalogue No. 71-201, annual).

TABLE 2-3

The Unemployment Rate, Canada and by Region, 1975-1983

Year	Canada	Atlantic Region	Quebec	Ontario	Prairie Region	British Columbia
			(per cent)			
1975	6.9	9.8	8.1	6.3	3.9	8.5
1976	7.1	10.9	8.7	6.2	4.1	8.6
1977	8.1	12.6	10.3	7.0	4.9	8.5
1978	8.4	12.5	10.9	7.2	5.2	8.3
1979	7.5	11.8	9.6	6.5	4.3	7.7
1980	7.5	11.2	9.9	6.9	4.3	6.8
1981	7.6	11.7	10.4	6.6	4.5	6.7
1982	11.0	14.4	13.8	9.8	7.4	12.1
1983	11.9	15.0	13.9	10.4	9.7	13.8

Source: Canada, Department of Finance, *Economic Review April 1984*, Reference Table 32, p. 164
(Catalogue No. F1-21/1984E).

Regional unemployment rates are a reflection of two related phenomena: employment opportunities generated by economic growth, and the region's migration experience. While all regions of the country were affected severely by the recession that began in the autumn of 1981, during the past two decades there has been a fairly consistent pattern of regional unemployment.

Slow economic growth in the Atlantic region and Quebec has resulted in above average unemployment rates, as shown in *Table 2-3*. In the Atlantic region unemployment rates would be even higher except that many residents involuntarily emigrated from the region to seek employment in Ontario and Western Canada. Emigration of the unemployed from Quebec has been limited to some extent by the linguistic and cultural barriers to mobility that exist for French-speaking Québecois, while a certain number of English-speaking Québecois have moved West in response to unemployment in Quebec, as well as a belief that employment opportunities would be better for them in predominantly English-speaking regions.

Unemployment rates in British Columbia tend to fluctuate around the national average despite the fact that there has been impressive economic growth in the province. This can be explained by the cyclical sensitivity of the demand for wood products and other raw materials, the inflow of new and temporary residents seeking work, and the unemployment associated with the shifting of economic activity from agriculture and resource-based industries to manufacturing and service industries.

In the Prairie region high levels of activity in agriculture and the growth of exploration and production in the energy and mining industries contributed to relatively low unemployment rates. This was accompanied by a considerable amount of interprovincial migration, with Alberta receiving job-seeking immigrants from all across the country. Since 1981, a general economic down-turn, accompanied by reductions in the demand for and world prices of energy products, has reduced dramatically economic growth in Alberta and Saskatchewan and has contributed to higher unemployment rates in the region.

In Ontario the growth of broadly based economic activity in manufacturing and service industries as well as in the public sector has kept unemployment rates consistently below the national average. Unusually high unemployment in 1982, which extended into 1983, was caused by poor performance in manufacturing industries and in metal mining.

HIDDEN UNEMPLOYMENT

Members of the potential labour force, who would work if jobs were available but are not looking for work because they believe jobs are not available, are not counted as unemployed. This group includes those who are laid off for more than 26 weeks or have lost their jobs permanently as well as housewives, youths, and elderly persons who are able and willing to work if jobs are available. These persons are called **"discouraged workers."**[43]

The monthly Labour Force Survey also does not take account of the number of persons who are working part-time involuntarily or of the number of persons who are employed at jobs whose requirements are beneath their level of training and competence.

These three groups of workers — discouraged workers, involuntary part-time workers, and those workers employed at jobs beneath their level of training and competence — are the **hidden unemployed**. In 1982, the annual average unemployment rate for Canada would have been 15.3 per cent instead of the official 11 per cent reported by Statistics Canada, if hidden unemployment was taken into account.[44]

THE UNEMPLOYMENT RATE AND UNEMPLOYMENT INSURANCE CLAIMS

Published estimates of unemployment and unemployment rates are based on information gathered in the Statistics Canada monthly household Labour Force Survey. They are **not** based on applications or payments for unemployment

---

[43] In March 1983 there were 335,000 persons counted as **not in the labour force** who wanted to work and were available for work, but were not seeking work because they believed none was available or were awaiting recall from layoffs of more than 26 weeks and therefore were **not in the labour force**. Statistics Canada, *The Labour Force*, March 1983, pp. 143-145 (Catalogue No. 71-001, monthly).
[44] Statistics Canada, "Supplementary Measures of Unemployment," *The Labour Force*, April 1983, pp. [83]-95 (Catalogue No. 71-001, monthly).

32

insurance. Unemployment insurance claims cannot be used to measure unemployment because many people classified as unemployed under Statistics Canada definitions are not eligible to collect unemployment insurance. One example is new entrants to the labour force who are seeking jobs or who have been laid off before they had worked a sufficient number of weeks to qualify for unemployment insurance payments. There are also persons who are eligible for unemployment insurance whom Statistics Canada would not count as unemployed. Part-time workers with extremely low incomes fall into this category.

THE EMPLOYMENT-POPULATION RATIO

In January 1978, Statistics Canada introduced a new data series entitled the employment-population ratio, which represents the proportion of the potential labour force that is engaged in the production of goods and services in the Canadian economy. It is defined as the ratio of the number of persons employed, as determined each month in the Labour Force Survey, to the size of the potential labour force, which is estimated from other sources. The ratio can be calculated each month as follows:

$$\text{The Employment-Population Ratio (in per cent)} = \frac{\text{Employed}}{\text{Potential Labour Force}} \times 100.$$

In March 1983, employment in Canada was 10,236,000 and the potential labour force was 18,746,000. Therefore,

$$\text{The Employment-Population Ratio} = \frac{10,236,000}{18,746,000} \times 100 = 54.6\%.$$

This ratio received much attention during the May 1979 federal election campaign. Faced with the fact that Canadian unemployment had been among the worst in the industrialized world, the reigning Liberal party argued that its record in creating new jobs had been excellent.[45] One piece of evidence the Liberals used was *Chart 1-3*, which shows that the employment-population ratio for all Canadians 15 years of age and over increased between 1966 and 1977. However, further investigation reveals that the same ratio for males 25 years of age and over shows a marked decline while that for females 25 years of age and over rises sharply. These relationships are shown in *Charts 2-3* and *3-3*. What has happened is clear. Rising unemployment was accompanied by a falling employment-population ratio for adult males who for the most part hold full-time jobs when they are employed. However, adult female employees, many of whom

---

[45] Table 8, p. 29 in the July 1977 issue of *OECD Economic Outlook 21*, published by the Organization for Economic Co-operation and Development, shows that during the period 1962-1976 the average unemployment rate in Canada was 5.4 per cent compared to 5.1 per cent in the United States and 3.2 per cent for all the industrialized countries taken together.

CHART 1-3

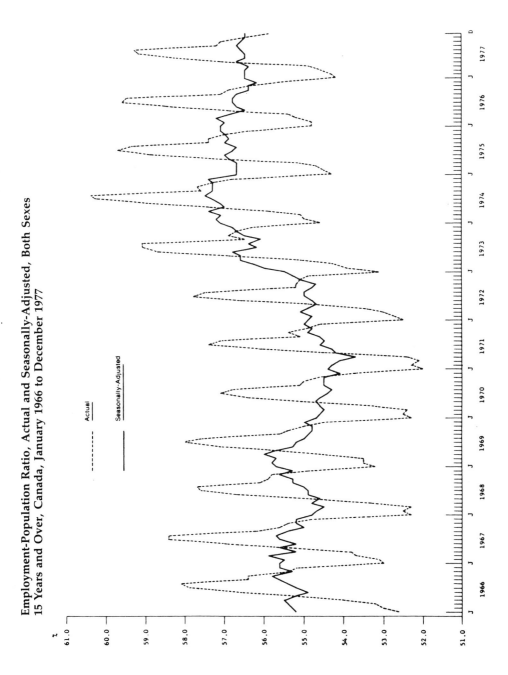

Employment-Population Ratio, Actual and Seasonally-Adjusted, Both Sexes
15 Years and Over, Canada, January 1966 to December 1977

Actual

Seasonally-Adjusted

Source: Statistics Canada, *The Labour Force*, January 1978 (Catalogue No. 71-001, monthly).

34

CHART 2-3

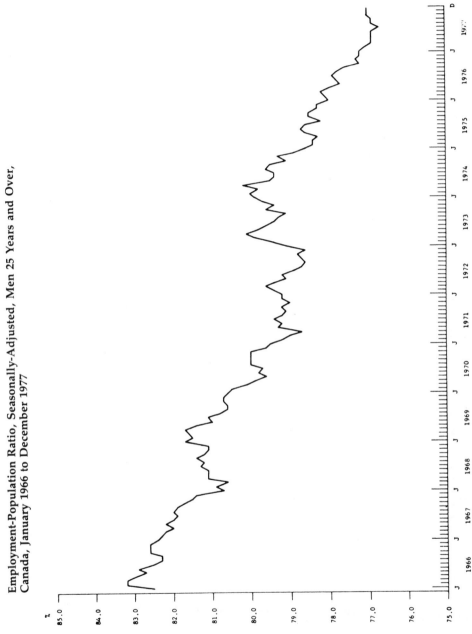

Employment-Population Ratio, Seasonally-Adjusted, Men 25 Years and Over, Canada, January 1966 to December 1977

Source: Statistics Canada, *The Labour Force*, January 1978 (Catalogue No. 71-001, monthly).

35

CHART 3-3

Employment-Population Ratio, Seasonally-Adjusted, Women 25 Years and Over, Canada, January 1966 to December 1977

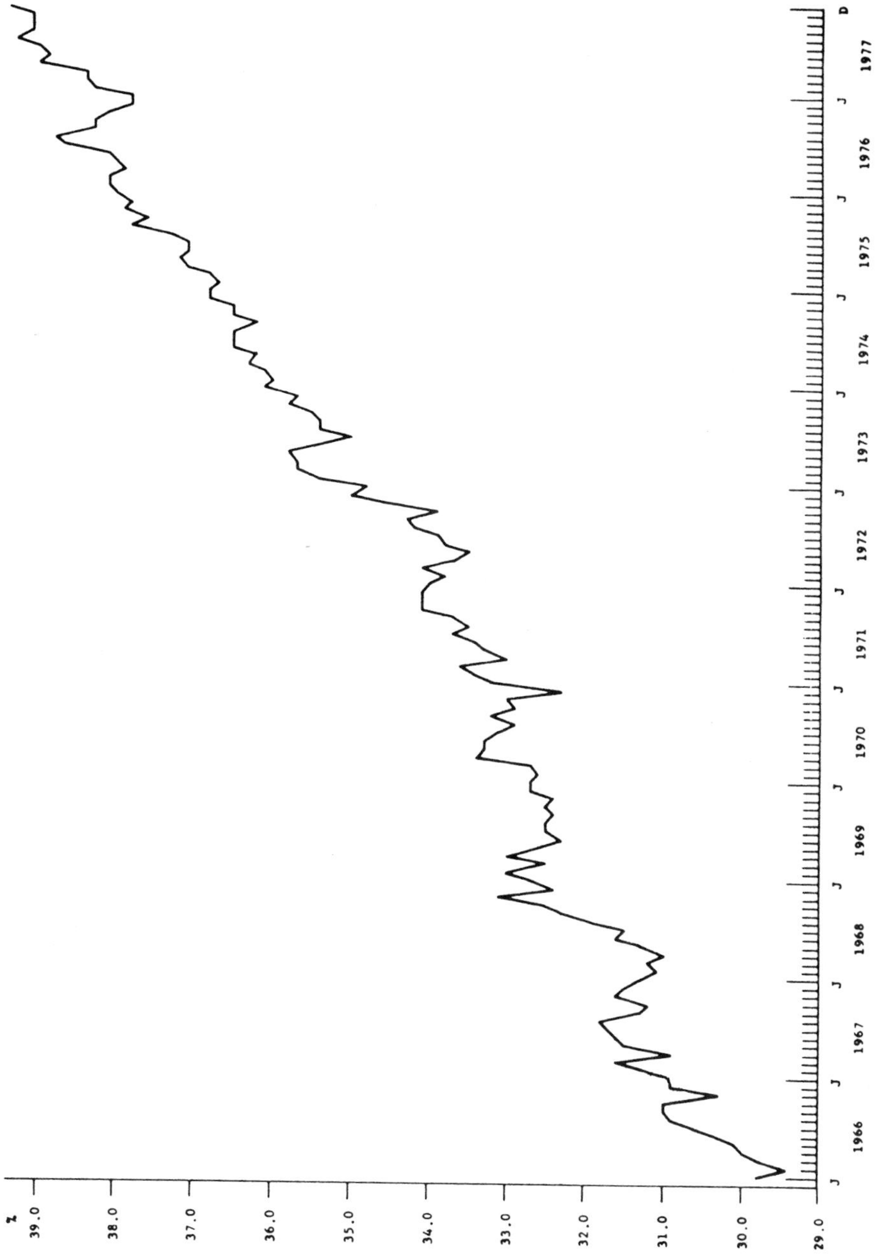

Source: Statistics Canada, *The Labour Force*, January 1978 (Catalogue No. 71-001, monthly).

hold part-time jobs, entered the labour force in large numbers during this period. Their employment-population ratio rose, but much of this employment creation was part-time employment.

THE LABOUR FORCE PARTICIPATION RATE

"Everyone who wants to work" has been defined as the **labour force**. The labour force is the sum of those members of the potential labour force who are employed and unemployed. It was shown in Chapter 2 that the size and characteristics of the population and thereby of the **potential labour force** are determined by natural population growth and net migration. The size and characteristics of the **labour force** are in turn influenced by the **proportion** of people in the potential labour force who want to work. The proportion of people in the potential labour force who want to work is called **the labour force participation rate**, and is expressed as follows:

$$\text{The Labour Force Participation Rate (in per cent)} = \frac{\text{Labour Force}}{\text{Potential Labour Force}} \times 100.$$

The sum of individual decisions by members of the potential labour force produces an overall labour force participation rate. In addition, the labour force participation rates of groups within the potential labour force as defined by sex, age, skill, national origin, and region are often of interest. Labour force participation rates by age and sex for selected years from 1901 to 1983 are presented in *Table 3-3*.

Until 1961, overall labour force participation rates were constant except for the sharp increase between 1901 and 1913, which was caused by a massive wave of immigrants, many of whom were men of working age. In this period the tendency for male labour force participation rates to fall was more or less balanced by the rise in female labour force participation rates. Between 1961 and 1971 male rates continued to fall, but there was an extraordinary 10.2 per cent increase in female rates, which raised the overall labour force participation rate by 4 per cent.

After 1971, male labour force participation rates, which had been falling for about 60 years, began to rise while female rates continued their spectacular increase. Marked changes in the labour market behaviour of the potential labour force clearly have occurred. To understand the nature of these changes, female, male, and regional labour force participation rates must be examined.

The labour force participation rate of a particular group of persons is the number of persons in that group who are in the labour force as a percentage of the number of persons in that group who are in the potential labour force. For example, to obtain the labour force participation rate of married women, divide the number of married women in the labour force by the number of married women in the potential labour force and multiply the dividend by 100.

TABLE 3-3

Labour Force Participation Rates, by Age and Sex, Canada, for Selected Years, 1901-1983

Year	Both Sexes 14 years and over %	Men All Ages 14 years and over %	14-19 %	20-24 %	25-34 %	35-64 %	65 and over %	Women All Ages 14 years and over %	14-19 %	20-24 %	25-34 %	35-64 %	65 and over %
1901	53.0	78.3	—	—	—	—	—	14.4	—	—	—	—	—
1911	57.4	82.0	—	—	—	—	—	16.6	—	—	—	—	—
1921	56.2	80.3	68.4	94.3	98.0	96.9	59.6	17.7	29.6	39.8	19.5	12.0	6.6
1931	55.9	78.4	57.4	93.9	98.6	96.7	56.5	19.4	26.5	47.4	24.4	13.2	6.2
1941	55.2	85.6	54.6	92.6	98.7	96.1	47.9	22.9	26.8	46.9	27.9	15.2	5.8
1951	54.5	84.4	53.7	94.2	98.2	95.0	39.5	24.4	33.7	48.8	25.4	19.8	4.5
1961	55.3	81.1	40.6	94.4	98.4	95.3	30.6	29.3	31.7	50.7	29.2	29.9	6.1
1971	58.1*	77.3*	45.4*	82.8	96.3	92.7	20.0	39.4*	40.4*	62.3	40.7	38.3	5.1
1981	64.8*	78.4*	58.2*	86.5	95.3	89.2	13.8	51.7*	53.0*	72.9	65.5	52.5	4.0
1983	64.4*	76.7*	52.9*	84.3	93.7	88.0	13.0	52.6*	50.1*	74.0	67.6	54.6	4.6

*15 years of age and over.

Sources: 1901-1961, F.H. Leacy, ed., *Historical Statistics of Canada*, 2nd edition, Series D107-122 (Catalogue No. CS11-516E).

1971, 1981, and 1983, Statistics Canada, *Historical Labour Force Statistics . . . 1983*, Section 6, pp. 213-241 (Catalogue No. 71-201, annual).

1971, 1981, and 1983, (for age groups 25-34, 35-64, and 65 and over), Statistics Canada, Labour Force Survey Division, (unpublished data).

The increasing labour force participation rate of women has affected dramatically the size and character of the labour force. This rate rose from 14.1 per cent in 1901 to 52.6 per cent in 1983.[46] In 1983, 5,026,000 women constituted 42 per cent of the total Canadian labour force. Increases in the female labour force participation rate were steady relatively between 1901 and 1961, as revealed in *Table 3-3*. However, between 1961 and 1983 this rate increased 1.7 times more than it had during the previous 60 years.

The increase in female labour force participation rates since the early 1960's has taken place among women of all age groups and marital status. However, as *Table 4-3* reveals, there have been particularly large increases in the participation rates of married women. The influx of married women into the labour force has changed the traditional pattern of female labour force participation. In earlier years young women entered the labour force and remained there until they married or became pregnant, at which time they assumed household and child-rearing responsibilities. After children grew up, many women would re-enter the labour market. However, by the mid-1970's fewer women were leaving the labour force because of marriage or to stay at home to raise children.[47] There are

---

[46] For a detailed discussion of this subject see, Paul Phillips and Erin Phillips, *Women and Work: Inequality in the Labour Market* (Toronto: James Lorimer & Co., 1983), pp. 31-51.
[47] *Ibid.*, pp. 36-37.

TABLE 4-3

**Female Labour Force Participation Rates by Marital Status,
Canada, 1951, 1961, 1971, and 1981**

Status	1951	1961	1971	1981
		(per cent)		
Single	58.1	51.4	49.2	64.6
Married	11.2	21.1	32.8	50.6
Other (widowed, divorced, separated)	19.3	27.8	28.3	35.6
Total	24.0	29.2	36.6	51.7

Sources: 1951 Census; 1961, 1971, and 1981, Statistics Canada, *The Labour Force.*

also a significant number of women who are the heads of single-parent families and who must work to support their families adequately. Paul and Erin Phillips have pointed out that:

> By 1975 there were almost 400,000 female headed, single parent families. With rates of divorce and separation approaching a third of marriage rates, the number of such families is increasing and is bound to continue to do so. These are women who must work to support themselves and/or their families. The alternative is to rely on usually insufficient welfare payments, support payments, widows' pensions or some other form of transfer payment. For the most part, they work just to put bread upon the table.[48]

Women have entered the labour force in growing numbers because of the increased demand for their services. This increased demand was caused by the short supply of male workers to meet the production needs of the Second World War and the rapid growth of output in Canada after the war. Later, increased employment opportunities for women became available because of the expansion of sectors of the economy in which the proportion of women employees was substantial already. Examples of these sectors are education, government, commerce, finance, and health, as well as in the light manufacturing industries like electronics and communication equipment where women are thought to be well-suited for employment.

---

[48] *Ibid.*, p. 38.

In all these sectors women constitute a pool of high-quality labour that is available at relatively low wage rates.

> In 1911 the average wage of employed women stood at 53 per cent of the average of male wages. In 1931 it was 60 per cent. By 1978 the average earned income of women who worked the entire year was 58 per cent of men's full year earnings, . . .[49]

Women have become more willing and able to work or, as economists would say, "the supply of female labour has increased." This has occurred as average family size has decreased, as labour-saving devices (washing machines and dryers, vacuum cleaners, etc.) have entered the home, and as more and more domestic tasks are commercialized (T.V. dinners, prepared frozen foods, commercial laundry and dry cleaning establishments, etc.).[50] Equally important, women have demonstrated increased determination to be rid of their second class status in society by achieving more creative lives with greater individual independence through employment, among other things.

While female labour force participation rates have risen since the turn of the century, the overall male labour force participation rate declined from 82 per cent in 1911 to 76.7 per cent in 1983. (See *Table 3-3.*) The most important reasons for the decline in the overall male participation rates were the tendency for young men to stay in school longer and for older men to retire at an earlier age.

In the 1970's male participation rates began to rise, though not as dramatically as female rates. These increases took place mainly among younger workers. The cause of these increases seems to have been an increase in part-time work by both male and female students and a shift away from longer years of schooling towards full-time labour force participation by younger males who dropped out of the educational system to seek jobs with the intention of later going back to school or continuing their education in part-time and evening school programs that became more available. However, the severe restriction of employment opportunities for young people, beginning in mid-1981, has resulted in young people staying in school longer and returning to school when this is possible.

The labour force participation rates of older males has fallen since 1921. (See *Table 3-3.*) This fall reflects the decline of employment in agriculture and in small independent businesses where workers tend to remain employed longer, the increased availability of pensions, and the enforcement of compulsory retirement rules in collective agreements and by individual employers.

---

[49] *Ibid.*, p. 52.

[50] A number of studies contest the assertion that the amount of time women spend on household tasks has been reduced considerably. Time budget studies made in the United States show that the total time women spend on their domestic tasks has declined little in the last half-century; full-time housewives living in urban areas were found to spend an average of 53 hours a week on domestic tasks. What has changed is the way in which their time is distributed between various tasks: the proportion spent on child care has increased, and the time spent on cooking and cleaning has decreased. See, A. Leibowitz, "Women's Work in the Home" in *Sex, Discrimination and the Division of Labour*, C. Lloyd, ed. (New York: Columbia University Press, 1975), pp. 223 and 230.

40

The labour force participation rate of the population of a particular geographic region is the number of persons in the labour force as a proportion of the potential labour force in the region.

Labour force participation rates differ among the various regions of the country. The most important factor affecting regional labour force participation rates is the existence of employment opportunities. These opportunities are related to the industrial structure of the region and to the existence of seasonal and part-time employment. In addition, the age distribution and cultural characteristics of the population affect labour force participation rates. For labour force participation rates for Canada and by province in 1983, see *Table 5-3*.

TABLE 5-3

Labour Force Participation Rates for Canada and by Province, 1983

	1983
	(per cent)
Canada	64.4
Atlantic Region	
Newfoundland	52.1
Prince Edward Island	60.2
Nova Scotia	57.4
New Brunswick	55.5
Quebec	60.9
Ontario	67.1
Prairie Region	
Manitoba	65.6
Saskatchewan	65.2
Alberta	71.6
British Columbia	64.1

Source: Statistics Canada, *Historical Labour Force Statistics . . . 1983* (Catalogue No. 71-201, annual).

UNEMPLOYMENT AND LABOUR FORCE PARTICIPATION RATES

"Everyone who wants to work" has been defined as the **labour force**, but the **size** of the labour force is influenced by **labour force participation rates**. However, participation rates are influenced in turn by employment opportunities. When jobs are scarce some unemployed workers who cannot find jobs or know none are available become discouraged and do not actively seek work. When the monthly household Labour Force Survey is made, many of these workers are recorded as **not in the labour force**. They are no longer considered unemployed because they are not actively seeking work. Under these conditions the unemployment rate understates the seriousness of the absence of employment opportunities.

Scarce employment opportunities for the main breadwinner in a family may cause other members of the family (housewives, teenagers, retired persons) to seek work, thus adding to the size of the labour force and adding to both the number of employed and unemployed. These workers are called "additional" workers.

A complete analysis of the labour market situation during a particular period of time requires examination of what is happening to **the potential labour force**, the **labour force participation rate**, and the **process of job creation**. This can be done for the nation as a whole, for a particular age-sex group in the potential labour force, for a region, or for other labour force categories for which Statistics Canada has collected data. (Appendix A to this chapter illustrates the interdependence of the various labour market concepts that have been discussed.)

SEASONAL VARIATION

Seasonal patterns of economic activity are reflected in data collected in the Labour Force Survey as well as in other economic data. Seasonal factors cause month-to-month differences in employment and unemployment and therefore in estimates of employment, unemployment, and labour force participation rates. Seasonal variation in these statistics reflect the effect of **weather, established traditions**, and **institutional arrangements** on the production and sales of goods and services as well as on the number of people in the labour force.

Weather conditions during the year significantly affect employment in agriculture, fishing, logging, and other primary industries. Established traditions associated with holidays and vacations affect consumer purchases and therefore employment patterns in the production and sales of certain goods and services. Institutional arrangements, for example the time of year new automobile models go into production, create seasonal employment patterns.

The beginning and end of the school year have an impact on the labour force. Each May and June large numbers of permanent and temporary additions to the labour force take place when high schools, colleges, and universities end their regular instruction. Many of these students enter the ranks of the employed and unemployed. In September, large numbers of students leave the labour force and return to school.

Seasonal adjustment is a statistical technique used to determine whether **changes** in actual employment, unemployment, and other economic statistics reflect changes in fundamental economic conditions, or whether they merely reflect expected seasonal variation. A seasonally adjusted data series is one from which seasonal movements have been eliminated.

When a statistical series has been seasonally adjusted, data for any month can be compared with data for any other month or with an annual average to determine if anything more than a normal seasonal change has taken place.

The seasonal adjustment process essentially observes by how much monthly statistics have deviated from annual average statistics over a number of previous years. These past average monthly deviations are expected then to occur during the current year and are used to adjust the actual data in order to produce the "seasonally adjusted" monthly statistics.[51]

One way of interpreting the seasonal adjustment process is to see this process as answering the question: what do the actual data for a particular month imply about what the average will be for the year? For example, actual unemployment in a summer month will be below the expected average unemployment for the year and will be seasonally adjusted upward, while actual unemployment in a winter month will be above the expected average for the year and will be seasonally adjusted downward.

The unadjusted or actual unemployment rate for Canada in February 1983, a winter month, was 14.4 per cent; the seasonally adjusted rate was 12.5 per cent. The unadjusted unemployment rate for July of the same year, a summer month, was 11.2 per cent; the seasonally adjusted rate was 12 per cent. The annual average unemployment rate for Canada in 1983 was 11.9 per cent.

An interesting example of the importance of understanding the difference between seasonally adjusted and unadjusted data was an event that took place during the summer of 1970. On June 16, Statistics Canada released the **seasonally adjusted** and **seasonally unadjusted** labour force report for Canada, but only unadjusted figures for the country's economic regions.

The report created the impression that between May and June 1970, Quebec unemployment improved even though unemployment was higher in the country as a whole. The impression was so strong that one Montreal newspaper ran a front page story (with headlines) that attributed the improvement to the newly-elected provincial Liberal government (although the government had been in power less than 30 days when the June monthly household Labour Force Survey was made). Nevertheless the impression was false. Relative to unemployment changes that usually occur from May to June in Quebec, the unemployment situation was worse rather than better. Unemployment **normally** drops between the months of May and June in Quebec and elsewhere in Canada, as summer

---

[51] Statistics Canada's seasonal adjustment technique is contained in a complicated computer program, which differentiates between seasonal, trend, and irregular movements in a series over a number of years and, on the basis of past movements, estimates appropriate seasonal factors for current survey data. These factors are published annually by Statistics Canada in *Historical Labour Force Statistics — Actual Data, Seasonal Factors, Seasonally Adjusted Data* (Catalogue No. 71-201).

employment rises to more than absorb new entrants into the labour force. In other words, actual unemployment tends to normally fall between May and June in Quebec. The economic situation was worse in June because unemployment had not fallen **enough** compared to other years.[52]

In general, if labour force data is available for the same month in two successive years, comparison of the **seasonally adjusted** data can be an indication of whether employment opportunities for the labour force are better or worse than a year ago. However, to compare two successive months or two different months to determine if the situation is fundamentally better or worse, a comparison must be made of the **seasonally adjusted** statistics.[53]

---

[52] When corrections for seasonal influences were made, it was found that between June 1969 and June 1970 seasonally adjusted estimates of Quebec unemployment rose from 163,000 to 193,000, or from 7.1 per cent to 8.2 per cent of the labour force. Furthermore, this 18.4 per cent annual rate of increase in the number of unemployed Quebec workers was not levelling off between May and June 1970. To the contrary, seasonally adjusted unemployment increased by about 2,000 workers.

[53] Although they are not seasonally adjusted, Canadian strike statistics illustrate this point. Strike activity usually is higher in summer than in winter. (Most workers would rather not walk picket lines in freezing weather, if they can avoid it.) Thus the fact that strikes increase from winter to summer of a given year is not necessarily evidence of a general deterioration of the industrial relations climate. The interesting question is whether or not the increase is more or less than normally occurs.

Appendix A

BASIC LABOUR MARKET RELATIONS

Basic labour market relationships can be examined using the following identities:

Let, P = potential labour force;
L = labour force;
N = not in the labour force;
E = employed;
U = unemployed;

$u = \dfrac{\text{unemployed}}{\text{labour force}}$ (When this ratio is multiplied by 100, it is the unemployment rate in per cent.)

$x = \dfrac{\text{labour force}}{\text{potential labour force}}$ (When this ratio is multiplied by 100, it is the labour force participation rate in per cent.)

Then, (1) $P \equiv L + N$;

(2) $L \equiv E + U \equiv xP$,

(3) $u \equiv \dfrac{U}{L}$.

Since $L \equiv xP$ and $U \equiv xP - E$ then,

(4) $u \equiv \dfrac{xP - E}{xP}$ and, by arithmetic manipulation,

(4a) $u \equiv \dfrac{xP}{xP} - \dfrac{E}{xP} \equiv 1 - \dfrac{E}{xP}$.

From (4a) it can be seen that the unemployment rate depends on the potential labour force (P), the labour force participation rate (x), and employment creation (E). Differences in these three factors will be associated with differences in the unemployment rate (u). Therefore, interpreting past or present unemployment rates or predicting future unemployment rates for a particular country or region requires that these factors be taken into account.

CHAPTER 4

HOW ARE FRICTIONAL UNEMPLOYMENT,STRUCTURAL UNEMPLOYMENT, AND WAGE RATES RELATED TO FULL EMPLOYMENT?

T he first part of this chapter examines the element in our definition of full employment that "everyone who wants to work **can
find a job within a reasonable period of time, without involuntary dislocation.**" Frictional and structural unemployment are two
concepts economists use in discussing the length of time necessary
for the unemployed to find employment.

This chapter also examines theories about the effects of different levels of the
wage rate on employment and unemployment in the economy. This discussion
is related to that part of our definition of full employment that "everyone who
wants to work can find a job . . . **at the established wage rate for his or her
skills.**"

FRICTIONAL UNEMPLOYMENT

A reasonable definition of full employment does not require that there be zero
unemployment. This is because there will be measured unemployment even in
labour markets where job vacancies outnumber individuals capable of doing
these jobs who are seeking work. Workers who have left one job require time to
find another. Students, housewives, the retired, and others who decide to seek

work take time (on average) to locate employment. Under these circumstances, the unemployment that is measured is called **frictional unemployment**. It reflects the time necessary for workers to move between jobs and in and out of the labour force when employment opportunities are available.

After the Second World War and until the late 1950's, economists defined the Canadian full employment goal as an unemployment rate of 2 per cent. This figure was accepted as the irreducible level of seasonal and frictional unemployment in Canada. The goal of a 2 per cent unemployment rate was determined by simply observing the unemployment rates that occurred between 1943 and 1953, that is, from the period of full mobilization for the Second World War through the periods of postwar reconstruction and the Korean War. These unemployment rates are shown in *Table 1-4*.

TABLE 1-4

Unemployment Rates, Canada, 1943-1953

Year	Unemployment Rate (per cent)	Year	Unemployment Rate (per cent)
1943	1.7	1948	2.3
1944	1.4	1949	2.9
1945	1.6	1950	3.6
1946	3.4	1951	2.4
1947	2.2	1952	2.9
		1953	3.0

Source: *Historical Statistics of Canada*, M.C. Urquhart and K.A.H. Buckley, eds. (Cambridge: University Press, 1965), Series C47-55, p. 61.

STRUCTURAL UNEMPLOYMENT

In later years economists introduced the concept of **structural unemployment** to explain the persistence of unemployment rates well above the frictional level. Structural unemployment is unemployment that exists because the "structure" of the economy is changing more rapidly than the labour force is able to adapt to it. Three important sources of the structural problem are thought to be: rapid changes in production technology (automation); unusual shifts in the sectoral composition of output (for example, the change in the relative importance of services as compared to goods in Canadian output); and major shifts in the geographical location of production from east to west.

Structural unemployment can be perceived as long-lasting frictional unemployment because it takes considerable periods of time for the labour force to adjust to new skill demands, working conditions, and training requirements in expanding sectors of the economy or to relocate to regions where job opportunities are becoming available.

One objective of government manpower training and mobility programs should be to speed up these adjustments, so that new entrants into the labour force and workers displaced by changes in the structure of the economy can find employment **within a reasonable period of time**.

The Economic Council of Canada in its *First Annual Review*, published in 1964, maintained that a 3 per cent unemployment rate — or a 97 per cent employment rate — was a realistic full employment objective over the remainder of the 1960's because of seasonal, frictional, and structural unemployment.[54] By the 1970's some economists had given a new interpretation to structural unemployment and were asserting that the full employment goal was nearer to a 7 per cent than a 3 per cent unemployment rate. The upward adjustment of ideas about the rate of unemployment to be associated with full employment is the subject of Chapter 5.

The Cost of Dislocation

Workers affected by changes in the structure of the economy must rearrange their lives in order to seek and obtain new employment. Economists are prone to discuss mobility between jobs, occupations, and regions made necessary by structural change as if it was without economic and social cost to the workers and their families. But such costs do exist, and governments have to take careful account of them within the framework of a full employment policy.

Structural change often is caused by forces that are uncontrolled, and these changes may or may not be in the perceived interest of the general population, that is, of the nation. When structural changes are deemed undesirable, government intervention is necessary to control them, and the costs of such intervention must be shared among Canadians.

A prime example is the tendency of Canadian firms in the cultural-communication sector (book publishing, movies, radio, television, theatre, newspapers) to fail because the size of their market is too small to allow them to use the most advanced production and sales techniques. Government subsidies or government operation of enterprises in this field may be necessary.

A more controversial example is the national commitment to balanced regional growth. In the short run at least, the more prosperous sections of the country

---

[54] Economic Council of Canada, *First Annual Review, Economic Goals for Canada to 1970* (Ottawa: Queen's Printer, 1964), p. 38.

are being called upon to support economic adjustment in the slower growing regions.

There are other cases where structural changes are clearly in the interest of the general population. The "costs" of these changes that will benefit the nation collectively should not be borne by individuals. Arrangements must be made through government legislation and in the industrial relations system (the rules governing union-management relations) to prevent the burden of adjustment to structural change from falling randomly on individual groups of workers.

Events on the railroads during the decade 1955-1965 provide a case in point. Dieselization displaced thousands of firemen and allowed trains to "run-through" towns that previously existed largely as repair and refuelling points.

The unilateral institution of these "run-throughs" in 1964 by the Canadian National Railways provoked large-scale resistance from running-trade employees and their unions. This resistance took the form of over 2,800 employees of the company "booking off" sick. Faced with the possibility of an interruption of the transcontinental operations of Canadian National Railways the Canadian government intervened and, with the agreement of the involved parties, appointed Mr. Justice Samuel Freedman of Manitoba as commissioner of an industrial inquiry commission. The report of this commission is now considered a pathbreaking document in the field of adaptation to technological change.

A quotation from this report, which deals with the question of who bears the burden or costs of technological change, follows.

> Economists tell us that the problem of technological change is not new but that it is simply the modern form of a process as old as the Industrial Revolution, if not older. Nor is it, many of them say, a cause of unemployment; it is rather a source for the creation of new jobs. They add that when economic conditions are buoyant and the demand for labour is brisk, technological changes can be introduced without any significant disruptive effects upon the work force. It is only when the economy is sluggish and when government action has been inadequate or ineffective to strengthen it that technological innovations bring unfortunate consequences to individuals. But in such circumstances the villain is not technology, which is an instrument for industrial progress, but rather government, which failed in its responsibility to keep the economy healthy and vigorous.

> This thesis is probably sound. The commission, however, would venture an observation concerning its practical application in a specific situation. A perfectly buoyant economy is always an ideal but rarely an attainment. When such an economy does not exist (a usual situation, one might say) and technological change is introduced with disruptive consequences, a worker whose job has become redundant is likely to find little consolation in the reflection that he is a victim not of technology but of government inaction. For him the stark and

immediate fact is that he is jobless. Admittedly if the total demand for labour happened to be great he could quickly move into other employment — in which case there would be less occasion for him to isolate or identify technology as the source of his trouble. Very often he might simply be reassigned to another job with the same employer. Even then, however, he might be confronted with the need to learn a new kind of work, his old skills having been made obsolete by technological advance. Taking a broad, national, long-range view and looking at employment in its totality the economists may be justified in contending that technology does not cause unemployment. Within the total picture, however, technology may bring about individual cases of difficulty and hardship, cases which will be multiplied if the general demand for labour is slack.

Moreover when a job becomes redundant the impact of the change may extend beyond those who seem immediately affected by it. A wise and benevolent employer may protect the present job holder either by retaining him in it until his retirement or by assigning him to another job. But what of the new entrant into the industry? For him the former job no longer exists. "Silent firing" is what this state of affairs is sometimes called. This new member of the labour force may perhaps have a different job available to him. But he may have to go elsewhere to obtain it, and so even in such a case some hardship would result from the technological change.[55]

Clearly the entire population benefits from increased efficiency of the railways, but these benefits should not require that the displaced firemen and uprooted townspeople pay the cost for general progress. The most important point made by Justice Freedman's report was that public policy must guarantee more equitable arrangements.

Thus, the requirement for full employment that "everyone who wants to work can find a job within a reasonable period of time. **without involuntary dislocation**" means that, when structural changes are taking place, **involuntary** dislocation should be minimized by appropriate training, mobility assistance, financial allowances, early retirement provisions, etc., that reduce to an acceptable minimum the number of persons who **involuntarily** change employment and geographical location.

Public policy that attempts to create employment without assuming responsibilities for the economic and social costs of the changes associated with its efforts is not an acceptable full employment policy, under our definition.[56]

---

[55] Canada, *Report of Industrial Inquiry Commission on Canadian National Railways "Run-Throughs"*, (Ottawa: Queen's Printer, 1965), p. 82. Condensation of the report in *Labour Gazette,* January/February 1966, pp. 4 to 6.

[56] An interesting discussion of Canadian and international experience in dealing with plant shutdowns can be found in Labour Canada, *Report of the Commission of Inquiry into Redundancies and Layoffs*, March 1979, A.W.R. Carrothers, Chairman.

EMPLOYMENT AT ESTABLISHED WAGE RATES

Economists once believed that if workers would accept lower money wage rates when unemployment appeared, full employment always could be attained. Historical experience has not supported this belief, and as a result of the work of British economist John Maynard Keynes most modern economists reject this theory for industrial capitalism. Nevertheless, from time to time, one hears the argument that if the unemployed and those threatened with unemployment would only accept lower money wage rates the unemployment problem would not exist. The argument usually goes like this: if workers who are unemployed or who are about to be laid-off would accept lower wages, firms' production and sales costs would be reduced. With reduced costs, firms could and would lower prices, sell more output, and would therefore need more workers to produce that output. Everyone who wanted to work at the appropriate lower wage then could find a job.

Keynesian economic theory rejects this approach on the grounds that **even** if all workers were willing and able to work for a lower wage at jobs that used their present skills, employers in general still would be unable to increase employment in the absence of a sufficiently increased demand for their products. Essentially, the argument is that with a general lowering of the money wage rate the additional goods and services that enterprises would try to produce could not be sold. It also is argued that a general reduction in wage rates would result in economic and social pessimism, if not revolt, which would create uncertainty about the future and thereby reduce new investment by entrepreneurs in machinery, plant, and equipment and by consumers in houses, cars, and other consumer durable goods. This reduction in investment would contribute to increased unemployment.

It is possible that a general wage reduction in one country, which results in lower prices of exported goods, may succeed in transferring unemployment to competitor nations in international trade. However, competitors are likely to retaliate with higher import duties or quotas, which will reduce Canadian exports, and/or policies to reduce their own wage rates in order to maintain their domestic production and employment in industries producing for export.

In any event average money wage rates have increased every year since 1933, and Canadian workers and their unions cannot be expected to accept **general** money wage reductions during periods of unemployment.[57]

There is the **isolated** case where in a particular region at a particular time a relatively low wage industry cannot easily fill its labour needs at existing wage rates in that industry. This situation provides a temptation to conservative politi-

---

[57] During the Great Depression money wage rates fell by approximately 15 per cent between 1930-1933. See, M.C. Urquhart and K.A.H. Buckley, eds., *Historical Statistics of Canada* (Cambridge: University Press, 1965), Series D1-11, p. 84. For current wage statistics see, Labour Canada, *Wage Rates, Salaries and Hours of Labour* (Ottawa: Information Canada), occasional and annual reports.

cians and the odd Chamber of Commerce representative to call on the unemployed to take jobs at wages and skill levels below those at which they usually have been employed.

Such a solution to local unemployment is unacceptable to unemployed workers because they would have to curtail their search for re-employment at their established skill and income level within and outside the region. Furthermore, employment in these low wage industries often pays little more than existing unemployment and social welfare benefits, thus providing little attraction for the unemployed. The article "Welfare Beats Picking Apples," reproduced as an appendix to this chapter, illustrates this situation.

Finally, specific observations of these relatively low wage industries reveal that the amount of additional available employment is usually small and transitory.

A reasonable definition of full employment requires that:

Everyone who wants to work can find a job within a reasonable period of time, without involuntary dislocation, at the established wage rate for his or her skills.

Appendix A
WELFARE BEATS PICKING APPLES

By Josh Freed

Excerpt from *The Montreal Star*, 7 October 1972

"Automne cometh ageyne — hevy of apples" reads the saying of the week at my favourite church at the corner of Sherbrooke and Simpson. But if Geoffrey Chaucer, the author of the words, had been alive today, he would likely have added a line dealing with the problem of getting the apples off the trees.

For the past two weeks, Quebec's leading apple centres, Hemmingford and Rougemont, have been faced with an acute shortage of apple pickers. The droves of unemployed who generally flock to the areas during harvest season have just not been prepared to come and work for $1.50 to $1.75 an hour wages usually paid to apple pickers.

Growers, fearful of losing their crops, were forced to handle the situation in different ways.

Some producers had already rid themselves of the problem last year, offering U-Pik services which invited families to "come down for an outing" and get "only the freshest apples from the trees — because you pick them yourselves."

Others went so far as to rent buses and provide transportation from Caughnawaga, where perhaps 50 Indians were prepared to do the labour at prescribed rates.

But most growers simply suffered with unpicked crops and laid the blame on increased unemployment insurance.

Alleviated

As a result of the publicity given the labour shortage earlier in the week, help eventually arrived. Manpower offered free bus service and hundreds of CEGEP (junior college) students took days off; consequently, the problem was alleviated and the apple crisis is over, for this year at least.

But the incident did serve to point up a growing phenomenon in Canada, one that struck the Quebec blueberry crop and New Brunswick logging industry earlier in the season and one that is certain to come up again. It is the matter of higher unemployment benefits which offer many inactive workers the luxury of refusing jobs that do not appeal to them, and last week's events had some people suggesting that unemployed labourers be obliged to accept apple-picking jobs or forfeit their unemployment insurance.

The apple producers of course, feel that the work should be mandatory, and much currency has recently been given to their views. Unemployment benefits are too high, they claimed that workers were deliberately turning down a job that could "net them as much as $175 a week."

But conversations with unemployed workers who have recently attempted apple-picking point to a different consensus.

Origene Deneault is a heavyset, greying 56-year-old welder recently left unemployed by the closing of the Domtar plant in Delson, Quebec. He had come to spend the day apple-picking in Hemmingford, something he had not done since he was a boy of 19. "It's hard to believe," he explained, "fourteen years I've been a welder with a good salary — and now here I am picking apples again, just as though I was a young boy."

On Strike

"We went on strike at Domtar for 5 months . . . and then suddenly — phfft! — the company was closed. I still can't believe it — it was like my home."

"I'm supposed to start collecting $75 unemployment pretty soon — and believe me I need it . . . this is no way to make a living. I'm here today because I haven't got $3 in my pocket and my family needs food — but as soon as I get my unemployment you can be sure I won't be doing this anymore."

Most apple pickers are paid by weight — 35 cents a bushel. At two o'clock Origene had worked five hours and collected 23 bushels, for an average of $1.60 per hour — which is the present minimum wage in Quebec.

"It's 20 miles from my home in Sherrington and I've got to get up at seven in the morning. Then I make about $13 for the day and spend $2 of it on gas — that's $11 for the day. Ever try to feed a family on $55 a week?"

At 56, climbing about in trees is no easy feat for Origene. Each time he climbs the ladder he puffs hard and wipes the sweat from his brow.

"Sure it's hard work," he conceded, "I was pooped out by 12 o'clock and I'm always scared of falling off the ladder. But I could take the hard work if I was being paid for it — I made $3.50 an hour as a welder and didn't work half this hard."

His friend Louis Boyer, a fellow ex-employee of Domtar, was also working that day in the orchards. He was 35, supported two children and was visibly upset with the notion that unemployed people should be obliged to do this sort of work.

"Sure I've heard what some of these guys on the radio said about us unemployed being lazy — about how we should be forced to work. But you tell me after I've worked 10 years at $3.05 an hour why should I have to work like this for the crummy $1.75 an hour I pull in?"

"Jobs in Quebec are tough to come by and and I shouldn't have to settle for this just because some company decided it would pull out of Delson."

"These guys on the radio make a lot of noise — but I'd like to see some of them out here picking apples if their jobs suddenly fell through."

Origene and Louis' attitude was shared by many. Workers at several orchards expressed their dissatisfaction with present wages, and unemployed workers in one Montreal unemployment office were quick to say they would rather remain on unemployment insurance.

"Why should we want to drive 35 miles to Hemmingford, just to make 10 or 12 bucks for the day? For a steady, decent-paying job . . . sure but for money like that I'm a lot better off with my unemployment insurance."

For those who make little money in their work, unemployment insurance benefits are really too low to live on. But for men, like Origene and Louis, who have earned a decent living, the benefits have given them a security they have not known before — the right to refuse low pay, heavy labour jobs which are a blow to both their dignity and pocketbooks.

"Look," explained Francis White, an ex-carpenter's assistant and one of the 50 Indians bussed in that day from Caughnawaga to help out with crops. "We heard that this might be a good way to make some money so we came down here today."

"I guess it's all right for some spare cash, but you can't make a living at it unless you've had a lot of experience picking."

"I'm young and healthy and can scamper around those trees pretty fast and I still only make about $2 an hour during my best periods. I was up at six this morning to catch the bus and won't be home until six tonight — and all I've got to show for it is $13."

"One hundred and seventy-five dollars! . . . they must be kidding," he reacted to one of the producer's claims, but then pausing for a moment he reconsidered and smiled. "Yeah . . . I guess it's possible — if you work from six in the morning to ten at night, seven days a week."

"Look, I'm not saying that this work is all that hard — but I've been a carpenter's assistant for the last year at $2.50 an hour and since I was laid off, I have $70 a week coming to me."

"I came down here because I like to work and thought maybe I'd do this for awhile — but it's ridiculous. You'd have to be crazy to do work like this when there's a decent unemployment plan you're paying money into."

None of which is to suggest that apple producers are deliberately underpaying their workers. While some of the larger and more vociferous growers can indeed afford to pay higher wages, there are many other small growers who just cannot afford any more. Like Mrs. Frank Peche, whose husband is an elementary school teacher in a nearby town, they simply do not make a great deal from their apple orchards.

"We do this on the side," she explained, "and it doesn't get us very rich. At the present market value for apples we just can't afford to pay anymore."

What it all comes down to is that apple growers cannot afford higher wages than they are now paying, yet many workers feel that the work to be done is not worth the wage; consequently it will have to be performed by anyone willing to accept the given pay, and no one, employed or otherwise, should really be chastised for choosing not to.

"Face it," offered Francis. "This is okay for youngsters, particularly students looking for some spare cash and it's all right for locals who want to work in the fields some days — but it's no answer to unemployment."

CHAPTER 5

THE POLITICAL ECONOMY OF FULL EMPLOYMENT

A full employment goal has disappeared from the programs of the main establishment parties. From time to time, in the 1970's, the federal Liberal government would mention the term full employment, but by the mid-1970's what they were referring to was an annual average unemployment rate in the 5.5 to 6 per cent range. By the 1980's goals had been replaced by forecasts, and the February 1984 federal budget predicts a 9 per cent average annual unemployment rate between 1985 and 1988.[58] The Progressive Conservatives, in recent years, rarely have spoken about full employment nor have they challenged the Liberals' formulation of what full employment should be. Meanwhile, there has been no shortage of economists to produce excuses for successive governments' failures to bring down the unemployment rate to frictional levels.

A revealing insight into the political pressures that are exerted on economists to justify government's acceptance of high rates of unemployment can be found in an article in the October 20, 1973, issue of *The Financial Post*.

> Ottawa — Any unemployment figure much under 6 per cent probably represents a realistic measure of practical full employment in Canada in the mid-1970's.

---

[58] Canada, Department of Finance, The Hon. Marc Lalonde, Minister of Finance, *The Canadian Economy In Recovery*, February 1984, Table 8, p. 16.

This was a view fast gaining support in senior policy making circles, even before this week's announcement that the jobless rate reached 6 per cent in September as against 5.5 per cent in August.

The backroom advisers argue that for a host of different reasons — from more generous unemployment benefits to a more casual attitude to changing jobs among the young and even the influence of Women's Lib . . . — the measurements that made sense over the last 20 years no longer apply.

And, they warn, if the government keeps desperately trying to get the unemployment figures down to the mystical 4 per cent that seems to have become accepted as full employment — or even lower, it is doomed to keep overheating an already uncomfortably hot economy.

But who is to say this in public?

It probably won't be Finance Minister John Turner. . . .

Perhaps, then Prime Minister Trudeau? Insiders say that once upon a time — to be precise, prior to the last election — he wouldn't have hesitated if his advisers could have made a convincing case of the need to speak out.

. . . .

What the cabinet **hopes** is that someone or some organization with undisputed authority, but at the same time not directly and politically connected to them will do the job. And they had just the organization in mind — the Economic Council of Canada.

Some months ago they asked its chairman, André Raynauld, to undertake a special study of the whole situation, with particular attention to the effects of different work habits, in an era of changing social conditions and attitudes. It was a thinly disguised invitation to revise the previous ECC view that Canada could, and should, do better than 4 per cent in unemployment levels.[59]

In fact, in subsequent years the Economic Council of Canada produced a number of studies that suggested that their previous view of what the level of unemployment at full employment should be was too low.[60] When one observes studies emerging in response to political pressures or producing results that justify political performance, care must be taken in evaluating them. Much good and interesting work may emerge from such exercises, but both the **questions asked** and the **conclusions derived** from these studies may be misleading or

[59] Clive Baxter, "Ottawa talks up acceptance of new jobless rate goal," *The Financial Post*, 20 October 1973, p. 5.
[60] See, for example, Economic Council of Canada, *People and Jobs: A Study of the Canadian Labour Market* (Ottawa: Information Canada, 1976).

wrong. Those who effectively serve the establishment are well rewarded. Economists like other mortals are not without social conscience nor self-interest.

Economists enter political debate by the presentation and evaluation of economic theories that are the basis for economic policies. Economic theories are attempts to explain the way the economy or parts of the economy function. When an economist wants to explain how the economy worked in the past, how it is presently working, or how it can be made to work in the future, the argument usually is made on the basis of an economic theory. The tendency for unemployment rates to rise since the 1950's (see *Table 1-3,* page 29) has been "explained" by the following theories: the appearance of structural unemployment; the inflation-unemployment trade-off; insurance induced unemployment; minimum wage unemployment; and, the natural rate of unemployment. Actual unemployment rates have been consistently above the continuously changing pronouncements by most economists and politicians about what constitutes full employment.

New theories, if they are to be tested, often require new kinds of statistics. In 1972, Statistics Canada began publishing job vacancy statistics.[61] It was hoped that this new data series together with unemployment statistics would provide a better view of how labour markets function and allow some of the new theories to be tested. In 1978, under peculiar circumstances the federal government announced that the collection of job vacancy statistics would be terminated in 1979.

The following sections of this chapter survey and evaluate theories that have been put forward to explain growing unemployment, and comment upon the lessons to be learned from the appearance and subsequent termination of job vacancy statistics.

THE STRUCTURALIST ARGUMENT

Cyclical unemployment — sometimes called deficient demand unemployment — occurs periodically when consumers, enterprises, and governments do not spend enough on goods and services to maintain adequate employment. In the previous chapter, it was indicated that unemployment also could be explained by frictional and structural factors in the economy. Frictional and structural unemployment reflect the fact that it takes time to match jobs to workers.

Frictional unemployment is unemployment that is measured when there are unemployed workers in a given local labour market with the appropriate skills to fill existing job vacancies. It takes time for the enterprises and the workers to find each other.

---

[61] Actual gathering of job vacancy statistics began in 1971 and data are available beginning in that year.

Structural unemployment reflects the fact that there are fundamental changes in the economy that require adjustments that take a considerable amount of time. Old industries are closing and new industries are springing up, new technology is being introduced making old skills obsolete and demanding new skills, some geographic areas are developing and others are contracting. These "structural" changes are always going on, sometimes more rapidly, sometimes more slowly in one sector or another. The unemployment associated with these changes, historically known as **technological** unemployment, was considered to be a contributor to frictional unemployment.

When average annual rates of unemployment began to rise well above the 3 per cent level in the late 1950's and 1960's, the explanation offered for the increases was that in addition to cyclical and frictional unemployment there was a new kind of **structural** unemployment. The essence of the structuralist argument was that **as compared to a previous period** the structure of the economy was changing more rapidly. This more rapid change, it was asserted, increased the minimum level of possible unemployment, that is, the full employment level of unemployment.[62] The Economic Council of Canada, in its 1964 annual report, declared that seasonal, frictional, and structural factors taken together created an irreducible unemployment rate of 3 per cent.[63] A decade later economists were talking about a **natural rate of unemployment** of 6 per cent made up of frictional and structural unemployment.[64]

THE UNEMPLOYMENT-INFLATION TRADE-OFF: THE PHILLIPS CURVE

When unemployment rates began climbing above 4 per cent in the late 1960's, economists provided a new way of looking at the problem of unemployment and a new definition of full employment. In this view unemployment and inflation are related closely so that high unemployment results in low rates of inflation and low unemployment is associated with high rates of inflation. Full employment is said to exist when government has influenced economic activity so as to achieve **acceptable combinations** of both unemployment and inflation. Acceptable to whom? Acceptable to the government.[65]

---

[62] The technical argument was that rapid change in technology, the growth of service industries, and the movement of production opportunities from east to west had not been matched by appropriate worker training and mobility programs. Therefore, enterpreneurs were investing less than they did when such mismatches were less common because the abundance of mismatches created expectations of higher costs of production and therefore lower profits. This lower level of investment slowed down the process of job creation and thereby raised unemployment.

[63] Economic Council of Canada, *First Annual Review, Economic Goals for Canada to 1970, op. cit.*

[64] See, J.A. Sawyer, D.P. Dungan, J.W.L. Winder, *The Ontario Economy 1978-1987* (Toronto: Ontario Economic Council, 1978), p. 20.

[65] This approach is presented in an article by Richard G. Lipsey, "Structural and Deficient — Demand Unemployment Reconsidered," Arthur M. Ross, ed., *Employment, Policy and the Labor Market* (Berkeley: University of California Press, 1965), pp. 210-255. Some formal training in economics is necessary to read this article.

60

The diagramatic apparatus for the argument is presented in *Charts 1-5, 2-5,* and *3-5.*

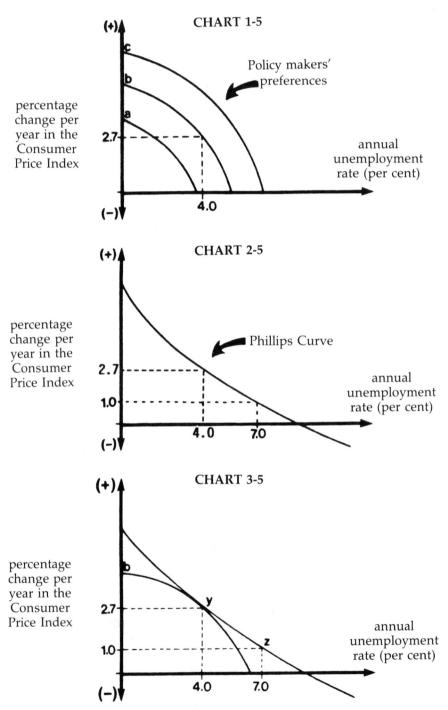

The annual average unemployment rate on the horizontal axis and the annual average percentage **change** in the Consumer Price Index (CPI), which is a measure of inflation, on the vertical axis is shown in *Chart 1-5*. Curves "a", "b", "c", etc., represent combinations of unemployment and inflation. It is argued that each of a possible infinite number of such curves represent **combinations** of unemployment and inflation that are acceptable equally to government policy makers.[66] For **any** combination of unemployment and inflation (for example, a 4 per cent unemployment rate and a 2.7 per cent rate of increase in consumer prices) there are also other **combinations** of unemployment and inflation that are acceptable equally to the policy makers. Each curve in *Chart 1-5*, for example curve "b", joins together these equally acceptable combinations. Of course, policy makers would prefer to be operating on combinations with less unemployment and inflation like "a" than with more unemployment and inflation like "b" or "c".

While *Chart 1-5* shows combinations of unemployment and inflation on each curve about which policy makers are "indifferent" or find equally acceptable, *Chart 2-5* shows **predicted** combinations of unemployment and inflation that will exist in the economy. This curve is called a Phillips Curve.[67] (The reader will note the horizontal and vertical axes of *Chart 2-5* are the same as that of *Chart 1-5*.) It predicts that at high rates of unemployment the rate of increase in consumer prices will be low or even negative and at low rates of unemployment the rate of increase in consumer prices will be higher. For example, a 7 per cent unemployment rate would be associated with a 1 per cent annual average rate of increase in consumer prices, while a 4 per cent unemployment rate would be associated with a 2.7 per cent annual average increase in consumer prices.

Chart 3-5 amalgamates *Charts 1-5* and *2-5*. In this chart point "y", at which the Phillips Curve just touches the curve with the lowest combinations of unemployment and price changes about which government policy makers are "indifferent," defines the "acceptable" level of unemployment and therefore **full employment**. In *Chart 3-5*, this is shown as an annual average unemployment rate of 4 per cent and an annual average percentage change in the Consumer Price Index of 2.7 per cent.

Thus, if the economy was at point "z" in *Chart 3-5* with a 7 per cent annual average unemployment rate and a 1 per cent annual average increase in the Consumer Price Index, government policy would be to stimulate economic activity, moving the economy along the Phillips Curve, until the unemployment was down to 4 per cent. Further stimulation of the economy, which would lower

---

[66] These curves are called "indifference" curves.

[67] This curve, which is supposed to predict the **current** relationship of price changes to levels of unemployment, receives its name from the British economist A.W. Phillips, who investigated the relationship of wage changes to the unemployment rate in England. A.W. Phillips, "The Relationship Between Unemployment and the Rate of Change of Money Wage Rates in the United Kingdom, 1861-1957," *Economica*, 25 November 1958, pp. 283-299.

unemployment, would be unacceptable because it would create undesirable inflation as the economy reached points on the Phillips Curve to the left of point "y".[68] The only policy option open to the government to lower the unemployment rate would be to institute policies that would affect the structure of the economy itself. These policies would shift the Phillips Curve downward to the left, that is, closer to the origin of *Chart 3-5*.

Two basic aspects of the Phillips Curve, or inflation-unemployment trade-off, argument should be noted. First, the determination of the acceptable combination of unemployment and inflation is a political judgement that responds to political pressures. Prime Minister Trudeau was willing to condone national unemployment rates between 6 and 7 per cent prior to the 1972 federal election in order to fight inflation.[69] Indeed on December 22, 1969, he launched a "War Against Inflation" by declaring:

> There are a lot of people in this country who are bargaining that, oh well, the government can't hang tough for too long because it will only get frightened when it sees unemployment go up to six per cent. But if people think we are going to lose our nerve, they should think again. We're not.[70]

However, when the Liberal majority government was returned as a minority government, John Turner, in his first Commons speech as Minister of Finance, committed the government to the pursuit of full employment for Canada:

> My first and most urgent priority is to provide continuing and well-paying jobs for those Canadians seeking work.[71]

Though the government continued to express concern about inflation, its relative importance, as reflected in Mr. Turner's speech, had diminished.[72]

Also, the assumption that there is a stable Phillips Curve that the Canadian economy "moves along" is not substantiated by available evidence. Indeed, in the period 1972-1980, contrary to *Chart 2-5*, inflation and unemployment were **both increasing**.[73]

---

[68] These points would be on indifference curves further from the origin and therefore less desirable.
[69] The average Consumer Price Index rose 4.6 per cent between 1968 and 1969.
[70] Press conference held 22 December 1969. Reported in David Crane, "Keep up inflation fight at any cost, PM warns," *Globe and Mail*, Tuesday, 23 December 1969, p. 1.
[71] John Turner, throne speech debate, *House of Commons debates*, Vol. 1, 24 February 1972, p. 214.
[72] *Ibid*, pp. 214-217.
[73] Some Phillips Curve advocates argue that the curve was "shifting" upward and to the right during this period. However, if the curve shifts about, that is, the curve is unstable, its ability to provide a guide to economic policy is doubtful. Some economists maintain that there are short-run and long-run Phillips Curves for the economy. The short-term curve resembles *Chart 2-5* while the long-run curve is much steeper or even vertical. These economists believe that the long-run Phillips Curve is a determinant of a **natural rate of unemployment**, which is discussed on page 61.

INSURANCE INDUCED UNEMPLOYMENT

When it became obvious that, while there was at best only a small cause-effect relationship between recently experienced unemployment and inflation and that the unemployment-inflation trade-off definition of full employment was dangerous politically, economists inevitably would discover new rationalizations for persistent Canadian unemployment rates above 5 per cent. The core idea of a more recent rationalization is that a significant proportion of measured unemployment does not reflect inadequate unemployment opportunities but rather overly generous unemployment insurance and other social welfare payments.[74] Therefore, if we discount this so-called **insurance induced unemployment**, we are not too far from full employment.

Two economists at Simon Fraser University in British Columbia maintain that "Canada's jobless rate of 6.3 per cent in 1972 would, in the absence of unemployment insurance, have been only about 4.3 per cent."[75] They argue that an important reason for increased unemployment is the result of improvements in Canada's unemployment insurance in 1971, which raised maximum weekly benefits from $50 to $100, permitted receipt of benefits not only upon layoff but also upon "quitting with just cause," and lowered requirements of prior employment before eligibility. Workers' reactions to their claim that it is less costly now to be out of work have been:

> To quit jobs more readily when work, hours, pay or personal job relationships are unsatisfactory.

> To become more selective in the choice of a new job — type and hours of work, pay, type of boss, commuting distance from home, etc.

> To resist retraining expenses and efforts to qualify for new types of jobs.

> The changes in the UIC laws furthermore have no doubt induced some workers to enter the labour force for short times in order to qualify for unemployment insurance benefits for the subsequent period.[76]

A number of comments can be made about this set of rationalizations for increased unemployment. First, no convincing evidence has been produced to substantiate the allegation that an **important part** of unemployment is caused by improvements in either welfare or unemployment insurance payments and

---

[74] For a detailed presentation of this position see, Economic Council of Canada, *People and Jobs: A Study of The Canadian Labour Market, op. cit.,* pp. 148-162.
[75] Herbert G. Grubel, "Cheating or Economic Rationality?" *The Financial Post,* 16 February 1974, p. 6.
[76] *Ibid.*

regulations.[77] Second, unemployed workers' ability to more carefully seek jobs that fit their skills, tastes, and personality should result in lower quit-rates (and incidentally higher productivity) and therefore should lower unemployment rates. Third, just as wage rates, fringe benefits, and conditions of employment for employed workers have improved over the years, it is only natural to expect that benefits for the unemployed and those receiving social welfare payments should improve. However, while wages, fringe benefits, and working conditions of the employed rise continuously as a result of changes that are being made in agreements between enterprises and wage and salary earners, unemployment insurance and social welfare payment changes take place less frequently. Undoubtedly a small fringe of marginal workers can be affected in their labour market behaviour by **either** improvements or deterioration of social insurance benefits relative to the advantage of working. However, it is the average long-run relationship between these two factors, not "one shot" changes, that is relevant.

With more young people and women in the labour force, the number of persons who are in a position to choose between employment and unemployment has grown. The improvement in unemployment insurance in 1971 initially made employment relatively less advantageous for that group, but once again, as wages, fringe benefits, and conditions of work continue to improve, the relative "attractiveness" of unemployment will be diminishing until the next time improvements are made in the unemployment insurance legislation. In fact, changes in the benefit formula and the administration of the granting of benefits have made it more difficult to collect unemployment insurance in recent years.[78]

Those who allege that an increasing part of measured unemployment, over a period of time, results from these **periodic** increases in social welfare payments must demonstrate first that, on average over this period of time, the overall benefits of being employed for those who can choose potentially to be unemployed exceed the **overall** benefits of working for these people. No convincing evidence has been produced to show this.

---

[77] The Economic Council of Canada study *People and Jobs: A Study of the Canadian Labour Market, op. cit.*, pp. 153-158, reviewed the main studies of the effect of the change in the unemployment insurance law and in no case found that the effect explained more than 0.8 percentage points of unemployment. However, none of these studies took account of the effect of increased spending on the level of unemployment because of the increased payments received by claimants. One of the most widely quoted of these studies neglected to take into account the fact that after 1972 unemployment insurance payments were taxable. When this correction was considered, the authors reported: "We originally presented a point estimate of the effect of the 1971 revisions to the unemployment insurance legislation on the unemployment rate of 0.8 percentage points. Equations (1) and (2) herein provide point estimates of this magnitude of 0.5 percentage points and zero respectively. These estimates thus indicate that **if** the average income tax applicable to benefits in 1972 was 20 per cent, the 1971 revisions in the Act had no effect on unemployment rates." Herbert G. Grubel, Denis Maki, Shelly Sax, "Real and insurance induced unemployment in Canada: a reply," *Canadian Journal of Economics*, Vol. VIII, No. 4, November 1975, pp. 603-605.

[78] See, Lars Osberg, "Unemployment Insurance In Canada: A Review of the Recent Amendments," *Canadian Public Policy*, Vol. 2, Spring 1979, pp. 223-235.

UNEMPLOYMENT AND MINIMUM WAGE LAWS

Federal and provincial minimum wage laws and other employment standards legislation protect workers who have little or no bargaining power.[79] Young workers employed by giant fast food chains, workers in industries competing with imports produced in low-wage foreign industries, and many workers employed in small non-union enterprises are protected from exploitation by the existence of minimum wage laws. One study has shown that women "working full-time or part-time in stores, hotels, and small industries are the ones principally affected by provincial minimum wage legislation."[80] It also is clear that immigrant workers and especially women immigrant workers often need the income protection provided by this legislation.[81]

It is estimated that 10 to 15 per cent of the Canadian labour force works for the minimum wage.[82]

Minimum wage rates for enterprises in the federal and provincial jurisdictions as of January 1, 1982, are shown in *Table 1-5*. In this table minimum wage rates

TABLE 1-5

Minimum Wage Rates for Experienced Adult Workers*, January 1, 1982; Average Hourly Earnings in Manufacturing in 1981 and Minimum Wage Rates as a Percentage of Average Hourly Earnings in Manufacturing, for Federal and Provincial Jurisdictions

Jurisdiction	(1) Minimum Wage per Hour January 1, 1982	(2) Average Hourly Earnings in Manufacturing 1981	(3) Minimum Wage as a Percentage of Average Hourly Earnings in Manufacturing
Federal	$3.50	$ 9.17	38.2%
Alberta	3.80	10.49	36.2
British Columbia	3.65	12.19	29.9
Manitoba	3.55	8.04	44.2
New Brunswick	3.35	8.46	39.6
Newfoundland	3.45	8.60	40.1
Nova Scotia	3.30	8.16	40.4
Ontario	3.50	9.13	38.3
Prince Edward Island	3.30	**	**
Quebec	4.00	8.47	47.2
Saskatchewan	4.25	10.12	42.0

*Various jurisdictions have lower rates for younger workers and certain other categories of workers.
**Data is not available.

Sources: Labour Canada, *Labour Standards In Canada, 1982* (Catalogue No. L-2-7/1982E).

Statistics Canada, *Employment, earnings and hours*, Vol. 60, No. 2, Table 18, p. 108, and Table 19, p. 112 (Catalogue No. 72-002).

[79] In addition to minimum wage laws employment standards legislation covers the use of child labour, excessive working hours, and advance notice of layoffs.
[80] Economic Council of Canada, *People and Jobs: A Study of the Canadian Labour Market, op. cit.*, p. 117.
[81] See, Sheila McLeod Arnopoulous, *Problems of Immigrant Women In The Canadian Labour Force* (Ottawa: Canadian Advisory Council on the Status of Women, January 1979).
[82] Economic Council of Canada, *People and Jobs: A Study of the Canadian Labour Market, op. cit.*

66

also are compared with average hourly earnings in manufacturing for each jurisdiction.

Some economists maintain that increases in minimum wage rates are the cause of growing unemployment in Canada and in some provinces. They advocate lowering minimum wages or at least preventing further increases in these rates as a cure for unemployment. Lower minimum wages, they argue, would allow certain producers to hire more labour and still produce at a profit. This argument is thought to be particularly relevant to youth unemployment, which has become an important part of total unemployment.[83]

Another variation of this argument is that minimum wages in Canada are rising faster than they are in the United States, thereby discouraging certain kinds of investment in new production facilities in Canada and also making it more difficult for Canadian producers to compete with their American counterparts.[84]

Most studies of the impact of minimum wage legislation on employment growth in both Canada and the United States reveal either small or no overall effects.[85] This is not to say that increases in the minimum wage may not affect employment in certain enterprises or even industries. But the evidence that minimum wage increases have significantly affected employment is not clear.[86]

Increases in the minimum wage have complex effects on economic activity in both the short and long run. While higher labour costs accompany increased minimum wages for some firms, these firms may be able to pass on the increased costs in higher prices or may have to be satisfied with lower profits. In the long run, these firms may be spurred to invest in more modern or technolog-

---

[83] See, Pierre Fortin and Keith Newton, "Labor Market Tightness and Wage Inflation in Canada" in Martin Neil Baily, ed., *Workers, Jobs and Inflation* (Washington, D.C.: Brookings Institute, 1982), pp. 252-253.

[84] The following are minimum wage rates, in U.S. dollars, in the United States federal jurisdiction and a sample of states in the United States in 1982.

Federal: $3.35	Arkansas:	$2.80	North Carolina:	$3.10
	Minnesota:	$3.35	Rhode Island:	$3.10 to $3.35
	Montana:	$2.50 to $2.75	South Dakota:	$2.30 to $2.80
	New Mexico:	$3.10 to $3.75	West Virginia:	$2.75 to $3.05

Source: United States Department of Labor, Bureau of Labor Statistics, *Monthly Labor Review*, January 1983, pp. 44-56.

[85] See, Robert Swidinsky, "Minimum Wages and Teenage Unemployment," *Canadian Journal of Economics*, Vol. XIII, No. 1, February 1980, p. 159, especially footnotes 2 and 3. In a similar vein see, Robert S. Goldfarb, "The Policy Content of Quantitative Minimum Wage Research" in Industrial Relations Research Association Series, *Proceedings of the 27th Annual Winter Meeting*, December 28-29, 1974, San Francisco, pp. 261-262 and 268. Both papers refer to studies of the effects of changes of minimum wages on teenage employment and claim to find evidence of such an effect for teenagers.

[86] See, Robert Swidinsky, "Minimum Wages and Teenage Unemployment," *op. cit.*, and F. Ray Marshall, Allan M. Cartter, and Allan G. King, *Labour Economics, Wages, Employment, and Trade Unionism*, 3rd edition (Homewood, Illinois: Richard D. Irwin, 1976), pp. 233-240.

ically advanced plants and equipment. An increase in the minimum wage also may increase consumer demand and thereby raise the level of output and employment.

There is no clear-cut theoretical reason why an increased minimum wage should affect employment in one direction or another.

THE NATURAL RATE OF UNEMPLOYMENT

When it became apparent in the 1970's that there was no evidence of a stable Phillips Curve of the type presented in *Chart 2-5* and that insurance induced unemployment and minimum wage caused unemployment provided at best only partial rationalizations for growing unemployment, a new theory that attempts to provide an overall explanation of unemployment took centre stage. The essence of this theory is that changing expectations of inflation make the traditional (now called "short-run") Phillips Curve shift up or down, but underneath all this shifting there is a **natural rate of unemployment** that would exist when all markets in the economy were in equilibrium.[87] In one version of this theory there is a long-run stable vertical Phillips Curve that determines this natural rate of unemployment.

Under these circumstances there is still frictional and structural unemployment that determines the natural rate of employment. Furthermore, this theory asserts that, even when the economy is functioning at the natural rate of unemployment, inflation can be high or low, depending on the population's expectations about what inflation will be in the near future.

Proponents of this complicated theory assert that, in the present period, frictional unemployment is high because of the presence of large numbers of women and young people in labour markets, the existence of unemployment insurance, and high minimum wages. Furthermore, these proponents claim that any attempt by government to bring unemployment below its natural rate will touch off an inflationary spiral. Claims are made that the natural rate of unemployment in Canada is in the 5 to 10 per cent range.[88]

---

[87] Equilibrium in this case means that **all** buyers and sellers of products and factors of production, including labour, are making the best of the situation facing them and there is a non-accelerating rate of inflation. For this reason some economists call the natural rate of unemployment, the non-accelerating inflation rate unemployment (NAIRU).

[88] The 3rd edition of R.G. Lipsey, G.R. Sparks, and P.O. Steiner, *Economics* (New York: Harper & Row, 1979), p. 708, asserts that "because of frictional unemployment the natural rate of unemployment will certainly be positive; it may well be as high as 5 or 6 per cent in Canada." S. Ostry and M. Zaidi, *Labour Economics in Canada*, 3rd edition (Toronto: Macmillan, 1979), p. 274, write: "Some estimate the natural rate of unemployment for Canada as ranging from a little over 7 per cent to close to 10 per cent. Some deny its existence altogether or consider the evidence for its existence as very weak."

68

This theory appeals to conservatives because it implies that government can do little about lowering the "natural" rate of unemployment. It also promotes the idea that individuals' expectations of increasing prices are an important cause of inflation and, therefore, the way to cure inflation is to affect expectations. One way to lower expectations of rising prices is to apply the stiff medicine of a recession and high unemployment until inflationary expectations are broken. If that path is not feasible politically, another solution to inflationary expectations that is advocated is wage-price controls.

The question of the nature, causes, and remedies for inflation are dealt with in Chapter 10. It is argued that expectations are part of the **transmission** mechanism of inflation and cannot be changed unless and until basic **causes** are changed.

JOB VACANCIES

Explanations of the causes of growing Canadian unemployment since the mid-1950's have centred on theories that stress either the unwillingness or inability of the unemployed to seek and find jobs. Implicit in most of these theories is the assumption that the **fundamental problem is not a shortage of job opportunities**.

In 1972, Statistics Canada began to publish data on job vacancies in Canada. Annual job vacancy statistics for all job categories, as well as the ratio of job vacancies to the number of unemployed expressed in percentage terms for Canada from 1971 to 1978, are presented in *Table 2-5*.[89]

Unemployment (of 514,000) and the national unemployment rate (of 5.3 per cent) were at their lowest levels in 1974 for the period 1971-1978. Nevertheless, in this year there were only 101,700 job vacancies for 514,000 unemployed. The job vacancy-unemployment ratio in 1974 was 19.8 per cent. From 1975 to 1978 job vacancies contracted and the number of unemployed increased. (See *Table 2-5*.) In 1978, only 44,500 job vacancies were reported while 911,000 persons were unemployed. The ratio of job vacancies to unemployed was 4.9 per cent. These data give little support to theories that seek to explain growing unemployment by the unwillingness of the unemployed to take available jobs.[90] Obviously, **the main problem is inadequate job opportunities for those who want to work**. The Canadian economics establishment has spent two decades diverting attention from this reality and thereby deflecting political pressure from governments that progressively have abandoned the goal of full employment.

---

[89] For a full explanation of the survey technique and data see, the technical notes in Statistics Canada, *Annual Report On Job Vacancies 1978* (Catalogue No. 71-203).
[90] Job vacancy statistics were discontinued in 1979. The only public explanation given by Statistics Canada for singling out this data series for elimination was that it was part of the federal government's efforts to cut back on government spending. At the time the Canadian Labour Congress and the Confederation of National Trade Unions criticized the discontinuance of these statistics.

TABLE 2-5

Job Vacancies All Categories*,
Unemployment, and Job Vacancies as a Percentage of Unemployment,
Canada, 1971-1978

	Job Vacancies All Categories (thousands)	Unemployment (thousands)	Job Vacancies All Categories / Unemployment (per cent) x 100
1971	37.4	535	7.0
1972	66.2	553	12.0
1973	85.8	515	16.7
1974	101.7	514	19.8
1975	63.3	690	9.2
1976	51.4	727	7.4
1977	44.4	850	5.2
1978	44.5	911	4.9

*Categories include full-time, casual, part-time, seasonal, and temporary jobs.

Sources: Statistics Canada, *Annual Report On Job Vacancies 1978*, p. 8 (Catalogue No. 71-203), and Statistics Canada, *The Labour Force* (Catalogue No. 71-001, monthly).

CHAPTER 6

EMPLOYMENT AND ECONOMIC GROWTH

T he achievement and maintenance of full employment and improvements in the nation's standard of living require **adequate economic growth**. The relationship between employment and economic growth as well as concepts and measures of economic growth are examined here.

GROWTH OF THE LABOUR FORCE

In the 1970's the Canadian labour force grew at an average annual rate of 3.2 per cent. For the period 1984-1988 the predicted rate of growth of the labour force is 1.9 per cent.[91] The exact amount of growth will be determined by:

1. the size of natural increases in the potential labour force as determined by birth and death rates;
2. net migration of persons of working age; and,
3. labour force participation rates.

During the 1970's, about two-thirds of the average annual increase in the labour force was due to growth in the potential labour force, while the remaining one-third was due to increased labour force participation rates. The rapid increase in the size of the potential labour force was due mainly to the post-World War II

---

[91] Canada, Department of Finance, The Hon. Marc Lalonde, Minister of Finance, *The Canadian Economy In Recovery, op. cit.*, p. 12.

"baby-boom" generation reaching working age. Lower labour force growth in the 1980's is expected because of a much slower growth rate of the potential labour force, which will more than offset expected increases in the labour force participation rate of women 25 years of age and over.[92]

In each of the coming years, purchases of goods and services by consumers, business, and government (economists call this **aggregate demand**) must expand sufficiently to provide employment for the growing labour force.[93] If output of goods and services, and thus employment, does not grow **at least** as fast as the labour force, the unemployment rate is expected to rise above present levels.[94]

But, even if output increases at the same rate as the labour force grows, will the unemployment rate remain the same? The answer is, most likely, no. Let us examine why.

INCREASED PRODUCTIVITY

The average Canadian worker's productivity — the amount of output of goods and services produced per hour of work — is rising. The increased productivity comes from workers whose skill, education, and physical well-being is improving as well as from the fact that on average Canadian workers have more and better equipment to work with each year. However, this increase varies from period to period. When the economy is approaching full employment, productivity and productivity increases are higher than when the economy is functioning with high unemployment, excess overhead personnel, and idle plant and machinery.[95]

From 1954 to 1974 — a period of general economic expansion — output per hour worked in all commercial industries increased at an average annual rate of about 3.3 per cent per year.[96] Slow economic growth since 1975 brought down the average annual productivity growth in these industries to 1.3 per cent per year in the period 1975-1981. If we assume that in the coming years each employed worker will be able to produce on average 2 per cent more output per hour worked, purchases of goods and services (that is aggregate demand) must rise on

---

[92] *Ibid.*, p. 14.

[93] Unless otherwise specified, the expression "goods and services" means consumer goods and services and capital goods. Capital goods result from investment in machinery, plant, and inventories as well as residential construction.

[94] This discussion assumes average hours of work per employee remain constant.

[95] Managerial, sales, and certain skilled personnel may be maintained in employment even when there is inadequate work to keep them fully occupied. In this sense they can be described as overhead personnel. Enterprises have such policies in order to promote the loyalty of these employees and to prevent them from permanently transferring to other enterprises.

[96] Output per hour worked (output per person-hour) is different than output per employed person. Output per employed person has increased less in recent years than output per hour worked because of the growing number of persons who are employed part-time. For a discussion of Canadian productivity measures and data on productivity during this period see, Sidney H. Ingerman and Ruth Rose-Lizée, "The Estimate of Productivity Growth in Canada's Prices and Incomes Policy," *Industrial Relations*, Vol. 32, No. 1, 1977, pp. 127-132.

average by at least 2 per cent a year, or fewer workers will be needed to produce each year's output if average hours worked remain the same.

To recapitulate: If output per worker is rising, previous levels of output can be produced with fewer men and women at work. Additional output must be demanded and produced if the present employment level is to be maintained.

THE PREVENTION OF INCREASED UNEMPLOYMENT

If the labour force is growing on average at about 1.9 per cent per year and output per worker is increasing at about 2 per cent per year, purchases of goods and services must increase by roughly 3.9 per cent (1.9 per cent plus 2 per cent) per year just to maintain the existing ratio of employed to the labour force, that is, if the unemployment rate is to be no higher than it has been.

If one starts from full employment, a 3.9 per cent growth rate of purchases of goods and services will maintain it more or less. However, if one begins with unemployment at over the full employment level, the growth rate of output must be **higher than** 3.9 per cent if full employment is to be achieved.[97]

The benchmark for **adequate** economic growth in Canada in the current period is an average annual growth rate in excess of 3.9 per cent, that is, economic growth that is sufficient to reduce unemployment and ultimately to achieve full employment. But how is economic growth measured?

THE MEASUREMENT OF ECONOMIC GROWTH

A satisfactory estimate of economic growth requires a measurement of the total production of a country for successive years. Total production is estimated by Statistics Canada in the *National Income and Expenditure Accounts*. In this estimate, any process that creates **value** or **adds value** to already existing goods is production. Thus, **transformation** of raw materials into finished goods as well as the **transportation** of these goods from the factory to the market where they can be sold creates value and constitutes production. The **distribution** of these goods through wholesale and retail trade to the consumer makes them accessible and therefore creates value. The **services** provided by teachers, lawyers, advertising people, physicians, and exotic dancers are considered to create value by Canadian government accountants (because people voluntarily pay for them) and are therefore part of the national product.

---

[97] In the 1st edition of this book the growth rate of purchases of goods and services necessary to maintain existing rates of unemployment was set at 5 per cent. This was because at that time labour force growth and productivity growth were expected to grow at average annual rates of 2 per cent and 3 per cent respectively. It is important to note that both of these variables are in part determined by how fast the economy is and is expected to grow.

The **value** of a given amount of output is equal to the sum of the **quantity** of each good or service produced, multiplied by its **price**.

The use of **value** to estimate production allows us to add together different goods and services and to compare different groups of such goods and services. For example, comparison of the total output of two countries, or the output of one country in different years, is not possible by comparing physical quantities of output. Such comparisons are possible if total value comparisons are made.

The measurement of Canadian output takes account of certain goods and services that are **not** bought at a price in regular markets, but are nevertheless considered part of total output. These goods and services include (but are not limited to) food and fuel produced and consumed on the farm and services of owner-occupied dwellings. The value of these so-called "imputed" items are estimated and added to total output.

GNP EQUALS GNE

Gross National Product (GNP) and Gross National Expenditure (GNE) are estimates of total output during a given year.

In the Canadian National Accounts, the method that adds up all **incomes** (wages, salaries, interest, rent, and profit) generated through production in a given year is called **Gross National Product** — GNP. The method that adds up the value of all **final products** produced and **subtracts the value of imports** is called **Gross National Expenditure** — GNE. The two totals are equal by definition because every dollar's worth of **final** product (which includes both sold and unsold production) yields a dollar's worth of income (including profits) to someone in the course of production, distribution, and sales.

The GNE for a particular year is estimated by adding together:

1. personal expenditures on consumer goods and services (C);
2. expenditures on business and government gross fixed capital formation (machinery, equipment, residential and non-residential construction) and the value of the physical change in business inventories (I);[98]
3. government expenditures on consumer goods and services (G); and,
4. spending on goods and services produced in Canada by purchasers in foreign countries (exports), minus expenditures by Canadians on goods and services produced abroad (imports). Exports minus imports, or net exports, can be abbreviated as (En).

---

[98] All expenditures on machinery, equipment, and buildings are included in investment. In addition, enterprises may produce output in a given year that is not sold and becomes part of inventory. The net addition to or subtraction from the inventory that existed at the end of the previous year is considered as investment in the current year.

Thus, the sum of consumption expenditures, investment expenditures, government expenditures, and the difference between export and import expenditures is defined as, or is identical to, Gross National Expenditure:

$$GNE \equiv C + I + G + En.$$

For actual values for each of these annual expenditure elements in 1982, see *Table 1-6*. Note that all figures are in **current dollars**, reflecting prices that existed in 1982.

GNE equals GNP. This can be observed by comparing *Table 1-6* and *Table 2-6*.

TABLE 1-6

1982 Gross National Expenditure, Canada
(in millions of current dollars)

Consumption Expenditures		205,952
Investment Expenditures		
Business		
Gross Fixed Capital Formation	53,039	
Inventory Change	−8,692	
Government		
Gross Fixed Capital Formation	10,620	
Housing	12,734	
		67,701
Government Expenditures on Goods and Services		75,748
Exports − Imports (100,395 − 99,150)		1,245
Residual Error of Estimate*		−1,721
Gross National Expenditure		348,925

*The statistical estimate of GNE and GNP for a given year always differs somewhat because of measurement problems. In the system of national accounts GNE is made to exactly equal GNP by dividing the measured difference between the two estimates by two (2) yielding a quantity called the **Residual Error of the Estimate**, and adding this quantity to the lower number and subtracting it from the higher number.

Source: Canada, Department of Finance, *Economic Review April 1983*, Reference Table 3, p. 122 (Catalogue No. F1-21/1983E).

TABLE 2-6

1982 Gross National Product, Canada
(in millions of current dollars)

Wages, salaries, and supplementary labour income	201,736
+	
Corporation profits before taxes	21,777
+	
Deduct: dividends paid to non-residents	− 3,356
+	
Interest and miscellaneous investment income	29,704
+	
Accrued net income of farm operators from farm production	4,646
+	
Net income of non-farm unincorporated business including rents	14,031
+	
Inventory valuation adjustment	− 3,784
=	
Net national income at factor cost	264,754
+	
Indirect taxes less subsidies	40,588
+	
Capital consumption allowances	41,862
+	
Residual error of estimate	1,721
=	
Gross National Product	348,925

Source: Canada, Department of Finance, *Economic Review April 1983*, Reference Table 9, p. 132 (Catalogue No. F1-21/1983E).

THE CALCULATION OF
CONSTANT DOLLAR VALUES OF GNE

To compare total **physical** output of one year with another, the effect of changing prices on the estimate of output must be eliminated. For example, imagine physical production is identical in two successive years, but prices rise considerably from the first to the second year. Under these conditions, GNE will be higher in the second year, even though we know physical output has not changed. Therefore, a measure of output is needed in which prices are held constant (for computational purposes) so that changes in quantities can be used as a guide to change in total output. For this reason, government statisticians produce **constant dollar** GNP, GNE, and other statistical series using base year prices of certain years. Appendix A of this chapter presents a simplified example of a conversion from a current to a constant dollar estimate of GNE.

Constant dollar GNP and GNE statistics (as well as other economic statistics such as the Consumer Price Index) are recalculated periodically and published on a more current base year. This is necessary because, as time passes, products enter into national output that did not exist when earlier estimates of output were made and products become more or less popular, which affects their relative price and therefore the accuracy of the previously used base year prices.

To construct an economic data series from data in tables with different base years, **splicing** is necessary. Appendix B of this chapter demonstrates such a procedure.

THREE MEASURES OF ECONOMIC GROWTH

A number of different approaches to the statistical description of economic growth exist. The following are among the most important.

1. Change in the constant dollar GNE is a measure of the growth of a nation's overall production.
2. Change in constant dollar GNE **per capita**, that is, GNE divided by population in each year, provides an indication of the potential for change in the standard of living of individuals.
3. Changes in constant dollar GNE per hour worked, per employed person, or per member of the labour force give an indication of trends in national productivity.

Canadian GNE and GNE per capita (in constant 1971 dollars) for selected years from 1950 to 1982 are presented in *Table 3-6*. The non-availability of total person-hour data for the entire Canadian economy does not permit a computation of real GNE per person-hour, and comparisons of data for real GNE per **employed person** over the last 20 years are not an accurate measure of national productivity because of the growing number of persons employed at part-time jobs.

TABLE 3-6

GNE and GNE Per Capita for Canada, Selected Years 1950 to 1982
(in constant 1971 dollars)

Year	1950	1955	1960	1965	1970	1975	1980	1982
Real GNE (billions of constant dollars)	33.8	43.9	52.2	70.0	88.4	113.0	130.5	128.1
Real GNE per capita (thousands of constant dollars)	2.47	2.80	2.92	3.56	4.15	4.98	5.42	5.21

Source: Canada, Department of Finance, *Economic Review April 1983*, pp. 119 and 124 (Catalogue No. F1-21/1983E).

ECONOMIC GROWTH AND THE DISTRIBUTION OF INCOME

The use of GNE and GNP statistics to measure national output, well-being, productivity, and economic growth does not take account of the **distribution** of income and therefore output among the population. Nor does it take account of the relationship between the distribution of income and the level of output. This is the result of the ingrained belief among most contemporary economists that it is possible to determine first how much is to be produced and then to consider how this output is distributed.

Two erroneous ideas underlie the separation of the determination of national output from the nature of income distribution. The first idea is that economists can only give "technical" advice on methods of achieving various levels of national output and that value judgements that are made through the political process should determine who gets more or less in terms of wages, profits, interest, dividends, and rent. The second idea is that, to the degree that incomes are made more equal, output will grow more slowly.

The first idea is wrong because the well-being and incentives of the persons engaged in organizing and carrying out production obviously will affect the amount of production.[99] The second idea is contradicted by observed experiences. For example, over 40 years of social reform and movement towards greater income equality in Sweden has resulted in remarkable advances in total production and one of the highest standards of living in the world. Turning to countries that more recently have adopted fairly radical income distribution schemes under socialist governments of one form or the other, there is no evidence that their economic performance has deteriorated. Indeed, a number of these countries including China, North Korea, East Germany, and Romania seem to have had remarkably high growth rates relative to countries in similar stages of economic development.

A thesis propounded by the world famous Swedish economist and Nobel prize winner Gunnar Myrdal is that wisely planned social reforms resulting in a more egalitarian distribution of income in both developed and underdeveloped countries "can have the character of 'investments', leading not only to greater 'justice', but also to higher production. Such 'investments' often require considerable time before maturing in the shape of returns, but should not for this reason be forgotten more than other long-term investment."[100]

THE UNDERGROUND ECONOMY

A certain amount of production and income result from activities that are not recorded in the National Income Accounts and therefore are not included in

---

[99] The relationship between income distribution and output is discussed in Chapter 9.
[100] Gunnar Myrdal, *Against the Stream, Critical Essays on Economics* (New York: Pantheon Books, 1972), pp. 192-193.

measures of national output. These activities take place under conditions where tax and social insurance responsibilities are avoided and work typically is performed at below prevailing wage rates. These activities are illegal and therefore are said to take place in the underground economy.

ECONOMIC GROWTH, GNP, AND THE QUALITY OF LIFE

Many social scientists have become skeptical of measures of economic growth based on GNP.[101] An article by Sylvia Ostry in the *Montreal Star* indicates two ways in which revisions of estimates of economic growth are possible.

New Indicators

by Sylvia Ostry

The notion that Gross National Product provides a questionable or misleading measure of economic performance has an ancient lineage in economic doctrine. It has a strain deriving from Marxism, another from the neoclassical school which led to modern welfare economics and another from contemporary economics and statistics of national accounting. What is new about the present attack on economic growth is its intensity, its growing popularization and the direction of its thrust. The GNP has become a household term . . . but at the same time it is used almost as a term of opprobrium.

Galbraith, in *The Affluent Society* (not a book favoured by academics), pointed to what was to become a familiar litany: the distinction between the quantity of output and the quality of life. He first brought to the attention of a large and diverse audience the question "does bigger mean better?"

The popular thrust of "anti-growthmanship" is not likely to abate soon. By and large it has been stimulated by problems of environmental pollution, though it is not confined to that issue.

But GNP is still the best indicator of economic activity available.

But even its most ardent defenders are troubled by the increasingly glaring paradoxes which emerge when it is used to estimate levels of, and changes in, economic and social well-being. For example, air pollution doesn't enter the accounts as a cost or negative item but air pollution equipment is dutifully registered as a plus. Littered parks require more park attendants and equipment: up goes GNP.

More crime involves more policemen and police cars: GNP solemnly records an increase. Mr. X buys a bottle of liquor a day and GNP rises

---

[101] *Ibid.*, pp. 184-196.

and rises again as hospital space for the treatment of alcoholics is expanded. The knowledge invested in human beings is one of the most important elements in real growth: it is not directly recorded in the accounts.

These and other worrisome examples have led to two important developments. One involves a careful and painstaking attempt to revise the concepts of economic accounting to deal with some of the deficiencies in the present measure. This work is proceeding now in a number of countries and in a number of international agencies. It will not be accomplished quickly but, when completed, will certainly reveal a very different picture of the economy than that which we presently hold.

The other development stems only in part from dissatisfaction with the GNP, and will not be satisfied by an improved measure of economic activity. This is the movement to develop what have been called "social indicators", direct measures of social welfare or distress such as indexes of mental and physical health; social mobility; public order and safety; the quality of the environment; participation and alienation, etc.

The social indicator idea developed first in the U.S. but in the past couple of years has caught fire in many countries in Europe and in Japan.

The social indicator movement reflects the same kind of concern which provokes questions about equating affluence with "the good life" — quantity with quality. Much of the work produced thus far is primitive and disappointing; hardly surprising when one considers the magnitude of the task and the infancy of the movement.

Social indicators will, their proponents claim, enable us to take stock of our social condition and, hopefully, "forsee and forestall incipient social crises." We cannot act if we do not know. Knowledge, however, does not ensure action. Social data are also required for another reason: to meet the principle of accountablility by governments — to allow the public to evaluate the results of government actions.

The author of the U.S. Government's document "Towards A Social Report", one of the earliest publications in this area, sums it up very well; "For a social report we need information about the condition of our society; about how much children have learned, not about the time and money used for schooling; about health, not about the number of licensed doctors; about crime, not about the number of policemen; about pollution, not about the agencies that deal with it."[102]

---

[102] *Montreal Star*, 16 June 1971, p. 71.

Appendix A

CURRENT AND CONSTANT DOLLAR ESTIMATES OF GNE

Assume there is an economy with only two products: apples and oranges.

LET:
Pa_1 = price per apple in year 1 = \$.05
Pa_2 = price per apple in year 2 = \$.05
Qa_1 = quantity of apples sold in year 1 = 3
Qa_2 = quantity of apples sold in year 2 = 2
Po_1 = price per orange in year 1 = \$.10
Po_2 = price per orange in year 2 = \$.07
Qo_1 = quantity of oranges sold in year 1 = 4
Qo_2 = quantity of oranges sold in year 2 = 5
V_1 = value of oranges + apples in year 1 = GNE 1
V_2 = value of oranges + apples in year 2 = GNE 2

	Apples	Oranges		GNE in Current \$'s
YEAR 1:	$Pa_1 \times Qa_1$	$+ \; Po_1 \times Qo_1 = V_1$		$= GNE_1$
	\$.05 × 3	+ \$.10 × 4	= \$.15 + \$.40	= \$.55
YEAR 2:	$Pa_2 \times Qa_2$	$+ \; Po_2 \times Qo_2 = V_2$		$= GNE_2$
	\$.05 × 2	+ \$.07 × 5	= \$.10 + \$.35	= \$.45

If we compute the percentage change in **current dollar** GNE, we find:

$$\frac{GNE_2 - GNE_1}{GNE_1} \times 100 = \frac{\$.45 - \$.55}{\$.55} \times 100 = \frac{-\$.10}{\$.55} \times 100 = -18.2\%$$

That is, GNE measured in current dollars fell 18.2 per cent. But was this because of price changes (the price of oranges fell from \$.10 to \$.07 apiece) or quantity changes?

We now compute the change in GNE holding prices constant at year 1 levels.

	Apples	Oranges		GNE in Year 1 \$'s
YEAR 1:	$Pa_1 \times Qa_1$	$+ \; Po_1 \times Qo_1 = V_1$		$= GNE_1$
	\$.05 × 3	+ \$.10 × 4	= \$.15 + \$.40	= \$.55

YEAR 2: $\text{Pa}_1 \times \text{Qa}_2 + \text{Po}_1 \times \text{Qo}_2 = V_2 \qquad\qquad = \text{GNE}_2$
$\qquad\qquad \$.05 \times 2 \ + \$.10 \times 5 \ = \$.10 + \$.50 = \$.60$

If we now compute the percentage change in **constant** year 1 dollars or **real** GNE, we find:

$$\frac{\text{GNE}_2 - \text{GNE}_1}{\text{GNE}_1} \times 100 = \frac{\$.60 - \$.55}{\$.55} \times 100 = \frac{\$.05}{\$.55} \times 100 = \quad 9\%$$

The real output or constant dollar GNE increased by 9 per cent.

Appendix B

SPLICING GNE ESTIMATES

Assume you have available constant dollar GNE on a 1957 base extending to 1967, and on a 1971 base from 1967 to 1977, and you want a real output series on the **1971 base** extending from 1965 to 1977. Here is a simple way to do this.

In 1967, the GNE is estimated at $49 billion on the 1957 base and $77.3 billion on the 1971 base. Obviously, physical GNE is the same in 1967 regardless of the base used to estimate it. Therefore, the estimate of 1967 GNE in 1971 constant dollars is

$$\frac{1967 \text{ GNE in 1971 constant dollars } = \$77.3 \text{ b}}{1967 \text{ GNE in 1957 constant dollars } = \$49.0 \text{ b}} = 1.58$$

larger than the estimate of 1967 GNE in 1957 dollars. To estimate 1966 and 1965 GNE in 1971 constant dollars, you multiply

$$1.58 \times \$47.7 \text{ b (1966 GNE on 1957 base)} = \$75.37 \text{ b.}$$
$$1.58 \times \$44.8 \text{ b (1965 GNE on 1957 base)} = \$70.78 \text{ b.}$$

These values can then replace the question marks in *Table 4-6* for the 1966 and 1965 GNE in 1971 constant dollars.

TABLE 4-6

Year	GNE in billions of 1957 constant dollars	GNE in billions of 1971 constant dollars
1965	44.8	?
1966	47.7	?
1967	49.0	77.3
1968		81.9
1969		86.2
1970		88.4
1971		94.5
1972		100.2
1973		107.8
1974		111.7
1975		113.1
1976		119.4
1977		122.6

CHAPTER 7

EMPLOYMENT THEORY AND POLICY I

e are concerned with the problem of making real output, as measured by GNE in constant dollars, grow rapidly enough to allow the economy to approach full employment. Each year a given amount of real output is produced. This output is measured after the year is over. Thus, as discussed in Chapter 6:

$$GNP \equiv GNE \equiv C + I + G + En.$$

The sum of personal consumption expenditures on goods and services (C), expenditures on gross fixed capital formation and the physical change in inventories (I), plus government expenditures on consumer goods and services (G), plus exports minus imports (En), is a measure of what total output **has been**. The question is, how can the amount of these expenditure streams be increased in the coming year in order to increase output and employment? Another way of saying the same thing is, how can **aggregate demand** be increased where aggregate demand is the sum of **expected** expenditures resulting from consumption, investment, government spending, and net exports?

It is important to stress that in measuring GNP and GNE one looks back at what happened in a previous year. However, in developing a theory of aggregate demand, the economist asks what will determine the demand for output in the period to come. More specifically, the economist is interested in changes in each of the four expenditure streams and therefore in the change in aggregate demand. The theory of aggregate demand usually is expressed by the formula

$$Y_D = C + I_g + G + En$$

where:

Y_D = aggregate demand;
C = consumer demand;
I_g = gross investment demand;
G = government demand for consumer goods and services; and,
En = net export demand.

For the moment, let us consider an economy without foreign trade and post-pone a discussion of net exports until Chapter 11.

CONSUMPTION DEMAND

Consumption demand is determined by the level of income received in the aggregate by persons. The higher the level of the national income, the greater the amount people will want to consume, assuming that credit availability to consumers, tax structures, expectations about future employment, income and prices, and income and wealth distribution remain unchanged.

However, not all the national income is consumed at any moment; part of it is saved. If national income should rise, only a part of each additional dollar received (the marginal propensity to consume) would be used for additional purchases of consumption goods.

If the government wants to increase consumption spending **per dollar of income received** next year compared to this year, it might make consumer credit cheaper and easier to get, or it might institute income tax cuts on personal income so that individuals will be able to spend more on goods and services.

Individuals' expectations about the future also will influence their spending habits. For example, if people came to believe a major depression was likely next year, it surely would affect their present consumption activity.

The distribution of income and wealth normally does not change much from year to year, but to the degree it does shift from rich to poor we can expect consumer demand in general to increase because the poor spend a larger per-centage of their income on consumption than do the rich. (Their marginal pro-pensity to consume is higher.) For example, if the government instituted a guaranteed annual income plan, this might affect income distribution and con-sumption demand.[103]

---

[103] A detailed discussion of guaranteed income plans can be found in, John Munro, Minister of National Health and Welfare, *Income Security of Canadians* (Ottawa: Queen's Printer, 1970).

In 1982, personal expenditures on consumer goods and services in Canada was $205,952,000,000. These purchases constituted 59 per cent of the $348,925,000,000 Gross National Expenditure.[104]

INVESTMENT DEMAND

When economists talk about investment they are not talking about trading in stocks and bonds, nor are they referring to the purchase and sale of already existing properties. These are all financial transactions (sometimes called financial investment), which are basically exchanges of assets. For example, when individuals buy Canadian Pacific Limited stock they exchange one claim on assets — paper money — for another claim on assets — a piece of paper that represents a claim on Canadian Pacific Limited's assets. Clearly, nothing new is created by this transaction.

However, if Canadian Pacific Limited builds new plants, machinery, or other equipment or increases its inventory holdings, something has been created by existing labour and machinery that will contribute to production in future periods. For economists, **this** is investment.

It may be the case that Canadian Pacific Limited will float a new stock issue to **finance** this investment, but the issue of the stock and its purchase is **not** investment.

The most important factor determining business investment is the **expectation of satisfactory future profits**. (What is "satisfactory" is a complicated question which cannot be dealt with here.) All factors — political, sociological as well as economic — that influence expectations will influence current investment decisions. Among the most important government policies that are used to influence investment are monetary policy, depreciation allowance policy, and tax and subsidy policies. The availability of finance to enterprises also plays a role in determining the level of investment during particular periods.

INTEREST RATES AND MONETARY POLICY

One important cost of investment is the **interest cost** of credit (borrowing money). If interest rates are high (other things remaining the same — which they seldom do), the cost of a particular investment will be raised and the expected rate of profit will be lower than if interest rates were lower. Therefore, at higher interest rates, certain investments that would be attractive at lower interest rates do not take place because the higher cost of financing the investment is associated with a lower **expected** rate of profit.

---

[104] See, *Table 1-6*, p. 74.

86

Short-run **fluctuations** in interest rates are influenced by the supply of money in the economy. If there is a surplus of money in the economy relative to current needs, chartered banks will find that they have higher reserves than legally are necessary, and interest rates will tend to be bid down as banks seek to loan out the money rather than have it remain idle. If money is scarce, banks will find their reserves tending to approach their legal minimums, and they will be inclined to raise interest rates.

Government **monetary policy**, which is implemented by the Bank of Canada, seeks to regulate interest rates, and thereby regulate investment demand[105] by manipulation of the money supply.

To recapitulate: The money supply influences short-run fluctuations in the interest rate, which in turn influences the rate of investment.[106]

The Bank of Canada uses two main policy instruments to regulate the money supply:

(a) the buying and selling of government securities, called **open market policy**; and

(b) manipulation of the interest rate charged by the Bank of Canada to chartered banks when chartered banks make short-term loans from the Bank of Canada. This interest rate charged by the Bank of Canada to chartered banks is called **the bank rate**.

Open market policy works this way: if the government wants to increase the money supply, it buys outstanding government securities from institutions and individuals that hold them. In doing this, the Bank of Canada lays claim to pieces of paper (the securities) and replaces them with money in the hands of previous security holders. Thus, the purchase by the Bank of Canada of outstanding securities increases the overall money supply.

When the government sells its securities so that more are outstanding than previously, it gives people pieces of paper (the securities) and takes their money in return. In this way the money supply is reduced.[107]

Changes in the bank rate make loans from the Bank of Canada more or less expensive to the chartered banks because of the higher or lower interest costs to those banks that need loans from the Bank of Canada, and thus tend to raise or

---

[105] International short-term capital flows also are affected by interest rates. See Chapter 11.

[106] There is a great deal of debate among modern economists about this theory. Two basic questions are at issue. The first is whether the money supply has much influence on interest rates, and the second is whether fluctuations in short-run interest rates have much influence on investment. Students who go on to more advanced training in economics and teachers should see, Victoria Chick, *The Theory of Monetary Policy* (London: Gray-Mills, 1973).

[107] The fact that the government is in the market buying its own securities will tend to raise the price of these securities, thereby creating a situation where there are persons willing to sell their securities. When the government is selling its securities, it tends to lower prices of the securities, thereby making them attractive to additional buyers.

lower interest charges that the chartered banks demand from their borrowers. This means that fewer or more loans are made and less or more money is available for investment and consumer credit.[108] When changes in the bank rate are sufficient to affect the interest rate charged by the chartered banks, the chartered banks will indicate they are changing their interest rates by announcing changes in their **prime rate** of interest. The prime rate of interest is the rate of interest a chartered bank charges to its best customers — usually large successful corporations. Interest rates charged to other borrowers also are likely to be changed when the prime rate changes.

In many cases, changes in the bank rate have little or no effect on chartered banks because they do not need to borrow from the Bank of Canada. However, changes in the bank rate are taken as a signal that the Bank of Canada believes interest rates need adjustments.

DEPRECIATION ALLOWANCE POLICY

A depreciation expense represents an estimate of the portion of the total value of an investment that is used up each year in producing products and/or services. It provides a stream of available funds to the enterprise over the expected useful life of the investment equal to the original cost of the investment.[109]

The government can use its administrative power to regulate the length of time (the expected useful life) over which particular kinds of investment can be depreciated as an instrument of aggregate demand policy.

Lengthening or shortening the period during which firms can write off investments as a depreciation expense decreases or increases production costs as recorded in the firms' accounts and thereby the portion of total revenue that must be paid in taxes to the government over specified periods of time.[110]

If, at a given level of output and revenue, depreciation **expense** is larger (even though actual depreciation has not changed), the recorded profits before tax are

---

[108] In addition to using open market policy and manipulating the bank rate, the Bank of Canada can influence the supply of money by changing the banks' **required cash reserves**. Under the *Bank Act* each chartered bank must hold a certain amount of cash reserves. The minimum cash reserve requirements for the period March 1984 to August 1984 are 10¼ per cent of reservable Canadian dollar demand deposits, 2 per cent of reservable Canadian dollar notice deposits plus 1¼ per cent of reservable Canadian dollar notice deposits in excess of $500 million, and 3 per cent of Canadian residents' foreign currency deposits in branches and offices in Canada. Changes in these ratios are rarely used as an instrument of monetary policy.

[109] A similar principle applies to depletion allowances and amortization allowances. Depletion allowances are estimates of the value of natural resources that are used up, e.g., oil, coal, timber, metals, etc. Amortization allowances arise from the writing-off to expenses of assets such as copyrights, leases, etc.

[110] The period that the government allows to write off an investment may differ markedly from the useful economic life of the investment. For example, the government may allow 10 years to write off a machine, but technological change may make it obsolete in three years. On the other hand, a machine that can be written off in 10 years may still be in operation after 15 years.

smaller and therefore corporate taxes on profits are lower. The result is that firms' **cash flow**, that is, net profits plus depreciation allowances, rise. Thus, changing the period over which firms can write off investments influences the flow of funds **available** for investment.

An example using a hypothetical company will help to show how this works.

1. Profits per year (P) = Revenue per year (R) − Costs per year (C)

OR

$$P = R - C$$

2. Depreciation is a cost.

3. Assume: R = $5.0 million
   C = $3.0 million of which
      $0.5 million is the "normal" depreciation expense.

4. Then P = $5.0 million − $3.0 million = $2.0 million profits, before tax.

CASE No. 1

5. Assume there is a 50 per cent corporate profits tax. Then:
   (a) profits after tax = profits
      before tax − 50 per cent
      of profits before tax =
      $2.0 million − (.50 × $2.0 million)   = $1.0 million.
   (b) From (3) above there is depreciation   = $0.5 million.
   (c) Therefore, there is a cash flow of (a) + (b)   = $1.5 million.

CASE No. 2

Now assume that everything else remains the same as before, but the government regulation governing the "useful life" of investments **raises** the annual depreciation by **lowering** the "useful life" of investments for purposes of calculating depreciation expenses.

6. Assume that the government allows $1 million in depreciation expenses as compared to the $0.5 million in Case No. 1. This raises the costs recorded on the companies' books from $3 million in Case No. 1 to $3.5 million. Before tax, profits are now equal to P = R − C.

   Therefore,
   P = $5 million − $3.5 million = $1.5 million.

7. We continue to assume that there is a 50 per cent corporate profits tax. Then:
   (a) profits after tax = profits before
   tax − 50 per cent of profits before
   tax = $1.5 million − (.50 × $1.5 million) = $0.75 million.

   (b) Depreciation   = $1.0   million.

   (c) Therefore, the cash flow of (a) + (b)   = $1.75 million.

Thus, with the same level of output, revenue, and costs for labour and materials used in production, the company finds itself with $0.25 million more in cash flow available to it as a result of government changes in depreciation regulations in Case No. 2 compared to Case No. 1. These funds may be invested or they may be disbursed in any way the firm sees fit.

If, as a result of changes in depreciation regulations, firms depreciate capital more quickly, in later years the depreciation part of total costs will be lower than it would have been if accelerated depreciation had not taken place, and therefore profits and corporate tax payments to the government will be higher while cash flow will be lower. Nevertheless, firms have had the **extra cash flow** of money in preceeding years as an interest-free loan from the government.

If government policy allows **existing** machinery, plant, and equipment to be written off more quickly, it is doing this because it **believes** that the increased cash flow will give companies incentives to invest. However, the government can limit fast write-off provisions exclusively to newly-purchased plant, machinery, and equipment, thus requiring **actual** investment before firms receive the tax benefits. This may provide incentives to invest for some companies that were unsure about the profitability of potential investment projects. However, companies that were going to invest anyway will receive an unexpected gain.[111]

Trade unionists dealing with firms that receive these fast write-offs should not be deceived by changes in the companies' profits. In Case No. 1, the profit after tax is $1 million, but after the change in the depreciation regulation shown in Case No. 2, the profit after taxes has fallen to $0.75 million.

Claims by these companies that they are worse off in the second situation are illegitimate. What has happened is that their **cash flow** — profits after tax plus depreciation allowances — has gone **up** from $1.5 million to $1.75 million. They clearly are better off with an interest-free loan of $0.25 million at their disposal.

---

[111] For a lively critique of government policy in the use of depreciation allowances see, David Lewis, *Louder Voices: The Corporate Welfare Bums* (Toronto: James Lewis and Samuels, 1972), especially the introduction by Eric Kierans and Chapter 1.

TAX AND SUBSIDY POLICIES

A reduction in tax rates on business income **may** stimulate spending on plant and machinery in two ways. First, it may strengthen investment incentives by increasing the after-tax profits that businessmen and women can expect to earn on new and improved productive facilities. Second, it may add to the supply of firms' internal funds (retained earnings), allowing them to carry out more readily investments when they believe there are opportunities for future profits.

In addition to indirect incentives to promote investment given to business through various tax breaks, federal, provincial, and municipal governments provide businesses with a wide variety of direct subsidies designed to promote investment. An article in the September 1979 issue of *Canadian Business* reports:

> The sheer scope and scale of government handouts to business today are staggering. The new and very handy red-and-white ABC (Assistance to Business in Canada) guidebook to federal aid programs proudly announces: "The federal government provides over $8 billion each year in grants, expenditures, contributions, loans, loan guarantees and insurance to promote economic development in Canada. Of this amount, more than $6 billion is provided in direct support to business." It is instructive to note, by the way, that the federal government's corporate income tax revenues amounted to $6.76 billion in 1976. Which means that the private sector, in effect, pays practically nothing to support the costs of the federal government.
>
> And don't forget the provinces, which now compete vigorously with one another for new investment by offering additional incentives of their own.[112]

AVAILABILITY OF FINANCE

Given certain expectations about profits, the **availability of finance**, that is, the ease with which businessmen and women can obtain credit, will influence the level of current investment. Indeed, certain economists believe that manipulation of the money supply, and through it interest rates, affects investment not mainly by changing the cost of investment but by affecting the availability of loans from banks and other credit institutions.[113]

[112] Mark Witten, "The Corporate Welfare Guidebook," *Canadian Business*, September 1979, p. 62.
[113] A summary of this debate can be found in, Victoria Chick, *The Theory of Monetary Policy, op. cit.*, Chapter 4. Beginners in economics will have difficulty with this reference.

GOVERNMENT DEMAND

Aggregate demand is influenced by government expenditures on currently consumed goods and services as well as on investment resulting in capital formation. In 1982, expenditures by federal, provincial, and municipal governments accounted for 22.2 per cent of Gross National Expenditures.[114] Of these expenditures, 19.7 per cent was for currently consumed goods and services and 2.5 per cent was for investment.[115] Other things remaining the same (and we repeat that this rarely is the case), an increase in government expenditures over the level of the previous year will increase employment and output as the government increases its purchases from private industry and increases employment in the public sector.

A reduction in government expenditures to a level below that of the previous year, other things remaining the same, will decrease employment and output.

SUMMARY

The overall demand for output or aggregate demand, assuming no foreign trade, is determined by consumer, investment, and government demand. Factors that affect each of these components of aggregate demand have been examined in this chapter. The choice of these components and a determination of their interrelationships constitute a theory of how the overall economy functions in the short-run.[116]

---

[114] See *Table 1-6*, p. 74.

[115] Total government spending each year reflects government activities in purchasing goods and services, including capital goods, as well as in making transfer payments. Transfer payments are those payments that take money from various segments of the population through taxation and distribute it to other segments of the population in the form of pensions, unemployment insurance payments, welfare, subsidies to business, etc. Total government spending, including transfer payments, in 1982 was 47.5 per cent of Gross National Expenditure.

[116] Technically, the short-run is defined as the period over which one can assume the size and nature of existing plant, machinery, and equipment (the capital stock) of a country does not change much. In practice, for purposes of economic policy, most discussions refer to a time period of one year.

CHAPTER 8

EMPLOYMENT THEORY AND POLICY II

I n the previous chapter consumption, investment, and government demand were discussed. These three sources of demand taken together were characterized as **aggregate demand** (in an economy without foreign trade). After the Second World War economic policy in industrialized capitalist countries has been directed at the adjustment of aggregate demand.[117] The main instruments of this approach have been the manipulation by governments of expenditures, tax receipts, and the money supply. Manipulations of expenditures and tax receipts is called **fiscal policy**. Government attempts to influence aggregate demand directly by adjusting expenditures and taxes is called **discretionary fiscal policy**. Governments also have at their service certain automatic tools of fiscal policy, which are known as **built-in stabilizers**. Manipulation of the money supply is called **monetary policy**.

The use of fiscal and monetary policy in Canada has been associated with an increased national debt. Is this a source of concern for present or future generations?

DISCRETIONARY FISCAL POLICY

In preparing its budget for the coming period, the government **plans** to have a certain level of expenditures and also **plans** to raise a certain amount of money through taxation to support government expenditures.

---

[117] Sweden has also made **labour market policy** a primary concern of overall economic policy in an effort to reduce frictional, structural, and seasonal unemployment.

Increasing or decreasing planned expenditures compared to actual expenditures made the previous year will tend to increase or decrease aggregate demand.

Changes in the planned amounts of taxes that individuals and businesses will have to pay also will affect aggregate demand.

If personal tax rates are raised over the previous year, other things remaining the same, less income will be available to consumers and consumption demand will fall. If personal tax rates are lowered below those of the previous year, other things remaining the same, more income will be available to consumers and consumption demand will rise.

If business tax rates are raised over the previous year, other things remaining the same, after-tax profits will fall, and corporate dividend payments to stockholders will tend to go down, thereby reducing to some extent consumption demand.[118] Lower profits after taxes also **may** reduce investment demand because of reduced rates of return on investment and because of a smaller supply of internal funds (retained earnings), which may be reinvested.[119]

DEFICIT, SURPLUS, AND BALANCED BUDGETS

Deficit and surplus budgets are the main instruments of fiscal policy. When planned government expenditure (G) in a given year exceeds planned tax intake (T), a **deficit budget** occurs and deficit spending is planned. When planned government expenditures are less than planned tax intake in a given year, a **surplus budget** occurs and the government expects a surplus of income over expenditures. When planned government expenditures equal planned tax intake, a **balanced budget** occurs. These relations can be expressed symbolically by:

$$G > T = \textbf{deficit budget;}$$
$$G < T = \textbf{surplus budget; and,}$$
$$G = T = \textbf{balanced budget.}$$

If the government wants to change the level of output and employment from one year to the next, it can attempt to do this by the use of fiscal policy.

For example, if in a given year the economy produced a $100 million surplus (G < T) for the government and a level of GNP was associated with 9 per cent unemployment, the government might choose to stimulate the economy by

---

[118] Corporate stockholders tend to be wealthy. Therefore, only a relatively small portion of additional dividend income would be expected to be consumed while a relatively large portion would be expected to be saved. Technically, the economist would say the marginal propensity to consume (MPC) of these persons is low while their marginal propensity to save (MPS) is high; where MPC + MPS = 1.

[119] But, it is **expected** profits that are the main incentive to investment. Lower levels of retained earnings are typically more of a problem for small rather than large enterprises.

bringing in a budget that planned a $100 million deficit (G > T) in the following year. This would mean a planned stimulus of $200 million to the economy, as the government moved from a position where it taxed away $100 million more than it spent in one year to a position where it plans to spend $100 million more than it receives in taxes in the coming year.

It could do this by either increasing government expenditure (G) or decreasing the tax intake (T), or by initiating a mixture of the two policies. In fact, **reducing** the level of the surplus, or running a balanced or a deficit budget compared to the previous year in this case would all **tend** to stimulate employment and output. The reason is clear. Any one of these policies would increase the level of aggregate demand, other things remaining the same, **compared to the previous year**.

If the government wants to reduce aggregate demand compared to a previous year, other things remaining the same, it would plan a budget in which either a smaller deficit or a larger surplus compared to the previous year is expected[120].

To summarize: The government budget is the main instrument of fiscal policy. The planned **change** in the government deficit or surplus can be used to influence aggregate demand and thereby the level of output and employment.

In discussing fiscal policy, we have referred to the **planned** change in the government deficit or surplus because the government can never be certain beforehand about either its future expenditures or tax receipts. If economic activity actually is better than expected, government expenditures on unemployment insurance, welfare, subsidies, etc., may be lower than anticipated, while tax receipts may be higher because of unexpected higher incomes and progressive personal tax rates. On the other hand, if economic activity turns out to be worse than expected, expenditures may be higher and tax receipts may be lower than expected.

The following excerpt from an article "How much stimulus is the question" by Hyman Solomon in the December 11, 1982, *The Financial Post*, illustrates the kind of discussion that has surrounded the preparation of recent federal budgets.

> Pressure on the Trudeau government is mounting to relax its stringent restraint policies and use the spring budget to start spending Canada out of recession.
>
> The prebudget "jobs vs inflation" struggle will intensify as unemployment — currently at postwar record levels of 12.7% and mounting — tests Ottawa's deficit-wary policymakers with proliferating examples of human misery and hard evidence of stubborn economic recession.

---

[120] One would not expect economic policy in the Canadian economy to have as its goal a year-to-year reduction in aggregate demand. More likely, policy would be directed toward slowing down the rate of increase in aggregate demand.

Although final budget decisions are still some time away, the government at the moment seems ready to consider a package of budget measures that would provide a mild dose of economic stimulation and several thousand more jobs over the near and medium term.

However, unless the economy takes a fresh dive to uncharted levels, indications are that Ottawa will resist anything beyond a modest increase in the already swollen budget deficit.

"We aren't going to have the money to do a lot of big things. Forget about another New Deal, or a spending blowout," a senior policy official told *The Post*.

But there clearly is still no consensus within government on how much stimulation to allow, or the best way to design it.

Some in Liberal Party circles, viewing the budget as an early election launch pad, want Ottawa to accept a substantial increase in the deficit in order to fund as many jobs as the economy can absorb.

Other factions think new fiscal and industrial incentives should be introduced to encourage an investment recovery, with Ottawa applying maximum leverage in the use of its money.

Still others think a combination of public works and tax cuts designed to initiate a classic consumer-led recovery is the preferred policy route.

Signals that the government is prepared to downgrade its hitherto single-minded attention to inflation in favor of a more balanced policy — may be encouraging for some policymakers, but it's creating consternation among others.

Bank of Canada Governor Gerald Bouey, for example, used a Toronto speaking engagement last week to refute claims that inflation should no longer be the nation's paramount concern.

Sensing, perhaps, the wavering or changing attitude within government, Bouey attacked "commentators (who) imply that the time has come to forget about the problem of inflation, and concern ourselves only with expansionary policies."

The governor urged continued support for his monetary-restraint policies as the best and quickest way to "end the Great Inflation."

BUILT-IN STABILIZERS

Instability of aggregate demand has resulted in significant variations in the growth of real output in the Canadian economy. The year-to-year changes in

96

real (constant dollars) GNE from 1948 to 1982 are shown in *Table 1-8*.[121] However, the extent of the variation in the growth of real output would have been larger in the absence of so-called automatic tools of fiscal policy, known as built-in stabilizers.

TABLE 1-8

Annual Percentage Change in Real Gross National Expenditure, Canada, 1948-1982

Year	Annual Percentage Change	Year	Annual Percentage Change
1948	2.5	1966	6.9
1949	3.8	1967	3.3
1950	7.6	1968	5.8
1951	5.0	1969	5.3
1952	8.9	1970	2.5
1953	5.1	1971	6.9
1954	− 1.2	1972	6.1
1955	9.4	1973	7.5
1956	8.4	1974	3.6
1957	2.4	1975	1.2
1958	2.3	1976	5.5
1959	3.8	1977	2.1
1960	2.9	1978	3.6
1961	2.8	1979	2.9
1962	6.8	1980	0.5
1963	5.2	1981	3.1
1964	6.7	1982	− 4.8
1965	6.7		

Source: Canada, Department of Finance, *Economic Review April 1983*, Reference Table 4, p. 125 (Catalogue No. F1-21/1983E).

Modern capitalist economies have these built-in stabilizers to adjust aggregate demand automatically in response to changes in economic activity. These changes are automatic in the sense that both government expenditures (G) and tax intake (T) change independently of specific government decisions to change

---

[121] There are a number of explanations for the instability of aggregate demand in this period. External events such as the wars in Korea and Vietnam in the 1950's and 1960's and the energy crisis in the 1970's were certainly important causes. However, the fundamental source of the unstable growth of aggregate demand and output, throughout the whole period, appears to be the volatility of foreign and domestic investment in the Canadian economy. For discussions of the relationship between investment behaviour and fluctuations in output and employment see, Howard J. Sherman, *Elementary Aggregate Economics* (New York: Appleton-Century-Crofts, 1966), pp. 64-108, and R.G. Lipsey, G.R. Sparks, and P.O. Steiner, *Economics*, 3rd edition, *op. cit.*, pp. 553-561.

them. These automatic adjustments tend to reduce the decrease of aggregate demand in a recession or depression and to reduce the increase of aggregate demand in an expansion.

There are three principal domestic built-in stabilizers: taxes, social insurance and welfare payments, and agricultural support policies.

Most taxes yield more to government as total output and income increase. The government's tax intake rises from sales and excise taxes as total sales increase.[122] Total taxes on payrolls for unemployment insurance, medicare (in some provinces), and the Canada/Quebec Pension Plan also rise as employment and income in the economy increase. In these cases the total amount of income siphoned off by the government in taxes increases even though tax rates remain the same.

The effect of taxes on income is even more marked with taxes that are progressive rather than proportional. When the **rate** of taxation increases as income increases, as is the case with personal income taxes, a tax is said to be progressive. In these cases the government tax intake changes more than proportionately with changes in income. If incomes are expanding, higher personal income tax rates associated with higher income "brackets" progressively increase the government's tax intake and thereby progressively limit personal expenditures by individuals out of their additional before tax earnings.

Just as an expansion of employment and income automatically increases the government's tax intake, a contraction of economic activity decreases the amount of money removed from the private sector by taxation. In general, changes in the government's tax intake tend to **increase** the government deficit (G-T) when the economy is **contracting** and to **decrease** the deficit when the economy is **expanding**. Thus, the existence of taxes provides an automatic stabilizing effect on employment and income.

When employment and income are falling, government expenditures (G) to the unemployed and the needy rise. These payments tend to maintain aggregate demand at levels above those that otherwise would exist.[123] When employment and income are rising, social insurance and welfare payments tend to be reduced, thereby tending to reduce aggregate demand resulting from these government expenditures. During periods of recession, payroll tax collections decrease, while

---

[122] An **excise tax** may be a given amount per unit of a product, such as a provincial gasoline tax, or it may be a percentage of the selling price of a product, such as a provincial sales tax. The former is called a specific tax; the latter is termed an **ad valorem** tax.

[123] Payments made to the unemployed come in large measure from the unemployment insurance fund to which employees and employers contribute through a tax on insurable earnings. In periods of severe unemployment the fund may be exhausted, and the government can supply additional money from its general funds or increase the tax rate on employees and employers. When the tax rate is increased, the spending power of employees and employers is reduced. In this case, spending power is being transferred between the unemployed, and employees and employers, and there may be no automatic net increase in aggregate demand associated with the operation of the unemployment insurance program.

payments to individuals under these programs rise. Thus, both the government payments and the receipts serve as built-in stabilizers.

When there is a downturn in economic activity, the demand for all goods and services, including agricultural products, declines. Because agricultural product prices are more sensitive to supply and demand in the market place than most product prices, agricultural prices are likely to fall (or not increase as quickly) during a downturn. When this happens, the government agricultural price support policy comes into play, and prices and thereby farmers' incomes are maintained above what they otherwise would be. The federal and provincial governments' quota and price support policies include arrangements for government to increase purchases of agricultural commodities for storage when prices are falling and to sell and decrease the storage of agricultural commodities when prices are rising.[124] These activities guarantee that government expenditures to support agricultural income tend to increase when economic activity is contracting and to decrease when economic activity is expanding.

The built-in stabilizers are not the result of conscious economic planning. Each of the stabilizers discussed above is the by-product of policies adopted for other purposes. The progressive personal income tax structure was based on notions of ability to pay and the idea that the distribution of income should be less unequal. Social insurance, welfare, and agricultural support programs were adopted because of the social and political pressures that developed in all advanced capitalist economies. None of these stabilizers were developed with the aim of attempting to stabilize economic activity so as to protect overall employment and income.

Furthermore, built-in stability is desirable if the economy is functioning close to full employment. It is undesirable to stabilize an economy when unemployment levels are high and when levels of GNP are far below its productive potential.

DEFICIT SPENDING

Before the Second World War, governments generally believed that they should try to reduce expenditures in order to avoid increased deficits when economic activity faltered. Where such a policy was possible the reduction of government expenditures (G) contributed to the tendency of aggregate demand to fall, which further lowered income and government tax receipts. Such a policy thus may have increased deficits. The modern approach, flowing from Keynesian theory,[125]

---

[124] For a good summary of the theory and practice of Canadian agricultural support policy see, A. Asimakopulos, *An Introduction to Economic Theory: Microeconomics* (Toronto: Oxford University Press, 1978), pp. 52-61.

[125] John Maynard Keynes, in a pathbreaking theoretical work *The General Theory of Employment, Interest and Money* (Toronto: Macmillan, 1967), argued that the private sector of the capitalist economy if left to itself could stagnate at high levels of unemployment of labour and capital. His solution was government intervention in the creation of aggregate demand.

is to use deficit spending to raise aggregate demand (with the hope that there will be a significant multiplier effect),[126] ultimately increasing income and tax revenues and thereby limiting government debt.

Both the magnitude and the timing of a deficit requires good judgement. If a recession is allowed to reduce output and employment too much and/or last too long, businessmen and women and consumers will become pessimistic about the immediate future, making it difficult to stimulate private spending and investment. On the other hand, a large deficit budget, the effects of which bear fruit when the economy already is expanding rapidly, may create unnecessary inflation if production cannot keep pace with the desire to increase expenditures.

Some economists believe governments cannot use monetary and fiscal policy effectively because they cannot know the correct moment to act or how forcefully to act, and will therefore disequilibrate the economy, causing deeper downturns and unnecessary inflation. These economists usually believe that uncontrolled market forces will produce the best possible results.

Other economists believe that Keynesian-type policies can at best only temporarily repair basic defects in the present system of monopoly capitalism.

The first of these two groups of economists is associated with the so-called Chicago School (from the University of Chicago), and their best-known spokesman is Milton Friedman. The second group presents a Marxist point of view. The best-known spokesman of this group in North America is Paul M. Sweezy, a professional economist who is editor of the journal *Monthly Review*.

Keynes, in the course of his argument against those who would have the government do nothing even when faced with the Great Depression, pointed out that **if there are unemployed resources** (labour, plant, and equipment) **even** nonproductive projects would have some positive effect. Thus, the building of pyramids, or the filling of holes with money, and having people dig it out were to him outlandish examples of means to increase aggregate demand and to improve employment and output (hopefully with multiplier effects).

Present-day right-wing Keynesians prefer this kind of deficit-spending (e.g., nonsense make-work projects or armaments spending). They also are opposed to spending that creates government enterprises, which will compete with or reduce the scope of the private sector of the economy. They typically argue that government enterprises are bound to be less efficient than private firms.[127]

Clearly, to the degree government expenditures are necessary, it is in the national interest that the spending both supports employment in the short-run

---

[126] Government policies that increase aggregate demand have **direct effects** on output and employment. However, in addition to the direct effects, those workers who received new jobs, or more income on present jobs, and those owners of firms that are now more profitable will in turn use their increased income to purchase more goods and services. This is called a **mulitiplier effect**.

[127] The election program of the victorious Progressive Conservative Party in the 1979 federal election included policies to return Petro-Can and other Crown corporations to private ownership.

and increases the productivity of the economy in the long run. We **must** be concerned with the **quality** of the projects created by a policy of deficit spending. Projects that contribute to the efficient production of both private and public goods and services are necessary to improve the nation's welfare. "Pyramids" and other wasteful uses of our resources are technically and politically indefensible.

Keynesian prescriptions for achieving high employment levels by government policies affecting aggregate demand assumed that these policies would and should be neutral with respect to income distribution. Perhaps Keynes chose not to raise the thorny question of what is a desirable distribution of income because he was trying desperately to convince other economists and governments that it was necessary to use fiscal and monetary policies to counteract the Great Depression. Nevertheless, different kinds of government expenditures, taxes, and methods of adjusting the money supply clearly do affect the distribution of income among different groups in society. There is also an important group of modern economists who believe that the way in which income is distributed affects the kinds of goods and services that are produced as well as the level of employment and output.

WHAT ABOUT THE NATIONAL DEBT?

Government budgets at the municipal, provincial, and federal levels affect economic activity. But the federal budget plays a dominant role in national fiscal policy because of the size and broad taxing and spending powers of the federal governments.

Federal expenditures and federal deficits and surpluses for each year from 1970 to 1982 are presented in *Table 2-8*. The preponderance of annual deficits, shown in this table, has produced a growing net federal debt.[128] However, the growth of this debt and the interest cost of servicing the debt were not considered problems by most economists until the mid-1970's. Just as large and successful businesses in the course of expansion of their facilities normally accumulate growing debt, which is accompanied by growing production, sales, and revenue, so too do economies normally increase their debt without ill effect when they are growing.

However, since the mid-1970's when the rate of expansion of the economy slowed down, economists and politicians who have been more concerned with inflation than unemployment, who have sought to restrict government expenditures on social programs, and who have favoured a reduction in the government's role in the economy have criticized deficit spending and claimed that the growing national debt is the cause and not the effect of poor economic perfor-

---

[128] "Gross debt is a comprehensive measure of federal liabilities. Net debt is defined as gross debt less financial assets. Changes in net debt are equal to budgetary deficits and surpluses. . . ." Canada, Department of Finance, *Economic Review April 1979*, p. 86 (Catalogue No. F1-21/1979).

TABLE 2-8

Federal Government Expenditures, Deficit or Surplus, 1970-1982

Year	Total Expenditures	Deficit or Surplus
	(millions of dollars)	
1970	15,262	266
1971	17,386	−145
1972	20,126	−566
1973	22,422	387
1974	28,869	1,109
1975	35,508	−3,805
1976	38,704	−3,391
1977	43,812	−7,303
1978	49,075	−10,685
1979	52,805	−9,264
1980	60,799	−10,153
1981	71,716	−7,979
1982	85,957	−21,083

Source: Canada, Department of Finance, *Economic Review April 1983*, Reference Table 51, p. 182 (Catalogue No. F1-21/1983E).

mance. They argue that deficits and the debt will "crowd-out" private investment, thereby preventing economic expansion, and that the interest burden of the debt somehow will bankrupt future generations. Let us examine these two arguments.

The "crowding-out" argument maintains that a limited amount of savings is available for investment and that the government will be competing with the private sector for these funds in order to finance its increasing debt. The result of this competition is higher interest rates, which discourage investment as well as consumer loans for durable goods.

In fact, there is no evidence of a "crowding-out" effect taking place in North American financial markets between the onset of the 1981 downturn and mid-1983.[129] A debt-ridden private sector, with few if any prospects for profitable investment, was not straining for funds either in Canada or elsewhere. An argument also is made that investment is being discouraged because private sector investors fear a "crowding-out" effect should a real recovery get underway. But this argument does not consider that a recovery will be accompanied by increased business profits and rising stock market values of shares, both of which reduce the need for the private sector to make demands for loans. Furthermore, govern-

[129] "Recovery Shrugs Off the Deficit, a $210 billion federal debt, and borrowers still are not 'crowded out'," *Business Week*, 6 June 1983, pp. 24-26.

ment revenues increase more rapidly than expenditures during a recovery as personal and business tax payments rise and social welfare and subsidy payments fall, resulting in lower deficits or surpluses that affect the relative importance of the national debt.

The second argument maintains that there is an onerous interest burden of the public debt that must be contained to maintain the current and future financial well-being of the population. Conservatives often will argue that, just as individuals cannot continuously spend more than they receive, neither can governments. Let us examine this contention.

Individuals who borrow money must give another party a claim on their income or property. Furthermore, the interest payments on the loans are an additional drain on their income.

Because lenders fear that some unfortunate event (layoff, sickness, or accident) will interfere with debt repayment, the amount of credit available to individuals is limited and terms of repayment are fairly rigidly fixed. The threat of illiquidity (inability to meet debt payments) always exists in both the lender's and borrower's calculations.

Similarly with business lenders, the threat of bankruptcy is present always. (This is especially true of small, rapidly growing firms that expand a bit too fast, run into short-run problems with cash receipts, and cannot meet bill collectors' demands.)

The Canadian federal public debt is held, in large part, by Canadians. The government borrows from some Canadians who have extra cash and pays interest out of taxes it collects from all Canadians. When the federal government runs deficits, it has financed them in recent years by selling bonds — on the average about 13 per cent to the Bank of Canada, about 80 per cent to Canadian business firms and individuals, and about 7 per cent to non-Canadians. An article in the February 18, 1984, *The Financial Post* describes the consequences of this financing for interest payments on the federal debt.

> The federal government owns the Bank of Canada; at the end of each year, the Bank turns over all its revenues to the government, deducting only its operating costs. Thus in 1982 when the Bank received $1,986 million as interest on bonds it held, it gave back $1,878 million.
>
> The Canadian business firms and individuals who buy government bonds are obliged to pay federal income tax. At minimum they would have to pay Ottawa in tax probably 40% of the money they receive as interest on their bonds.
>
> Save for the small fraction received by non-residents, what Ottawa does not get back is not lost to Canada for it is received by Canadians.[130]

---

[130] Ruben Bellan, "We agonize over wrong deficits," *The Financial Post*, 18 February 1984, p. 10.

Given the federal government's control over the monetary system and its superior access to credit, it is not forced to retire the national debt unless there are good economic reasons for doing so. It merely can refinance both new and old debts by issuing new bonds to replace the old ones. The same is true of large, growing, and healthy corporations.

The payment of interest on public debt, which comes from taxes paid by all Canadians, is paid to a relatively small group of large, financially powerful corporations and wealthy individuals. It thus tends to redistribute national income from the less to the more wealthy. This may be considered the real burden of the debt.

Those who argue that the growing federal debt and debt servicing costs are not a problem point out that this growth has been accompanied by growing output as measured by GNE and GNP. Net federal debt as a percentage of GNP was affected markedly by the Great Depression and World War II and then decreased to lower levels thereafter. (See *Table 3-8*.) During the Great Depression decreased output and rising government expenditures to support the needy coupled with lower government tax revenue increased deficits dramatically. During World War II government expenditures on war production and maintenance of the armed forces increased net debt as a percentage of GNP to 95.4 per cent in 1945. However, this percentage was reduced in subsequent years as the economy grew and as smaller deficits and occasional surpluses occurred. These economists argue that slow economic growth since 1975 and the return of depression-like conditions in mid-1981 again are raising net debt as a percentage of GNP. Net public debt interest charges as a percentage of GNP for selected years between 1952 and 1982 also are presented in *Table 3-8*.[131]

Those who would paralyze expansionary economic policy because of current levels of the national debt ignore the economic policy lesson so painfully learned during the Great Depression, that government deficits and the resulting government debt are **instruments** of economic policy and not **objects**.

The experience of the Trudeau Liberal government with three successive budgets — October 1980, November 1981, and June 1982 — provide an object-lesson. Fiscal policy in the October 1980 budget was to provide expenditure restraint and deficit reductions. The November 1981 budget attempted to reinforce this approach by increasing the pace of deficit reduction. It **planned** for a decline in the deficit from $13 billion in the 1981-1982 fiscal year to $10 billion thereafter. However, the June 1982 budget forecasted a $19.6 billion deficit for 1982-1983, $9.6 billion more than forecast the previous November. And by October 1982, the new Minister of Finance, Marc Lalonde, raised the 1982-1983 deficit estimate to $23.6 billion.

What went wrong? The lessons of Keynes and the depression were ignored. Government economic policy, faced with economic stagnation in both the do-

---

[131] Public debt includes municipal, provincial, and federal debt.

104

TABLE 3-8

Net Federal Public Debt, Net Federal Public Debt, and Net Public Debt Charges As a Percentage of GNP for Selected Years 1929 to 1982

Year	Net Debt (millions of dollars)	Net Debt as a Percentage of GNP	Net Public Debt Changes as a Percentage of GNP
1929	2,225	36.2	—
1939	3,153	55.9	—
1945	11,298	95.4	—
1952	11,185	51.7	1.9
1957	11,009	34.3	1.0
1962	14,767	37.2	1.3
1972	18,811	19.9	1.1
1973	19,810	18.8	1.0
1974	21,194	17.2	0.9
1975	22,927	15.5	1.0
1976	28,390	17.2	1.1
1977	34,600	18.1	1.2
1978	44,889	21.5	1.4
1979	57,115	24.8	1.7
1980	68,594	26.2	2.0
1981	81,263	27.8	2.2
1982	94,869	28.6	3.0

Sources: 1929, 1939, 1945, André Raynauld, *The Canadian Economic System* (Toronto: Macmillan, 1967), Table 14:6, p. 348.

1952, 1957, 1962, 1972-1982, Canada, Department of Finance, *Economic Review April 1983*, Reference Table 53, p. 184 (Catalogue No. F1-21/1983E).

mestic and international economies and wedded to monetarism and high interest rates, failed to counteract the downward pressures on Canadian production and employment. Efforts by the federal government to reduce deficits as average real wages (the purchasing power of wages) were falling and unemployment was rising contributed to inadequate domestic demand and the recession which developed into the 1981, 1982 depression.[132]

MONETARY POLICY: ONE MORE TIME

Monetary policy was discussed in Chapter 7. The main idea expressed there was that the government can try to influence the supply of money as a means to

[132] The foregoing three paragraphs are adapted from Sidney Ingerman, *6 & 5 The Bankruptcy of Liberal Economic Policy, op. cit.*, pp. 17 and 18.

affect interest rates and the availability of finance. Changes in interest rates and the availability of finance may affect **investment** demand.

Three additional comments can be added now to this earlier discussion.

First, different kinds of investment projects are more or less sensitive to the cost of finance — the interest rate. On the one hand, interest charges on mortgages seem to have an important influence on individual decisions to purchase homes, while interest charges alone seem less important in decisions to invest in new commercial building, plant, and equipment.

Second, with consumer spending providing an important element in aggregate demand, the interest cost of the credit needed to purchase consumer durable goods (automobiles, furniture, washers, dryers, etc.) ultimately must affect aggregate demand and thereby output and employment.

Third, changes in monetary policy, which affect the level of Canadian interest rates relative to the level of interest rates in other countries, may cause short-term financial flows among countries, which in turn can influence the value of these countries' currencies and thereby can affect both the rate of inflation and employment growth. This topic is discussed more extensively in Chapter 11, which deals with International Trade.

PART THREE

INCOME DISTRIBUTION AND INFLATION

CHAPTER 9

INCOME DISTRIBUTION
AND CORPORATE POWER

In earlier chapters, discussion centred principally on data, theories, and policies related to the determination of total output and employment. In this chapter, the division of output among various groups or classes in society will be examined. It will be shown that the way in which output is divided reflects the distribution of money in comes and affects the **kind** and **amount** of output that gets produced. Finally, special attention will be given to the various forms in which production and sales are organized and the role of corporate power in determining current Canadian income distribution.

THE FUNCTIONAL DISTRIBUTION OF INCOME

The economy's physical output, which is produced during a given period of time, becomes the property of individuals through the distribution of **money incomes**.[133] These incomes take the forms of **wages, salaries, and supplementary labour income and profit, interest, and rent.**

---

[133] This follows the National Income Accounts convention of measuring GNP by the market and imputed market value of goods and services produced. However, another concept of output might take account of working conditions, the amount of leisure accompanying production of a given amount of goods and services and "quality of life" considerations such as those discussed in Chapter 6.

Wages, salaries, and supplementary labour income are the payments to labour used in the production of goods and services. **Profits** are the payments to owners of enterprises that bring together labour and physical assets (capital) to produce goods and services. **Interest** and **rent** are the payments received by owners of assets who allow others to use these assets. Economists call them **rentiers. Interest**, received by those who loan money, can command consumer or producer goods and services. **Rent** is received by those who allow others to use physical assets (buildings, land, machinery) that they own.[134] Income classified in this way, by the nature of the ownership of the means of production, is called the **functional distribution of income**. A consolidated form of the functional distribution of national income presents two categories of income: labour income and non-labour income. Labour income is simply all wages, salaries, and supplementary income (fringe benefits). Non-labour income combines profit, interest, and rental incomes, that is, all income that comes from the control and ownership of assets.

LABOUR INCOME AND TOTAL COMPENSATION

Labour income statistics are computed from data on **total employee compensation**. Statistics Canada estimates total employee compensation by calculating employers' expenses for pay for time worked, paid absence, miscellaneous direct payments, and legally required and other payments to employee welfare and benefit plans. The categories of payments in each of these types of expenses and their relation to **gross payroll, employer contributions to employee welfare, and benefit plans**, and thereby to **total** employee compensation, are presented in *Chart 1-9*. The percentage of total employee compensation that each kind of payment contributed to total employee compensation in all Canadian industries in 1978 also is shown in *Chart 1-9*. (Comparable data for 1982 was scheduled to be released by Statistics Canada in 1983, but still was not available at time of publication.)

Data on the functional distribution of **net national income** for Canada in 1958, 1968, 1978, and 1982 are presented in *Table 1-9*.[135] It would appear from this table that labour's share of net national income has increased from 68 per cent in 1958 to 74.1 per cent in 1983. However, data on the functional distribution of income, such as that presented in *Table 1-9*, are difficult to interpret. Labour income includes executive salaries and lucrative fringe benefits, a large portion of which should be considered part of the share of profits. This part of labour income may or may not have increased at a faster rate than non-executive wages, salaries, and fringe benefits between 1958 and 1982. More importantly, the percentage or

---

[134] *Table 2-6*, page 75, gives some indication of the payments out of Gross National Expenditure in 1982 that went to those who possessed various factors of production.

[135] Net national income is equal to Gross National Product minus capital consumption allowances and indirect taxes less subsidies. See *Table 2-6* in Chapter 6.

CHART 1-9

Composition of Employee Compensation, All Industries, 1978, Canada

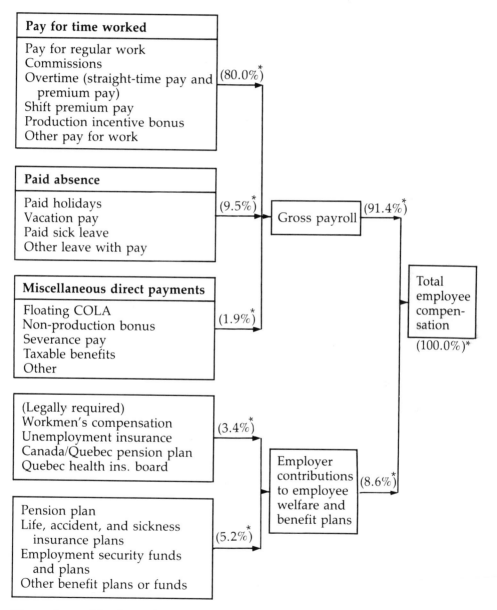

*Percentage of total employee compensation.

Source: *Employee Compensation in Canada: All Industries*, 1978, Statistics Canada, Figure 1 and Table 1
(Catalogue No. 72-619, annual/various).

112

relative share of labour income has risen because employment has shifted from individual proprietorships and small businesses to corporations and government. The *Economic Review April 1976* explains these changes:

> Over the longer run, workers have moved from farms and self employment in small enterprises so that the proportion of the labour force in paid non-agricultural employment has risen; thus there has been a secular increase in the proportion of income going to wages, salaries and supplementary labour income and a decline in the proportion going to net farm income and non-farm unincorporated business income.[136]

TABLE 1-9

The Functional Distribution of Net National Income (NNI), 1958, 1968, 1978, and 1983, Canada

Year	Labour Income		Non-Labour Income	
	Millions of $	% of NNI	Millions of $	% of NNI
1958	17,982	68.0	8,454	32.0
1968	39,318	72.0	15,288	28.0
1978	133,237	74.1	46,588	25.9
1983	222,199	74.1	77,578	25.9

Source: Canada, Department of Finance, *Economic Review April 1984*, Reference Table 9, p. 134, and Reference Table 12, p. 139 (Catalogue No. F1-21/1984E).

It may, therefore, be the case that labour's **share** of net national income has not improved or has even deteriorated in the sense that the average worker is receiving a smaller share of total output in 1983 than he or she received 24 years earlier. While sufficient statistical evidence is not available to make conclusive statements about workers' **share** of income, as will be shown in the following section, there **is** evidence that the distribution of income between the rich and the poor has not improved.

CORPORATE PROFITS

In the early stages of capitalism, individual entrepreneurs and enterprising families organized and managed production, and some amassed great fortunes. Although these capitalists lived exceedingly well, they typically also plowed much of their acquired profits into further expansion of enterprises. They thus ensured themselves prestige, power, and future profits. There are still individual tycoons and dynamic family businesses, but for the most part indus-

---

[136] Canada, Department of Finance, *Economic Review April 1976*, p. 51 (Catalogue No. F1-21/1976).

try and trade are now run by a form of managerial capitalism.[137] Companies are owned by a changing population of shareholders and are in fact managed by salaried staff,[138] often under the control of a small group of powerful financial manipulators.

This form of managerial capitalism has been made possible by the emergence of the **corporation** or **limited liability company** as the most important form of business organization.

A corporation is a distinct legal entity, separate from the people who set it up, own it, and manage it. Investors can buy shares in a corporation, while the assets that they have not invested in the corporation are shielded from the claims of possible creditors of the corporation. Under these conditions owners of wealth can spread their risks by holding shares in many corporations about which they know practically nothing except those things that may affect the value of their shares on the stock market.[139] For shareholders, the income from holding shares is similar to receiving interest on a loan. Even though they are nominally owners and receive **dividends** from profits of the corporation, shareholders function essentially as **rentiers**, just as if they owned government bonds or derived income from renting land.

This form of ownership and income distribution bears little resemblance to the mythology of dynamic, enterprising entrepreneurs who are rewarded for their efforts by profits. The net profits of companies now belong to shareholders, a significant number of whom have inherited their wealth from others. These shareholders receive earnings neither in the form of dividends or in the form of an increase in the value of their shares on the stock market.[140] In this way a large part of the wealth created by technological advances, investment in new plant, machinery and equipment, the labour of employees, and the skill of managers ends up under the control of those who do nothing economically productive, or those who occupy themselves in pursuits unrelated to the enterprises that provide them with part or all of their income.

While shareholders are not loyal to particular companies, managers are. Their salaries, fringe benefits, and prestige are linked to the success of the company. If they allow the stock market value of a company to fall below the potential

---

[137] An example of the fading breed of individual entrepreneurs and entrepreneuring families is the Irving Group, built and controlled by K.C. Irving and his three sons, which has its headquarters in Saint John, New Brunswick. "The group consists of something like one hundred separate enterprises, some very large even by Canadian standards, some very small even by provincial standards, all connected directly or indirectly by a labyrinth of holding companies." See, Royal Commission on Corporate Concentration, Study No. 16, *The Irving Companies*, 1978 (Catalogue No. Z1-1975/1-41-16).

[138] Another term for shareholders is stockholders.

[139] The only time shareholders are concerned with the fact that they are **owners** of a corporation is when the company goes bankrupt or when a "takeover bid" is in progress and the value of shares may change radically.

[140] The value of shares in an enterprise is influenced by its profits, which may be distributed to shareholders or may be used to increase the retained earnings of the enterprise.

profitability of its real assets, a **takeover bid** from another company can result in a change in the actual control of the company, that is, shareholders will sell their shares to the highest bidder who then may have a sufficient portion of ownership shares to control the company. The new controlling group may change management, consolidate operations, switch products, and in short do what it believes is necessary to make the enterprises' **overall** holdings more profitable.

INCOME INEQUALITY AND POVERTY

The distribution of income among households, without taking account of ownership of factors of production, is called the **size distribution of income**. Studies of the size distribution of income reveal how much of total income is accounted for by given proportions of a nation's families.

On **average**, the income of Canadian families has been rising. Between 1965 and 1981 the average annual income of family units rose from $6,536 to $30,440, or by 366 per cent. The increase in average real income of these families measured in constant 1971 dollars, that is, after taking account of inflation, was 58 per cent.[141] However, contrary to popular belief, there is considerable income inequality in Canada, and there has been no tendency for this inequality to decrease since 1965.

The National Council of Welfare estimates that approximately four million Canadians — one in six — lived in poverty in 1982.

> This estimate represents a substantial increase of half a million men, women and children over 1981. The risk of poverty went up for families especially those led by women and young people and those with children to support (the poverty rate for families with four or more children went from one in four in 1981 to one in three in 1982). About 1.2 million children are in low-income families.

> Poor Canadians have incomes substantially below average. The poverty line for a family of four is less than half of the average income for a family of four. The low-income line for a single person living in a metropolitan area is 44 per cent of the average industrial wage. Keep in mind that most poor people have incomes that are significantly less than the poverty line, so that the income gap between them and the average Canadian is even wider.[142]

Low levels of education, living in a rural area, living in the Atlantic provinces, living in a family headed by a woman, or being 65 years of age or over are some of the typical characteristics of those who are living in poverty.

Women are particularly disadvantaged. In 1979, the National Council of Welfare reported that three out of every five poor adults in Canada were women and

---

[141] Statistics Canada, *Income Distributions by Size in Canada, 1981*, Table 1, p. 45 (Catalogue No. 13-207, annual).

[142] Government of Canada, National Council of Welfare, *1984 Poverty Lines*, March 1984, pp. 4 and 5.

that one-and-a-quarter million women (one woman out of every six) were living in poverty, compared to only two-thirds of that number of Canadian men.[143]

The percentage of families and unattached individuals in various income classes in 1981 is shown in *Table 2-9*. Note that 9.4 per cent of all families and 47.9 per cent of unattached individuals had an **annual** income of less than $10,000.[144]

TABLE 2-9

Percentage Distribution of Families and Unattached Individuals by
Income Groups, 1981, Canada

Income Group	Families (per cent)	Unattached Individuals (per cent)
Under $5,000	2.0	15.8
$5,000 − 9,999	7.4	32.1
$10,000 − 14,999	10.2	16.5
$15,000 − 19,999	11.1	13.1
$20,000 − 24,999	11.9	9.7
$25,000 and over	57.2	12.8
Average Income	$30,440	$13,535

Source: Statistics Canada, *Income Distributions by Size in Canada, 1981*, Table 1, p. 45, families, and Table 28, p. 75, unattached individuals (Catalogue No. 13-207, annual).

It is often claimed that families are poor because they are lazy and prefer not to work. In fact, in 1977, there were 425,800 working poor families and single adults in Canada. They constituted 6 per cent of the country's "young" family units and 47 per cent of those living below the poverty line.[145] Counting together heads of households, spouses, children, and live-in relatives, 1,034,000 persons lived in working poor households in 1977.[146]

Poverty in Canada is accompanied by a significant degree of income inequality in the sense that a small number of rich families receive a disproportionately high percentage of annual income, while a large percentage of poor families receive a disproportionately low percentage of annual income. In 1981, families and unattached individuals, taken together, who were classed in the highest quintile (20 per cent) of income recipients received 41.8 per cent of total income,

---

[143] Government of Canada, National Council of Welfare, *Women and Poverty*, October 1979, p. 1.

[144] **Family unit** in this discussion refers to a group of individuals sharing a common dwelling unit and related by blood, marriage, or adoption. An **unattached individual** is a person living alone or in a household were he/she is not related to other household members.

[145] "Young" family units refers to unattached individuals under 65 and families with no member aged 65 or over.

[146] Government of Canada, National Council of Welfare, *The Working Poor: People and Programs: A Statistical Profile*, March 1981, p. 3 (Catalogue No. H68-3/1981E).

116

while families and unattached individuals who were classed in the lowest quintile received only 4.6 per cent of total income. (See *Table 3-9*.) Families and unattached individuals in the highest quintile received a considerably larger share of total income (41.8 per cent) than those in the three lowest quintiles taken together (33.1 per cent). Furthermore, as can be seen in *Table 3-9*, there has been little change in the unequal size distribution of income by families and unattached individuals between 1965 and 1981.

TABLE 3-9

Inequality in Families, Unattached Individuals, All Families, and Unattached Individuals, Income Distribution 1965 and 1981 (Shares of Total Income)

Income Rank	Families		Unattached Individuals		Families and Unattached Individuals Combined	
	1965	1981	1965	1981	1965	1981
Lowest Quintile	6.2	6.4	3.7	5.0	4.4	4.6
Second Quintile	13.1	12.9	8.3	9.5	11.8	10.9
Middle Quintile	18.0	18.3	16.6	15.7	18.0	17.6
Fourth Quintile	23.6	24.1	26.1	25.1	24.5	25.2
Highest Quintile	39.0	38.4	45.2	44.7	41.4	41.8

Source: Statistics Canada, *Income Distributions by Size in Canada, 1981*, Table 74, p. 146 (Catalogue No. 13-207, annual).

In all modern capitalist countries, governments intervene to prevent the worst excesses of the unequal distribution of income that would result from the uninhibited activities of individuals and firms seeking to maximize profits. This intervention results in programs such as unemployment insurance, welfare, public pensions, and medicare. Fundamentally, these programs provide **transfer payments** by using social insurance payments by employees and employers and tax revenues to redistribute income.

The tax system provides different rates of taxation on income from work and on income from the ownership of assets. There also is a progressive tax rate structure so that those with higher incomes and a greater ability to pay are taxed at higher rates. The avowed intention of these provisions is to reduce major income inequalities. In fact, this intention is to a large degree circumvented by the ability of the wealthy to influence the nature of tax law and to use high-priced tax specialists to find loopholes in the law.[147] During the 1984 federal

---

[147] See, *The Hidden Welfare System: A Report by the National Council of Welfare on the Personal Income Tax System in Canada* (Ottawa: National Council of Welfare, 1976), and David Lewis, *Louder Voices: The Corporate Welfare Bums, op. cit.*

election campaign the New Democratic Party (NDP) pointed out that, in 1982, 239 persons with annual incomes of more than $25,000 paid no personal income tax. Neither did 1,000 persons earning from $100,000 to $200,000, nor 6,500 persons earning from $50,000 to $100,000. Ed Broadbent, the NDP leader, called for a minimum tax rate of 20 per cent for all those earning $50,000 or more. Brian Mulroney, the Progressive Conservative (PC) leader who won the election, endorsed the principle of a minimum tax for persons with high incomes, but did not present a specific proposal to implement the principle.

INEQUALITY OF WEALTH

Income is called a **flow** concept by economists. It is the **rate** at which individuals receive control over money or other assets with a monetary value each year. Wealth is a **stock** concept. It is the value of the total amount of assets that a person or family has at a particular period of time. A family may have a large annual income but a modest amount of wealth. An example of this might be the family of a doctor just beginning to practise medicine. It also is possible to have a significant amount of wealth and a modest amount of income. Think of a farmer or a land speculator who owns valuable property but is holding on to it until some future date when he believes its value will rise a great deal.

Notwithstanding these examples, the usual relation between wealth and income is that those with high incomes are those who have much wealth and those with small incomes have little wealth. The control of wealth directly affects income through returns in the form of profits, interest, and rent.

Estimates of the distribution of wealth in Canada as measured by the **net worth** of families (total assets — total liabilities) in relation to their income rank is presented in *Table 4-9*.[148] In 1977, families ranked in the highest fifth of income distribution had 44.3 per cent of net worth, while families ranked in the lowest three-fifths of income distribution had only 36.8 per cent of net worth. There has been little change in the relation between net worth and income distribution between 1970 and 1977. (See *Table 4-9*.)

THEORIES OF INCOME DISTRIBUTION

Theoretical explanations of income distribution have always been a source of contention among economists and have been at the root of disagreements about the proper way to understand how capitalist economies function.[149] It is useful therefore to examine briefly the history of debates about income distribution theory and then to link the current state of this theory to the realities of modern industrial organization.

---

[148] Data on the distribution of wealth in Canada have many weaknesses as is indicated by the author of the study from which *Table 4-9* is derived.
[149] See, Maurice Dobb, *Theories of Value and Distribution Since Adam Smith* (Cambridge: University Press, 1973), pp. 31 and 32.

TABLE 4-9

Share of Total Net Worth* of All Family Units
Ranked by Size of Income, 1970 and 1977

Family Income Rank	1970 Percentage Share of Net Worth	1977 Percentage Share of Net Worth
Lowest fifth	10.4	9.0
Second fifth	13.8	12.8
Middle fifth	14.0	15.0
Fourth fifth	19.0	19.0
Highest fifth	42.8	44.3

*Total assets less total debts.

Source: Gail Oja, "Inequality of the Wealth Distribution in Canada 1970 and 1977," in *Reflections on Canadian Incomes* (Ottawa: Economic Council of Canada, 1980), p. 352 (Catalogue No. EC22-78/1980E).

RICARDO

In 1817, David Ricardo, an English political economist,[150] produced the first systematic theoretical work on how a capitalist economy functions.[151] For Ricardo, the laws that regulate distribution were seen as "the principal problem in Political Economy."[152] His theory of income distribution maintained that profits were what was left over after historical and social conditions determined wages. (Profits, in his argument, incorporated all non-labour income.) Capitalists owned the means of production, a large part of which was land in those days, while workers could be hired at a subsistence wage. The subsistence wage level in each country was decided by historically determined social conditions. If wages temporarily rose above the subsistence level, workers would live longer and reproduce more quickly, flooding the labour market and driving the wage back to its "natural" subsistence level.[153] In addition, Ricardo had a **labour theory of value**, which maintained that the **value** of a commodity was determined by the average **quantity** of labour necessary to produce the commodity. This implied that profits in general were the result of the confiscation by capitalists of value produced by labour.[154]

---

[150] Historically, people who are now called economists were known as political economists in explicit recognition of the close relationship between these two fields of human activity. Departments of political economy existed in most Canadian universities 10 to 15 years ago, and a few still live on.

[151] Adam Smith's *Wealth of Nations* was published in 1776. This book made available a detailed description of capitalist relations. It also provided theoretical reflections on various aspects of the functioning of the economy, but it did not provide a theory of distribution and its theory of price determination is incomplete.

[152] David Ricardo, *On the Principles of Political Economy and Taxation*, Preface, (in *Works and Correspondence of Ricardo*, P. Sraffa, ed. (Cambridge: University Press, 1951), Vol. 1, p. 5).

[153] This follows Malthusian population theory. See, Robert Malthus, *Essay on Population*, 1798.

[154] Labour created the machinery and developed the land that the capitalists own.

MARX

While Ricardo was part of the English financial and intellectual establishment, Karl Marx, a Prussian expatriate, functioned for a considerable period of time as a full-time revolutionary. When it became clear in the 1840's that revolution in Europe was not imminent, he settled in London where he wrote *Das Kapital*, which appeared in 1867. He and his close collaborator Friedrich Engels believed the book would provide the scientific analysis of capitalism, which would prove socialism was inevitable.[155]

Marx "was in a direct line of descent from Ricardo."[156] Distribution of income was a central element in his system. He differed from Ricardo in his stress on class and power relations. The process of **primitive accumulation** initially dispossesses workers from the land and control of the means of production and leaves them at the mercy of the capitalists with only their labour power to sell. Under these conditions the capitalists extract profits from workers in the form of **surplus value**, which is the difference between the value of what they produce and subsistence wages that they receive. But he rejects Ricardo's notion that workers remain at a subsistence wage because they live longer and reproduce too quickly when wages rise. For Marx, wages are kept at a subsistence level by the existence of a **reserve army of labour**, which is the product of recurrent capitalist crises and the displacement of workers by technological change, which progressively tends to replace workers with capital. Nevertheless, on the central question of income distribution they essentially agree: profits are what is left over after wages are paid, and the wage rate essentially is the result of historically determined power relations.

NEOCLASSICAL ECONOMICS

Criticisms of Ricardo and Marx play an important role in the development of economic doctrines. The rival doctrines downplay distribution as a central element in economic theory and push individuals' tastes and choices between consumer goods to centre stage. The main stream of this doctrine is developed by the English economist, W.S. Jevons, in his *Theory of Political Economy* (1871), the German economist, Carl Menger, in his *Grundsatze* (1871), and the French economist, Leon Walras, in *Eléments* (1874). The ideas in these works, progressively refined and elaborated, evolve into neoclassical economics, which is now the dominant theory in the Anglo-Saxon countries. In this system the initial distribution of income and wealth is taken as "given," that is, there is no question about how it got to be what it is. Economic actors, each trying to maximize their own welfare (utility), meet in free, that is, competitive markets where

---

[155] No discussion of Marx is complete without recognition of his co-worker and friend Friedrich Engels. The two are the co-authors of the *Communist Manifesto* (1848). For an excellent biography of Engels see, W.O. Henderson, *The Life of Friedrich Engels*, in two volumes (London: Frank Cass, 1976).

[156] Maurice Dobb, *Theories of Value and Distribution Since Adam Smith, op. cit.*, pp. 142 and 143.

prices are set by supply and demand. Income to workers and to owners of assets (capital) is determined by the value of these factors in producing final products. Workers in these markets are supposed to receive the value of their contribution to production of goods and services. Free competition is supposed to provide efficient production and the greatest possible output of goods and services, which are distributed equitably among the factors of production. Interference in free markets by unions or government is harmful. The same is true of the growth of monopolies and oligopolies, but, in practice, less concern is shown about this development, which is now characteristic of modern capitalism. Best of all, if not interfered with, this system is supposed to guarantee full employment.

THE CAMBRIDGE SCHOOL

The Great Depression, which racked the world for over a decade (1929-1940), made it clear that neoclassical theory did not deal with the "real world." It could not help to solve the economic crisis with its widespread unemployment, accompanied by idle machinery, plant, and equipment. Economic power was in the process of becoming highly concentrated in the hands of a relatively narrow group of powerful corporations and individuals. Government intervention was necessary if the system was to survive. Workers were organizing unions to defend and improve their conditions of life. Neoclassical economics became less and less believable and, though it still robustly survives in academia and its arguments are used in many forms to support the status quo, an alternative theoretical line of argument now challenges it. This alternative returns to the spirit of the Ricardo-Marx approach, but seeks to correct certain technical criticisms of this body of ideas and adapt it to modern capitalism in a world economy far different from that envisioned by either Ricardo or Marx.

The three economists who are associated most closely with this alternative theoretical approach are Joan Robinson, Piero Sraffa, and Michal Kalecki. This group often is referred to as the Cambridge School because Robinson, who was influenced strongly by Kalecki, and Sraffa taught at Cambridge University in England, and many of their followers have studied there.[157]

Robinson, an English economist, wrote widely and effectively against the fundamental tenets of neoclassical theory and especially against its assumption that the profits of those who own the means of production (capital) can be explained by the productivity of their capital.[158] This assumption is a key element in the neoclassical justification for capitalists' share of income.[159]

Sraffa, an Italian economist who came to Cambridge University in the 1930's, tried to establish the logical unity of Ricardo's distributional ideas that had been

---

[157] Joan Robinson and Piero Sraffa died within a few months of each other in 1983.

[158] The strict technical argument is that profits are not related to the **marginal productivity** of capital.

[159] Those who are comfortable with the material in this book may wish to read two of Joan Robinson's works, *Economics: An Awkward Corner* (London: George Allen and Unwin Ltd., 1966) and *Economic Philosophy* (New York: Doubleday, 1962).

criticized by others. His work is highly technical and therefore accessible only to a limited audience.[160]

Kalecki, a Polish exile during the Second World War, taught economics in the United States for a number of years and finally returned to Poland to take charge of economic planning in that country after the war. He developed a theory published prior to Keynes's *General Theory* that recognizes the role of aggregate demand. However, unlike Keynes, Kalecki maintains that the distribution of income affects the level of output and employment.[161]

A simplified version of Kalecki's theory would argue that the total output of a modern capitalist economy is determined by the amount of investment that takes place in a given "short period" and the ability of firms to mark up their prices over production costs. Kalecki's analysis assumes that actual investment is determined by capitalists' investment decisions in a previous period and that idle production capacity and unemployed workers are present in the economy. Capitalists' total profits are equal to the amount of investment that takes place plus capitalists' consumption. Total output, assuming a given level of investment and capitalists' consumption, is influenced by the general level of prices. If firms have the economic power to maintain high mark-ups on costs of production, and thereby high prices, workers can purchase fewer goods and services and there will be lower total output and unemployment.

At this point, union and political power enter his theory. Kalecki maintains that strong unions acting through collective bargaining and/or through the political process can limit the average mark-up by limiting the rate of profit.[162] Therefore, in their attempt to improve labour's share of income, unions are contributing to maintaining higher levels of production and employment.

INDUSTRIAL ORGANIZATION, PRICES, AND INCOME DISTRIBUTION

The "rules of the game" in the capitalist economy are such that individuals and groups struggle for as much of total output as they can get. But the amount of output that individuals and groups get is determined by the distribution of **money incomes** under given **price conditions**. Therefore, to understand income distribution it is necessary to understand how prices are determined. This can be done by recognizing two basic sectors in the private economy, which can be differentiated by the way prices are determined.[163] The first sector is made up of **competitive markets** where prices are determined by supply and demand. The

[160] Piero Sraffa, *Production of Commodities by Means of Commodities* (Cambridge: University Press, 1960).

[161] Kalecki's work is not easily accessible to beginners in economics, but when you are ready see, Michal Kalecki, *Selected Essays on the Dynamics of the Capitalist Economy, 1933-1970* (Cambridge: University Press, 1971).

[162] See, Kalecki's essay "Class Struggle and the Distribution of National Income," *ibid.*, pp. 156-164.

[163] Kalecki uses this approach. See, *ibid.*, pp. 43-61.

second sector is made up of enterprises that are in **imperfect competition** and prices are usually set by a **mark-up** over direct costs of production. The two sectors are linked by the purchase and sale of raw materials and finished products.

Competitive Markets

Competitive markets are significant in certain spheres of production, the most important of which are raw materials and food products. The **supply** of these products in any particular period is relatively fixed. This supply may be affected by events in nature such as bad weather and plagues, by government decisions to promote or restrict various crops, or by political instability that prevents production or distribution. The **demand** for these products, many of them now sold on an international scale, depends on the state of the economy, on techniques of production that affect raw materials inputs in manufacturing, and on consumer tastes. Large and often unpredictable changes in the supply and demand for these products cause significant price changes that affect the income of individuals, groups, and regions involved in their production and sales. These price changes also will affect **costs of production** in processing and manufacturing industries where raw materials are used in producing final products.

One of the characteristics of the products produced in the competitive sector is that by their nature they tend to be produced in particular regions so that significant price variations can mean prosperity or disaster for these regions. For this reason, Canada and other developed countries have introduced government regulations, subsidies, and marketing boards to smooth out extreme fluctuations in income, which result from unanticipated price changes. Undeveloped countries, which are typically suppliers of a limited range of agricultural products and raw materials, are affected most by changes in supply and demand for these products. Workers in these countries, still employed at subsistence or near-subsistence wages, are hardest hit when the prices of these products fall.

Joan Robinson has drawn an interesting analogy between countries that are primarily agricultural or raw material product exporters and problems of regional development and unemployment.

> Where a particular industry, such as shipbuilding, subject to foreign competition, is concentrated in a particular region, the situation there is somewhat similar to that of a primary-producing country. The income of the region fluctuates with the state of demand for a particular output. For this reason, a pre-condition for near-full employment was a policy for geographical development aimed at getting a mixed bag of industries in each district, and promoting the location of growing industries side by side with those that are shrinking. . . .[164]

---

[164] Joan Robinson, *Economics: An Awkward Corner, op. cit.*, pp. 54 and 55.

Imperfect Competition

Agricultural products and to a lesser extent raw materials are scheduled for production and produced before demand is known and must be sold at market prices.[165] Manufacturers, however, can regulate production more easily and within a certain range choose the price that will suit both the short- and long-run interests of the firm. The usual situation in manufacturing is one of **oligopoly** in which each industry is dominated by a few large companies operating with idle production capacity. These companies normally set prices on their products by adding a **mark-up** to **direct production costs per unit** of the product, which is sufficient to yield a net profit (profit after taxes) that the company considers acceptable and safe at which to aim.[166] (A more detailed discussion of mark-up pricing can be found in Appendix A of this chapter.)

Wholesalers and retailers in their turn will raise the product price to cover their direct production costs and to include a mark-up sufficient to produce acceptable levels of net profits. Raw material and agricultural product prices that are determined largely in **competitive** markets are a direct production cost input into manufacturing.

In oligopolistic industries, where there are fewer producers, mark-ups on direct production costs by each producer may be designed to produce the price set by a **price-leader**. The price-leader is usually a well established powerful firm in the industry. If it raises or lowers prices for various products, others usually will follow. Competition among firms is limited to marketing, packaging, and other non-price forms of competition. At given prices for similar products, the firms with the lowest costs of production make the highest profits.

In some situations **combines** are set up whereby firms in the industry agree both to the prices that will be charged and how much will be produced or how sales will be divided.[167] These arrangements almost always violate Canadian anti-combines legislation. However, efforts to prevent price-setting and division of markets have been ineffective.[168]

Competition in most spheres of production tends to result in the strong gobbling up of the weak. This can happen by voluntary **mergers** or forced **take-overs**. In the early stages of this process the struggle of firms for survival may result in improvements in efficiency and benefits to society as a whole. Left unchecked, this process results in a single firm or **monopoly** controlling an

---

[165] Raw material producers who are the sole producers of a commodity or who have formed a cartel, e.g., Organization of Petroleum Exporting Countries (OPEC), can to a certain extent control prices by agreements to limit production.

[166] Direct production costs vary according to the level of output of the firm. These costs include wages of production workers, raw materials, parts, etc.

[167] When all firms in an industry agree to both prices and division of markets, they have created a **cartel**.

[168] A summary of the history of Canadian competition policy can be found in R.G. Lipsey, G.R. Sparks, and P.O. Steiner, *Economics, op. cit.*, pp. 297-300.

industry. One natural check on this process is that, when the reduction of the number of firms in an industry leaves a few very large producers (oligopoly), the costs of war between the remaining firms may be high and the outcome unpredictable. Co-operation may be the safer course for managers and owners. A second check is that the removal of all competition in an industry may provoke government regulation, controls, or conversion to a state-owned Crown corporation.

There are certain industries in which technical considerations and efficient operations demand a monopoly by a single producer or a very limited number of producers in a given geographical region. Electricity, gas, and telephone services are examples of **natural regional monopolies**. Railway and airline transportation has been restricted to a limited number of firms by federal regulations. However, the federal government is moving toward **deregulation** of the airline industry and is talking about deregulation of the trucking industry. It is argued that promoting competition in these industries will lower prices to consumers and increase efficiency. Pressure for deregulation in Canada has come from the administration of President Ronald Reagan in the United States, who has instituted such a policy. Canadian opponents of deregulation have argued that short-run benefits to users of air and truck transport in major urban areas will likely occur at the expense of higher prices and poorer services to outlying areas with low population densities. American experience suggests that in the long run a few large companies will drive smaller companies into bankruptcy and gain control of the pricing process. These large American companies may be able to dominate a deregulated Canadian transportation industry.

Private firms that are given monopoly power by government usually are regulated to protect the public interest. Price regulation is an important aspect of this activity. Typically, a regulatory commission sets prices so as to provide a fixed rate of return on investment.[169]

CROWN CORPORATIONS

The government becomes a producer and seller of goods and services for diverse reasons.[170] The existence of **natural regional monopolies**, which are not profitable for existing private firms, or the unsatisfactory operation of a private firm may result in government ownership. In the communications field, government enterprises in radio and television broadcasting are deemed necessary to counteract the excesses of commercialism and to provide support for the development of an indigenous culture. In some cases, nationalization takes place

---

[169] In practice many regulatory commissions are staffed by past and future employees and executives of the firms being regulated. This raises questions about the arm's length relationship between the regulators and those being regulated.

[170] An excellent description and analysis of the operation of state-controlled Crown corporations in Canada can be found in, Allan Tupper and G. Bruce Doern, eds., *Public Corporations and Public Policy in Canada* (Montreal: Institute for Research on Public Policy, 1981).

when the private sector cannot sustain a high technology activity that is vital for national economic development or when military considerations demand government control. In a number of cases, provincial governments have nationalized enterprises to save jobs in the face of a private firm's bankruptcy or a decision to shut down an operation.

In some of these enterprises, prices are set to cover operating costs, and funds for expansion come from taxes. In other enterprises, prices do not even cover operating costs, but the good or service is considered important enough to the public to maintain its production. Some enterprises, especially in the natural resource field, are profitable and allow government to allocate funds to public services as well as to the further expansion of public production of marketable goods and services.[171]

Opposition to government ownership of enterprises that sell goods and services comes from those who believe that government ownership is inefficient and therefore costly to taxpayers. They advocate **privatization** of these enterprises, that is, their return to the private sector. One of the first acts of the Progressive Conservative federal government after its election in September 1984 was to announce its intention to sell Canadair, De Havilland Aircraft, Eldorado Nuclear, Teleglobe Canada, and other Crown corporation assets to the private sector.

CORPORATE POWER

The outcome of the struggle over the distribution of income has been influenced by both quantitative and qualitative changes in the nature of **corporate power**: quantitative in the sense of the increasing portion of employment and output that comes from the corporate sector, qualitative in terms of the centralization of power in conglomerate multinational corporations under the control of a limited number of individuals and families.[172]

Corporate power has been described on page 6 of the Report of the Royal Commission on Corporate Concentration (March 1978) as containing:

> . . . two major elements, economic power and political power, and a third element, social power, which derives its existence in part from the first two. The corporation is thought to have economic power if it can control the prices at which its products are offered, control the quantity of products produced, and through its ability, due to its size, to withstand losses, influence the prices at which it purchases labour, capital and raw materials. Large corporations are thought to have political power due to the resources at their disposal and their ability

---

[171] An excellent example of this can be found in the Crown Investment Corporation of Saskatchewan, "Chairman's Remarks," *Annual Report 1978*, p. 5.

[172] For an interesting discussion of control of the Canadian economy see, Jorge Niosi, *The Economy of Canada: A Study of Ownership and Control* (Montreal: Black Rose Books, 1978).

to inform and persuade the politicians and civil servants who make decisions in government. They are thought to have social power because of the influence they have directly over their employees and indirectly over consumers who are affected by their decisions and, in some instances, by their own ownership, or influence over, the mass media.

The acquisition of corporate power is a continuing and necessary activity for enterprises in the Canadian and other industrialized capitalist economies. In these economies, enterprises strive to survive, grow, and increase profits. Firms that do not grow and maintain acceptable profits often go bankrupt or are gobbled up in acquisitions and mergers by those that are growing and have corporate power.

In addition to the economic pressures on firms to expand size and influence, individuals and families who own and control firms are attracted by the personal power and prestige associated with corporate power. This attraction provides further stimulus to the acquisition of profits.[173]

The relentless economic and psychological drive for profits by the wealthy and their representatives inevitably brings them into conflict with workers and their unions. However, this conflict cannot be viewed simplisticly.

In certain periods the dominant corporations may have divided up markets and spheres of influence in one country and, if general economic growth is in progress, they may be satisfied with maintaining temporarily the status quo in their relations with labour. Profits may be growing because of the general expansion of production and because of the corporations' ability to exploit workers in less developed countries.

In other situations the domestic political situation may be such that the worst abuses of corporate power are being moderated by existing political power relations and political alliances. Sweden is cited often as being such a case.

Even when economic conditions are deteriorating domestically, some sections of the working class may be in occupations, industries, and regions that are doing relatively well. They may tend to forget that, if the more exposed workers and their unions are weakened, it is only a question of time until the system's insatiable thirst for profits affects all workers.

When a general downturn develops in the international and interdependent capitalist system, sharp conflict breaks out between the corporate establishment and the labour movement in each country. If the downturn is severe and prolonged, struggles also take place between various corporate giants, each allied with whatever political and governmental forces they can muster, to maintain and redivide profits. Corporate gentlemen's agreements are broken and pricing

---

[173] For an excellent description of individual and family ownership and control of industry in Canada see, Lars Osberg, *Economic Inequality in Canada* (Toronto: Butterworths, 1981), pp. 27-48.

policy, quotas, political pressure, and military aggression all become aspects of inter-corporate and international competition for profits.

The foregoing is certainly an accurate picture of economic events in the latter half of the 1970's and the early years of the 1980's.[174]

Economic instability, now typically characterized by high unemployment and bouts of inflation, sets the stage for a major assault on the labour movement. It is the labour movement that must be beaten if the standard of living of workers is to be sacrificed in order to protect corporate profits.

While the apparent contest takes place in particular negotiations, the corporate power centres organized in the course of horizontal and vertical integration, conglomerate expansion, and the growth of multinational corporations become the actual adversary of the labour movement. These power centres are more often than not in control of important centres of political power.

---

[174] One view of this situation can be found in the article, "Flexible Pricing, Industry's new strategy to hold market share changes the rules for economic decision-making," *Business Week*, 12 December 1977, p. 78.

Appendix A
MARK-UP PRICING

The determination of mark-up prices, under conditions of imperfect competition with idle capacity in industries, requires a discussion of the concepts of **direct production** and **overhead** costs of production.

Direct Production Costs

Direct production costs vary according to the firm's level of output from week to week. These costs would include wage costs, parts, and raw materials purchased from other firms, power, etc. These costs can be calculated with reasonable accuracy for a given production run and therefore provide a natural basis for estimating product prices. However, the firm has other expenses that must also be taken account of even though they are less easy to attribute to a particular product or a particular production run. These other costs are called **overhead costs**.

Overhead Costs

The cost of the upkeep of plant, machinery, and equipment, the wages of management personnel, interest and rent payments, as well as depreciation (or amortization) costs associated with the using-up of capital equipment are the main items an accountant would include in overhead costs.

The Price-Setting Formula

Mark-ups usually are set in such a way as to cover average overhead costs, when the firm is operating at or near its normal capacity, and to yield an "acceptable" or target level of profits.

In general, firms in the manufacturing and distribution sector set prices on particular products by adding a mark-up (a certain percentage) to the direct production cost per unit of the product.

For example, if the direct production cost per unit of producing a refrigerator is $300 and the mark-up is 30 per cent, the selling price of the manufacturer to the wholesaler or distributor will be calculated as follows:

direct production cost per unit + (mark-up × direct production cost per unit)
= product price per unit
or
$300.00 + (.30 × $300.00) = $390.00 per unit.

CHAPTER 10

INFLATION

I **nflation** is an increase in the average price level of goods and services in the economy. The opposite of inflation is **deflation**, which is a decrease in the average price level.[175] The problems associated with inflation, various measures and theories of inflation and, finally, remedies for inflation are discussed here.

The primary concern about inflation is that it redistributes income. Those with relatively fixed **money** incomes suffer a reduction in their **real** incomes, that is, in their standard of living, to the extent that the prices of goods and services they purchase go up faster than their money incomes. Hardest hit are the poor, the retired, and others who have little or no bargaining power with respect to their incomes.

Those who can protect themselves can arrange for contracts that are indexed to protect the "real" value of their agreements. For example, many unions negotiate cost of living allowance (COLA) clauses. Individuals or groups also can negotiate relatively short-term contracts so that unforeseen changes in prices can be corrected when contracts expire.[176] Failure to adopt one or the other or a

---

[175] The term deflation has disappeared virtually from popular usage since an annual decrease in the average price level in Canada has occurred only once since the Great Depression. In 1953 both the Consumer Price Index and the Implicit Price Index for Gross National Expenditure were less than 1 per cent below their level of the previous year.

[176] For a more detailed discussion of this subject see, Louis Ascah and Sidney Ingerman, "L'Indexation: remède à la mode," ed. Belzile et al.,*Inflation, Indexation et Conflits Sociaux* (Québec: Les Presses de l'Université Laval, 1975), pp. 127-152.

130

combination of these methods of protection means that there is a possibility of unintended gains to one party to a contract at the expense of the other when unforeseen inflation occurs.

The effect of inflation on employment is also a concern. If the prices of Canadian goods and services sold in international trade rise faster than those of competitors, Canada will lose sales and therefore domestic employment. Finally, it has been argued that inflation prevents the government from using fiscal and monetary policies to reduce unemployment.[177]

MEASURING INFLATION

Three price indexes are referred to in discussions of inflation:

1. **The Implicit Price Index of Gross National Expenditure (IPI)** estimates price movements in the **domestic** economy. It measures price levels affecting consumers, governments, business, and foreigners who purchase Canadian goods and services. The effect of changes in the prices of imported goods are kept out of the calculation of this index.

2. **The Industry Selling Price Index (ISPI)** estimates movements in both the costs of products sold by one manufacturer to another and the prices paid by distributors for finished manufactured products. Changes in this index are used often to predict the future course of consumer prices. However, these estimates must be used with caution because the same product may be bought and sold a number of times within the manufacturing and distribution process, resulting in "double-counting" in computing the ISPI.

3. **The Consumer Price Index (CPI)** is used to estimate price movements of a large number of goods and services purchased by consumers.

Changes in all three of these indexes indicate what has happened to prices in the past and may help to predict the behaviour of prices.[178] However, it is the CPI, which reflects changes in consumer prices and thereby indicates changes in **consumer purchasing power**, that is, of primary interest in discussions of inflation.

---

[177] For a more extensive discussion of arguments for fighting inflation see, J.C. Weldon, "Exorcising Inflation and Unemployment," *Labour Gazette,* September 1970 (Ottawa: Canada, Department of Labour), pp. 630-636.
[178] The use of these and other available price indexes for analyzing inflation is illustrated in Canada, Department of Finance, *Economic Review April 1979,* pp. 33-41 (Catalogue No. F1-21/1979).

The basic purpose of the CPI is to provide a measure of the change in living expenses that can be attributed to changes in the retail prices of consumer goods and services.[179]

The CPI presently in use is based on a survey of the market basket of consumer goods and services purchased by urban households in 1978.[180] The **average monthly price** of this market basket in 1981 is used as a base for comparison of prices in the months of other years and is assigned the base year index of 100.0.[181] For each month subsequent and prior to 1981 the price of the same market basket of goods and services is determined and then converted to an index number using 1981 = 100.0 as the base of comparison. For example, if the price of the basket of goods and services was $527 in January 1982 compared to an average monthly price of $500 in the 1981 base year, the CPI for January 1982 would be calculated as follows:

$$\frac{\text{Average monthly price of 1981 basket}}{\text{Price of January 1982 basket}} = \frac{\text{Average CPI 1981} = 100.0}{\text{CPI January 1982}}$$

$$\frac{\$500.00}{\$527.00} = \frac{100.0}{\text{CPI January 1982}}$$

$$\text{CPI January 1982} = \frac{\$527.00 \times 100.00}{\$500.00} = 105.4$$

Following this example, the CPI in January 1982 would be 105.4. Therefore, one could say that consumer prices were 5.4 per cent higher on average than they had been in the 1981 base year.

The CPI for Canada on a 1981 base extending from 1968 to 1983 with monthly indexes for 1982 and 1983 is presented in *Table 1-10*. The column headed "All items" is the overall price index, which takes account of the prices of goods and services in the categories of food, housing, clothing, transportation, health and personal care, recreation, reading and education, and tobacco and alcohol. There are also separate Consumer Price Indexes for 15 large urban centres in Canada.[182]

---

[179] "The Consumer Price Index (CPI) measures the percentage change through time in the cost of purchasing a constant 'basket' of goods and services representing the purchases made by a particular population group in a special time period. The 'basket' is an unchanging or equivalent quantity and quality of goods and services consisting of items for which there are continually measurable market prices over time." Statistics Canada, *Consumer Prices and Price Indexes*, October-December 1978, Appendix A, "Notes on the Consumer Price Index" (Catalogue No. 62-010, quarterly).

[180] See, Statistics Canada, *Consumer Prices and Price Indexes*, July-September 1983, p. 105 (Catalogue No. 62-010, quarterly).

[181] The base year for comparison is changed periodically. The previous base year was 1971. These changes can cause inconveniences for those using collective agreements that have cost of living allowance clauses in them that are expressed in terms of the formerly published base year CPI. In these cases special arrangements can be made with Statistics Canada to continue to receive the CPI as calculated on its former base year.

[182] The urban centres are: St. John's; Charlottetown/Summerside; Halifax; Saint John; Quebec and Montreal; Ottawa, Toronto, and Thunder Bay; Winnipeg; Regina and Saskatoon; Edmonton and Calgary; and Vancouver.

TABLE 1-10
Consumer Price Index for Canada, All Items, and Major Components
1968-1983, 1981 = 100, Annual Averages, and Monthly Figures
for 1982 and 1983

Years and months	All items	Food	Housing	Clothing	Trans- porta- tion	Health and personal care	Recreation, reading, and education	Tobacco and alcohol
1968	38.0	32.0	38.3	49.2	37.2	40.5	46.2	44.8
1969	39.7	33.3	40.3	50.5	38.9	42.4	49.0	46.4
1970	41.0	34.1	42.3	51.5	40.4	44.3	50.7	47.0
1971	42.2	34.4	44.2	52.2	42.1	45.2	52.4	47.8
1972	44.2	37.0	46.2	53.6	43.2	47.4	53.8	49.1
1973	47.6	42.4	49.2	56.3	44.3	49.7	56.1	50.6
1974	52.8	49.4	53.5	61.7	48.7	54.0	61.0	53.4
1975	58.5	55.8	58.9	65.4	54.4	60.2	67.3	59.9
1976	62.9	57.3	65.4	69.0	60.3	65.3	71.3	64.2
1977	67.9	62.0	71.5	73.7	64.6	70.2	74.7	68.7
1978	73.9	71.6	76.9	76.5	68.3	75.2	77.6	74.3
1979	80.7	81.0	82.3	83.6	74.9	82.0	82.9	79.6
1980	88.9	89.8	89.0	93.4	84.5	90.2	90.8	88.6
1981	100.0	100.0	100.0	100.0	100.0	100.0	100.0	100.0
1982	110.8	107.2	112.5	105.6	114.1	110.6	108.7	115.5
1983	117.2	111.2	120.2	109.8	119.8	118.2	115.8	130.0
(Not seasonally adjusted)								
1982 J	105.4	101.7	107.1	101.0	108.9	104.3	103.7	108.7
F	106.7	103.7	108.1	103.4	109.3	105.7	105.0	109.6
M	108.0	104.6	109.7	104.7	111.3	108.1	105.5	109.7
A	108.6	105.2	110.4	104.9	112.3	108.7	106.0	110.0
M	110.1	107.5	111.2	105.4	113.8	110.2	107.7	112.9
J	111.2	109.9	111.9	105.8	114.4	110.6	108.3	115.2
J	111.8	110.5	112.7	105.0	114.8	111.2	109.5	116.1
A	112.3	109.6	113.6	106.4	115.6	112.6	110.3	117.3
S	112.9	108.7	115.0	107.1	116.6	113.0	110.4	119.2
O	113.6	108.4	116.4	107.2	116.3	113.2	112.5	121.3
N	114.4	108.7	116.9	108.0	118.1	114.4	112.9	122.8
D	114.4	108.3	117.4	108.0	118.0	114.6	112.3	123.2
1983 J	114.1	108.5	117.5	105.5	117.0	115.1	112.1	123.5
F	114.6	109.2	117.9	108.5	115.9	115.9	113.5	124.1
M	115.8	108.9	119.0	109.6	119.7	116.6	113.8	124.6
A	115.8	110.0	119.3	110.0	116.8	117.7	114.1	125.6
M	116.1	111.8	119.3	110.1	115.3	118.2	114.9	128.1
J	117.4	112.0	119.5	110.2	121.4	118.2	115.3	129.3
J	117.9	112.7	119.9	109.7	122.0	118.8	116.9	129.5
A	118.5	112.6	120.8	110.3	122.6	119.0	117.3	130.6
S	118.5	111.5	121.4	110.6	121.6	119.5	117.7	133.7
O	119.2	112.7	122.2	111.1	121.1	119.7	117.9	136.7
N	119.2	112.1	122.3	111.4	121.3	120.1	118.0	137.3
D	119.6	112.5	122.7	111.1	122.7	120.0	117.5	137.3

Source: Statistics Canada, *The Consumer Price Index, December 1983*, Table 2, p. 9, all items, and Table 4, p. 14, major components (Catalogue No. 62-001, monthly).

The CPI for Canada and for the 15 large urban regions are estimated monthly, and the figures are released within two weeks of the end of the month to which they apply. The CPI for any year is the average of the 12 monthly indexes for that year.

Changes in the CPI may not reflect accurately changes in purchasing power for many individuals and groups in the population. The calculation of the CPI takes account of the relative importance of the different categories of purchases made by an **average** urban family. This is done by "weighting" the average price of each category of goods and services (food, housing, clothing, etc.) so as to reflect the importance of each of these categories in the average family's total purchases of consumer goods and services in computing the **All items** price index. The weights in use in computing the CPI as of April 1982 were based on a 1978 study of consumer expenditures and are shown along with the results of the 1974 and 1967 studies of consumer expenditure patterns in *Table 2-10*.[183] Note that **Food** has a weight of 21.1 per cent in the 1978 market basket. However, the

TABLE 2-10

Comparison of 1967, 1974, and 1978 Expenditure Weights Used in the Consumer Price Index, by Major Component, for Canada

Major Components	Weights (per cent)		
	1978	1974	1967
All items	100.0	100.0	100.0
Food	21.1	21.5	24.8
Housing	35.4	34.1	31.4
Clothing	9.6	10.1	11.3
Transportation	16.2	15.8	15.2
Health and personal care	3.7	4.0	4.5
Recreation, reading, and education	8.6	8.3	6.9
Tobacco and alcohol	5.4	6.2	6.0

Source: Statistics Canada, *The Consumer Price Index, December 1983*, Table 1, p. 32 (Catalogue No. 62-001, monthly).

---

[183] It is interesting to note in *Table 2-10* that as the standard of living has increased in Canada the proportion of consumer expenditures on food, clothing, and health and personal care has fallen, while the proportion of consumer expenditures on housing, transportation, recreation, reading, and education has risen. The increase in the proportion of consumer expenditures on tobacco and alcohol between 1967 and 1974 followed by the marked fall between 1974 and 1978 undoubtedly reflect the effects of higher standards of living being mitigated by increased provincial tax levies on these products and the growing consciousness of the health hazards associated with smoking.

average low income family spends more than 21.1 per cent of its income on food. If food prices rise more rapidly than the prices of other consumer goods and services, the change in the **All items** index will understate the loss in purchasing power of low income families.[184]

The CPI does not take account of income taxes. If personal income taxes are not indexed when wage increases take place, higher incomes result in higher taxes so that take-home pay does not increase as much as wages, and changes in the CPI would not provide an accurate indication of changes in the purchasing power of gross wages. Since 1973 the federal government and the nine provinces that allow the federal government to collect their taxes have indexed tax payments so that increases in the CPI result in proportionately lower tax payments as incomes rise into higher tax brackets.[185] Income tax payments were not indexed until 1979 for Quebec residents. Should the federal and provincial governments eliminate income tax indexation this inadequacy of the CPI will again be relevant.

Percentage changes in the CPI for Canada for each year from 1968 to 1983 and for each month in 1982 and 1983 are shown in *Table 3-10*. These changes are derived directly from the Consumer Price Indexes used in *Table 1-10*. The percentage changes in this table are in relation to the "same period a year ago." Thus, the 5.8 per cent increase in the **All items** index for 1983 means that the average **All items** index for the 12 months of 1983 of 117.2 (*Table 1-10*) is 5.8 per cent higher than the average **All items** index for the 12 months of 1982. Similarly, the 4.5 per cent increase in the **All items** index for December 1983 means that the December 1983 index of 119.6 (*Table 1-10*) is 4.5 per cent higher than the same index in December 1982.

When inflation is being discussed, it is necessary to differentiate **between the percentage change in the CPI from year to year** and **the percentage change in the CPI for the same month in two different years**.

If you want to calculate percentage changes between **different** months in the same year or in different years, you must make these calculations directly from data like that found in *Table 1-10*. An example of the use of the CPI to calculate a change in the purchasing power of the average money wage rate of a group of workers (often called calculating "real" wages) can be found in Appendix A of this chapter.

INTERNATIONAL COMPARISONS OF INFLATION

The performance of consumer prices in seven major industrial countries that were members of the Organization for Economic Cooperation and Development

---

[184] The opposite is true if food prices rise more slowly than the prices of other consumer goods and services.

[185] This indexation formula provides less than complete protection because corrections of tax brackets take place one year after prices have risen.

TABLE 3-10
Changes in Consumer Price Indexes for Canada, All Items, and Major Components 1968-1983, 1981 = 100, Annual Averages, and Monthly Figures for 1982 and 1983

Years and months	All items	Food	Housing	Clothing	Transportation	Health and personal care	Recreation, reading, and education	Tobacco and alcohol
(Percentage change from same period a year ago)								
1968	4.0	3.2	4.6	3.1	2.6	4.1	4.9	9.1
1969	4.5	4.1	5.2	2.6	4.6	4.7	6.1	3.6
1970	3.3	2.4	5.0	2.0	3.9	4.5	3.5	1.3
1971	2.9	0.9	4.5	1.4	4.2	2.0	3.4	1.7
1972	4.7	7.6	9.1	2.7	2.6	4.9	2.7	2.7
1973	7.7	14.6	6.5	5.0	2.6	4.9	4.3	3.1
1974	10.9	16.5	8.7	9.6	9.9	8.7	8.7	5.5
1975	10.8	13.0	10.1	6.0	11.7	11.5	10.3	12.2
1976	7.5	2.7	11.0	5.5	10.9	8.5	5.9	7.2
1977	8.0	8.2	9.3	6.8	7.1	7.6	4.8	7.0
1978	8.8	15.5	7.6	3.8	5.7	7.1	3.9	8.2
1979	9.2	13.1	7.0	9.3	9.7	9.0	6.8	7.1
1980	10.2	10.9	8.1	11.7	12.8	10.0	9.5	11.3
1981	12.5	11.4	12.4	7.1	18.3	10.9	10.1	12.9
1982	10.8	7.2	12.5	5.6	14.1	10.6	8.7	15.5
1983	5.8	3.7	6.8	4.0	5.0	6.9	6.5	12.6
(Not seasonally adjusted)								
1982 J	11.4	6.1	13.8	5.0	16.9	10.8	8.1	17.0
F	11.6	6.4	14.0	5.8	16.8	10.6	8.4	17.5
M	11.6	6.5	13.6	6.1	16.4	10.3	8.2	16.3
A	11.3	6.2	13.8	6.1	16.4	10.4	8.7	15.7
M	11.9	8.9	13.4	6.4	16.1	10.5	8.5	15.6
J	11.2	9.4	12.5	5.9	14.1	10.6	8.5	15.1
J	10.9	8.6	12.0	5.5	13.8	10.4	9.5	15.0
A	10.5	7.4	11.8	5.8	14.2	10.6	9.2	14.9
S	10.4	6.7	12.0	5.5	13.2	10.8	9.1	16.1
O	10.0	6.5	11.3	4.8	12.4	10.8	9.2	15.6
N	9.8	7.0	11.3	5.0	11.4	10.5	8.9	14.0
D	9.3	7.4	11.0	5.3	9.2	10.3	8.2	13.9
1983 J	8.3	6.7	9.7	4.5	7.4	10.4	8.1	13.6
F	7.4	5.3	9.1	4.9	6.0	9.7	8.1	13.2
M	7.2	4.1	8.5	4.7	7.6	7.9	7.9	13.6
A	6.6	4.6	8.1	4.9	4.0	8.3	7.6	14.2
M	5.4	4.0	7.3	4.5	1.3	7.3	6.7	13.5
J	5.6	1.9	6.8	4.2	6.1	6.9	6.5	12.2
J	5.5	2.0	6.4	4.5	6.3	6.8	6.8	11.5
A	5.5	2.7	6.3	3.7	6.1	5.7	6.4	11.3
S	5.0	2.6	5.6	3.3	4.3	5.8	6.6	12.2
O	4.9	4.0	5.0	3.6	4.1	5.7	4.8	12.7
N	4.2	3.1	4.6	3.1	2.7	5.0	4.5	11.8
D	4.5	3.9	4.5	2.9	4.0	4.7	4.6	11.5

Source: Computed from Statistics Canada, *The Consumer Price Index, December 1983*, Table 2, p. 9, all items, and Table 4, p. 14, major components (Catalogue No. 62-001, monthly).

(OECD) between 1974 and 1981 is illustrated in *Table 4-10*. This table clearly shows that there are differences in inflation among these countries in this period. It is worth noting also that Canadian inflation has been below the average rate of the seven major countries taken together. While the Canadian rate was somewhat above the United States rate for this seven-year period, an examination of Consumer Price Indexes in the two countries over a 25-year period shows that they are similar and tend to move together with some leads and lags over short periods of time.[186] The high degree of economic integration between Canada and the United States explains the similarity of price performance in the two countries. Important aspects of this integration will be discussed in Chapter 11, which examines international trade.

TABLE 4-10

Average Annual Increases in the Consumer Price Index in Seven Major OECD Countries, 1974-1981

Country	Average Annual Increase in the CPI
	(per cent)
United States	9.4
Japan	9.3
West Germany	5.2
France	11.4
United Kingdom	15.5
Italy	17.1
Canada	9.7
Seven major countries	9.9

Source: Canada, Department of Finance, *Economic Review April 1982*, Table 9.1, [p. 106] (Catalogue No. F1-21/1982E).

A THEORY OF INFLATION

Inflation has been attributed to: greedy and powerful unions raising wages; giant corporations raising prices; international cartels controlling energy prices, especially oil prices; government expansion of the money supply; and deficit

---

[186] See, J.C. Weldon, *Wage Controls and the Canadian Labour Movement* (Ottawa: Canadian Centre for Policy Alternatives, 1982), Appendix 2.

spending initiated to reduce unemployment. But each of these explanations only reflects an **aspect** of the inflationary experience. Inflation involves the whole economic process. It is related intimately to the struggle over control of output and thereby the distribution of income. What is needed to understand inflation is an explanation or theory of how prices are determined and how income is distributed in modern capitalist economies. The approach to understanding how prices are determined and income is distributed, which was introduced in the previous chapter, provides the best available theoretical framework (model) within which the many aspects of inflation can be explored. A brief review of this theory of price determination may be useful at this point.

THE PRICE SYSTEM

The price economy consists of two basic price determining sectors, which are linked to each other by the purchase and sale of raw materials and finished products.

In the **competitive sector**, land, agricultural, and raw material prices are set by market forces in the sense that the supply and demand for these commodities determines their price. An unforeseen change in supply as the result of unusual weather conditions, plagues, political upheavals, etc., with demand remaining the same, will cause changes in prices and incomes of those affected by these events. Some will gain while others will lose. For example, a drought that reduces agricultural production in one region may be a disaster for producers in that region, but it will be an advantage to unaffected regions that can sell their crops at more favourable market prices. Price changes in the competitive sector often are exaggerated by speculators who buy and sell control of commodities even though they may never actually take physical possession of them. (Speculation is discussed in Appendix B of this chapter.)

In the **manufacturing and distribution sector**, output is seldom sold under competitive conditions. The usual situation in manufacturing is that of oligopoly in which each industry is dominated by a few large companies operating with idle production capacity. Under these conditions firms can usually regulate production and within a certain range choose the price that will suit both the short- and long-run interests of the firm. These firms set prices using a formula in which **direct production costs** are marked up so as to produce an acceptable level of net profits.[187] Once a product is produced and enters the distribution system, wholesale and retail mark-ups are added in turn to the producer's price, yielding a final price to the consumer.

In addition to a producer's own **wage** cost, the producer's **direct production costs** consist of payment to suppliers of intermediate goods, which are used in

---

[187] See, Appendix A to Chapter 9 for a detailed discussion of this formula.

production, which cover the supplier's direct production costs plus the supplier's mark-up. Therefore, apart from imported parts and raw materials, direct production costs are influenced by wage costs that exist within the domestic economy. Therefore, the whole structure of observed prices is affected by direct production costs and existing ideas of enterprises about what are the necessary mark-ups to achieve acceptable rates of after tax (net) profits.

For a country like Canada, which imports a significant portion of consumer goods as well as intermediate goods used in production, a rise in the prices of these imported goods in exporting countries will tend to increase the prices of Canadian goods and services.

Once prices are rising for whatever reason, the money to buy goods and services at the higher prices is provided by workers raising their wage rates and by the higher profits that accompany the mark-up on increased direct production costs. This requires an expansion of the supply of money, which is to some degree controlled by government monetary policy. (See Chapter 7.) But the domestic and international banking system can generate necessary increases in the money supply through the expansion of loans and diverse forms of credit.[188]

CAUSES OF INFLATION

Imagine, if you can, a period of steady economic growth and stable prices, which reflect the smooth functioning of the **competitive** and **manufacturing and distribution** sectors of the economy. The relationship of wages to prices is associated with a certain distribution of income and also a level of output and employment.[189] Economic and political power relationships underlie the pattern of prices, income distribution, and employment that exists. These power relationships are embedded in the distribution of wealth (real assets), the nature of industrial organization and industrial relations, the control of domestic and international monetary institutions, and the nature of governments.

Inflation is **caused** by changes in or shocks to the system, which affect existing economic and political power relations. A change in power relations sets off an adjustment process throughout the **competitive** and **manufacturing and distribution** sectors, which when completed produces a new pattern of prices, income distribution, and employment.[190]

---

[188] See, Victoria Chick, *The Theory of Monetary Policy, op. cit.*, Chapter 2 for a technical discussion on this matter.

[189] The level of output and employment is influenced by the level of real wages. If expected profits do not fall and investment levels are unchanged, higher real wages associated with a smaller average mark-up will be associated with higher employment, that is, workers will be able to purchase more output.

[190] In "real life" a number of changes that interact with each other are likely to happen while this process is going on.

The study of the effects of changes in economic and political power relations is not well developed.[191] But what we can do is examine certain categories of change that have been associated with inflation. These are changes in aggregate demand, productivity, and political power relations.

Changes in Aggregate Demand

Moderate changes in aggregate demand normally cause output to vary, but firms in the manufacturing and distribution sector tend to leave their **mark-ups** unchanged. However, when there is a **substantial** increase in aggregate demand over a relatively short time period, some industries will find that at their "normal" mark-ups customers will want to purchase more of their product than they can produce with existing capacity. Some of these firms will extend the delivery dates of their products to customers, but others will increase their mark-ups by raising the prices of their products. Once this happens the new mark-ups tend to become the normal mark-ups and profits of these firms increase. In addition, a substantial increase in aggregate demand is likely to increase commodity prices in the **competitive sector**, which are inputs into the **manufacturing and distribution sector**, thereby increasing direct production costs on which mark-ups are applied. Usually, such a sequence of events will raise prices relative to money wage rates. Workers in turn will try to protect their **real** wage by increasing the money value of their wages when new agreements are negotiated. This in turn will increase direct production costs and will cause prices to rise as long as firms maintain their mark-ups.

There are relatively few cases in which an initial cause of inflation or a combination of causes produce an explosive wage-price spiral or hyperinflation.[192] Unemployment, the threat of unemployment, and/or weak bargaining strength may result in some workers not being able to raise their wages sufficiently to protect their real compensation. Inadequate demand for certain products or in certain regions may mean that producers and distributors in these industries and regions cannot completely pass on cost increases. This means that their **mark-ups** and therefore their profits will tend to fall. Eventually the effects of the initial change works its way through the system, producing a new pattern of prices, income distribution, and employment, which reflects altered power relations.

Since the Second World War, Canada, the United States, and the United Kingdom as well as other countries in the developed capitalist world have been subject to political trade cycles. These cycles are created by government policies designed to jazz up the economy, that is, to increase aggregate demand in order to reduce unemployment (especially close to election time) followed by policies to throttle down economic growth, that is, to reduce aggregate demand when

---

[191] A book that attempts to integrate economic and political power relations into the core of economic analysis is James O'Connor, *The Fiscal Crisis of the State* (New York: St. Martin's Press, 1973).
[192] The phenomenon of hyperinflation is discussed in R.G. Lipsey, G.R. Spark, and P.O. Steiner, *Economics, op. cit.*, p. 611.

inflation increases. This recurring **stop-go** activity creates inefficiencies in the form of high costs and increases in prices as many industries expand and contract their use of labour and other resources over relatively short periods of time.

Furthermore, inadequate aggregate demand during a **stop** phase may produce tendencies for many prices to rise, or at least not to fall. This will happen to the degree that **unit direct production costs** rise in oligopolistic industries when they operate at levels of output and specialization below those for which they were designed.

When aggregate demand is expanding rapidly and high levels of employment are being attained, changes in the composition of output between the production of investment goods and consumption goods often are associated with rising prices for consumer goods and services. In this situation optimistic businessmen and women (perhaps overly optimistic) create an investment boom, which shifts labour and other resources from the production of consumer goods to investment goods. With relatively full employment already existing, the shift of producing investment goods can restrict the supply of consumer goods and cause the prices of consumer goods and services to rise.

An investment boom and shifts in the composition of output can be provoked also by an election victory of a political party sympathetic to business interests, a war that creates new demands for productive facilities, or by a new breakthrough in science or exploration.

Productivity Change and Inflation

Net increases to the economy's stock of machinery, plant, and equipment, improvements in skill and motivation of the labour force, and innovations in the form of new products and in production technology all tend to raise output per person-hour, that, is, productivity at given levels of overall production. These changes occur more rapidly in some industries than in others. These changes also occur more quickly in different stages of the business cycle.

At **given** money wage rates, increased productivity lowers direct production costs per unit produced. If firms do not raise their mark-ups, prices will tend to fall. If workers receive higher money wage rates as productivity increases, mark-ups remaining the same, the effect of rising wages on prices is reduced. These relationships underlie the continuous struggle between labour and capital over how the fruits of capital accumulation and technological change are distributed, as well as the effect of productivity change in inflation.

Changes in Political Power Relations

Governments support and protect domestic economic interests. When political power relations change as a result of diplomacy or war, significant shocks are transmitted through the economic system. During the 1970's rates of inflation in almost all countries were markedly higher than they had been in the previous decade. The difference between these two periods is the change in political power relations, which neutralized the control of the United States and its allies over the Middle East. This allowed the oil-producing countries in this region to take control of the vast source of wealth in the form of oil. Change in the control of this wealth, and the income from it, sets off a world-wide struggle to determine how the new relationships would affect prices, income distribution, and employment.

The oil producers sought to reap the benefits of their newly acquired asset by forming the Organization of Petroleum Exporting Countries (OPEC), a cartel designed to raise well-head oil prices above the artificially low levels previously set by the foreign-owned private oil companies.[193] The oil companies, who maintained control of most of the processing and distribution system, were unwilling to accept reduced levels of income even though they lost control of this vast source of wealth. They used their considerable economic and political power to increase price mark-ups in the processing and distribution system. These increased prices became increased costs of production throughout the industrial world with a vast struggle breaking out to determine who would bear the burden of the redistribution of income implied by the new political power relations. Ultimately, workers were involved in this struggle as higher consumer prices appeared everywhere.

The so-called **energy crisis** provided a profound shock to the world economic system to which it still has not fully adjusted. If the continued development of Third World and non-capitalist countries restricts existing sources of income to the powerful corporations in the capitalist countries, inflation, caused by the struggle over the division of slower growing or even shrinking income, may be with us for some time even if Canada attains energy self-sufficiency.

INFLATION AND COLLECTIVE BARGAINING

The debate between labour and management about who **causes** inflation usually leads nowhere because of a failure to distinguish between the price transmission mechanism and the effects of changes and shocks acting through this mechanism. Management often will say that increasing wages cause inflation by increasing costs of production and therefore prices. Unions often will say that increasing prices cause inflation and therefore force unions to increase wages.

When the price of consumer goods and services is rising, unions attempt to protect the standard of living of their members by negotiating wage increases. Increased overall money wage rates increase **direct production costs** and thereby

---

[193] Well-head prices had been set artifically low because the private oil companies had paid royalties to the countries where the wells were located based on the dollar value of oil produced at the wellhead.

tend to further increase prices. This how the price transmission mechanism works. It does not explain what is the **cause** of a particular inflationary experience.

When employers argue that high wages cause inflation, they are arguing that power relations have changed so that unions can win a higher **share** of real output per worker than they could have in a previous period.

When unions argue that high profits cause inflation, they are arguing that **power relations** in the economy have **changed** so that firms have been able to increase mark-ups on direct production costs above the average level that previously existed. This argument maintains that inflation is being caused by **increases** in corporate power.

REMEDIES FOR INFLATION

Governments have used three kinds of policies to deal with inflation. One policy attempts to reduce the growth of aggregate demand and thereby to limit price increases. The most widely-used version of this policy is **monetarism**. A second policy attempts to limit increases in incomes by one form or another of wage, price, profit, interest, and dividend control and thereby to control prices and the distribution of income. This policy is called an **incomes policy**. A third policy attempts to limit price increases by increasing the supply of goods and services in markets. At the same time, the production of more goods and services would increase employment. This policy is known as **supply side economics**, or more popularly as **Reaganomics**. When he was first elected President of the United States, Ronald Reagan applied a version of supply side economics that he claimed would overcome both stagnation and inflation — **stagflation** — in the United States economy. Let us examine the theory, the application, and the problems associated with each of these policies.

REDUCTION IN THE RATE OF GROWTH
OF AGGREGATE DEMAND

The theory that underlies a policy to reduce the rate of growth of aggregate demand to fight inflation is that if consumers, business, and government purchase less, the lower demand for goods and services will keep down prices. Except for the rare situation in which workers on average are working more than normal hours, the inevitable result of a policy that succeeds in lowering aggregate demand is unemployment as fewer workers are needed to produce output.

Aggregate demand can be reduced by government through the use of fiscal and monetary policy. (See Chapter 8.) Reduction in government spending, increased taxes, direct control of consumer and business credit, and restrictions on the supply of money are among the actions government can take to reduce demand. However, the effectiveness of such a policy is dependent on what the fundamental causes of inflation are at a particular point in time. If the causes are relatively independent of domestic aggregate demand, an unacceptably high unemployment level may result from the large reduction in aggregate demand necessary to have an effect on prices.

For example, if a particular inflationary episode reflects the higher energy prices resulting from changing political power relations and the struggle over the redistribution of income associated with these changes, the amount of un-employment necessary to affect prices significantly may be politically unaccept-able to the government. Or if inflation is being caused by a general increase in corporate power associated with higher mark-ups in the manufacturing and distribution sectors of the economy, where price determination by oligopolies is not highly sensitive to changes in demand, reductions in aggregate demand and increases in unemployment may have a weak effect on prices.

In 1975, the Bank of Canada instituted a monetarist economic policy whose aim was to create unemployment and thereby reduce aggregate demand by reducing the rate of growth of the supply of money, driving up interest rates, and discouraging investment and consumer purchases of durable goods (auto-mobiles, washers, dryers, furniture, etc.). This policy followed similar policies in the United Kingdom and in the United States. This policy certainly succeeded in raising unemployment rates in Canada. (See *Table 1-3*, p. 29.) However, avail-able evidence indicates that this policy had no effect on Canadian inflation.[194] It **is** true that this policy, which was implemented in Washington, London, and Ottawa, contributed to the severe world-wide recession in 1981 that lowered the rate of inflation in most countries in 1982.

INCOMES POLICY

In an attempt to get out of the aggregate demand-unemployment dilemma, governments have tried one form or another of **incomes policy**. The essence of an incomes policy is that the government determines acceptable rates of increases in money incomes and acceptable rates of increases in prices and attempts to get individuals, unions, and enterprises not to exceed these increases. Some econo-mists believe that incomes policy should be used together with restrictive mone-tary policies to curb inflation.[195] And in 1975 a Canadian incomes policy was introduced by the Liberal government while the Bank of Canada was applying a restrictive monetary policy.

---

[194] For the period 1973-1979, Myron J. Gordon has examined: the average prime rate of interest charged by chartered banks; the annual rate of growth in the Consumer Price Index; and the rate of growth of the money supply as measured by the Bank of Canada's M1 and M3 definition of the money supply. He concludes that "it is difficult to infer . . . any systematic relation among the variables." Myron J. Gordon, *The Post Keynesian Debate, A Review of Three Recent Canadian Contribu-tions* (Ottawa: Canadian Institute for Economic Policy, 1980).
[195] See, for example, D.A. Wilton, "The Case for Wage-Price Controls," *Canadian Taxation: A Journal of Tax Policy*, Vol. 3, No. 2, Summer 1981, pp. 60-62.

Three variants of incomes policies have been used. The first produces a virtual **freeze** or **standstill** on increases in incomes and prices. The second allows incomes to increase in line with average increases in productivity while price increases are controlled. The third simply controls increases in incomes.

When rising domestic prices are linked to a crisis situation of one kind or another, increases in wages and salaries, as well as increases in the prices of a broad range of goods and services, are forbidden under a freeze or standstill policy. Such a policy is used for a limited and specified period of time (usually between three and six months) because it produces rigidities in the functioning of the economic system.

A freeze or standstill policy may be effective in limiting price increases in the short run. However, pressures for both income and price increases inevitably develop that are difficult to control afterward. Thus far, Canada has not used a freeze or standstill incomes policy.

A longer term incomes policy involves the overall relationship between incomes, prices, and productivity. Typically, the policy is put forward in terms of wage-price-productivity regulations that call for wage increases to be limited to **the trend rate** of increase in national productivity, while prices are held constant or allowed to increase only as fast as actual costs of production. Under these conditions, the benefits of increased productivity are expected to be shared between labour and owners of capital in the same proportion as income has been divided in the past.[196]

Assume there is a stable **labour force**,[197] all income is going to wages and profits, and real output per person-hour is growing on average by 3 per cent a year (i.e., the trend rate of productivity growth is 3 per cent per year).

If in a given year output and therefore income is equal to $300 billion and two-thirds of that income goes to wages and one-third to profits, the workers will receive

$$\tfrac{2}{3} \times \$300_b = \$200_b$$

and owners of capital will receive

$$\tfrac{1}{3} \times \$300_b = \$100_b.$$

Now, if output and income increase by 3 per cent, that is by 9_b and wages increase by 3 per cent following the productivity guideline, wage payments will go up by

$$.03 \times \$200_b = \$6_b.$$

[196] This result is predicated on the unrealistic assumption that there is a "fairly smoothly functioning competitive market economy subject neither to major excess demand nor major deficiency of demand." See, Robert M. Solow, "The Case Against the Guideposts," George P. Schultz and Robert Z. Aliber, eds., *Guidelines, Informal Controls and the Market Place: Policy Choices in a Full Employment Economy* (Chicago: University of Chicago Press, 1966), p. 45.

[197] Hours of work per year are assumed to remain the same.

This means that profit payments will increase by the total income increase minus the wage payment increase, that is, $9_b - $6_b = $3_b **OR**

$$\frac{\$3_b}{\$100_b} \times 100 = 3\%.$$

Therefore, following wage-price-productivity regulations, if prices remain constant and workers receive the trend increase in national productivity, wages and profits rise by the same **percentage**, maintaining the previously existing distribution of income.

At first glance, this approach to controlling inflation seems attractive. However, closer examination reveals a number of serious problems with this solution for inflation.

Problems With Wage-Price-Productivity Regulations

Incomes policies have had and continue to have considerable appeal to some economists and government policy makers despite the fact that experience with this approach to the unemployment-inflation dilemma in over a half a dozen countries, including Canada, has not been successful. Particular problems with wage-price-productivity regulations can be divided into two categories: administrative and technical, and economic.

Statistics Canada produces productivity measures of both **output per person-hour** and **output per person employed**.[198] Which is the proper measure to use? Experts would agree it should be output per person-hour.[199] However, the Government of Canada in its *1975 Anti-Inflation Act Regulations* used the average increase in output per person employed during the period 1954-1974 as its **national productivity factor** to regulate real wage increases during the 1975-1978 Canadian incomes policy. This meant that the national productivity factor was 2 per cent rather than a figure somewhat over the 3 per cent that would have resulted from using the output per person-hour measure. The main difference in these two measures results from the fact that the number of persons employed has grown at a faster rate than the number of hours worked during this period. The primary reason for this is the large increase in the number of part-time workers in the Canadian economy. Consequently, the ratio of output to employed persons has increased more slowly than the ratio of output to person-hours.

While output per person-hour is the generally accepted measure of productivity for an incomes policy, this measure can produce different results depending

---

[198] Prior to 1983, Statistics Canada described productivity measures of output per unit of labour-hour input as **output per manhour**. Recognition of the inaccuracy of this description resulted in this measure currently being described as **output per person-hour**.

[199] See, Sidney H. Ingerman and Ruth Rose-Lizée, "The Estimate of Productivity Growth in Canada's Prices and Incomes Policy," *Industrial Relations, op. cit.*

upon the **time period** chosen for measurement. For example, output per person-hour in Canada's commercial non-agricultural industries increased at an average annual rate of 3 per cent during the period 1961-1981. However, the same measurement for the period 1971-1981 produces an average annual increase in productivity of only 1.3 per cent. If the government had contemplated instituting an incomes policy based on wage-price-productivity regulations in 1982, there could have been significant disagreements about which was the appropriate productivity measure to use.

A policy of income and price controls inevitably requires elaborate research and administrative and enforcement support. In Canada, where a large proportion of collective bargaining activity is under provincial jurisdiction, the problems associated with organizing and running a national program are particularly difficult. Canadian experience with the high costs, arbitrary rulings, and inefficiency of the Anti-Inflation Board (AIB) during the 1975-1978 incomes policy illustrates the problem.[200] Perhaps even more troublesome than the high dollar and human capital costs of creating and running a large governmental apparatus is the disruption of collective bargaining (to be discussed below) and the bureaucratic tampering with a wide range of prices that inevitably accompany controls.[201]

Economic problems associated with wage-price-productivity regulations are centred around their effect on income distribution. An incomes policy that limits compensation changes to a fixed percentage increase, equal to the trend rate of increase in national productivity, **tends to freeze the existing distribution of income**. Thus, if the trend rate of increase in productivity is calculated as 3 per cent, persons with incomes of $10,000 a year would be allowed an increase in income of $300 per year, while persons with $30,000 a year income would be allowed $900 per year. The relative position of the two groups would remain constant.[202] In short, if you are poor and exploited, under a strict application of the productivity guidelines, you will remain so.

If workers receive the trend rate of increase in productivity, say 3 per cent, but prices continue to rise at say 8 per cent per year, **real labour compensation** would fall. Such a policy normally would provoke resentment among workers and resistance from unions. The 1975-1978 Canadian incomes policy attempted to meet partially this objection by permitting compensation increases equal to a

---

[200] Two articles in *The Financial Post*, 16 October 1976, one year after the AIB was introduced, illustrate the problems. See, Beatrice Riddel, "A chronicle of controls that cost $20 million," p. S-7, and Stephan Duncan, "Life is a steady siege for AIB's harried garrison," p. S-5.

[201] There is no inherent virtue in prices as they are set in the market place by enterprises acting in their own self-interest. The free enterprise world of Adam Smith in which pure competition was thought to lead to the best of all possible worlds does not exist presently (if it ever did). However, there is no reason to believe that bureaucratic manipulation of prices in an economy that is unregulated in most of its other functions can be successful in improving resource use and income distribution.

[202] $\frac{\$10,000}{\$30,000} = \frac{\$10,000 + \$300}{\$30,000 + \$900} = \frac{\$10,300}{\$30,900} = \frac{1}{3}$

national productivity factor, plus an **inflation protection factor** and an **experience adjustment factor.**[203]

A government that wants workers to accept wage and salary controls also must make an effort to control the profits of enterprises and thereby the non-labour income of owners of wealth. But profits are difficult to control.

Profits are a residual that result from the difference between a firm's revenue and costs of production. The demand for the company's products, the mixture of products sold, the efficiency of the enterprise, tax and depreciation regulations, and costs of production all affect profits.

Dividends are the payments out of profits to owners of capital. One way of selling an incomes policy to unions is to couple wage controls with controls on dividend payments. However, from the viewpoint of equity such controls do not mean very much. Profits that are prevented from being distributed in dividends turn up in increased retained earnings of the enterprise and ultimately in capital gains. (The value of the enterprise and therefore the value of its stocks rise.)

Even if dividends are controlled and capital gains are taxed, enterprises can use expense accounts, insurance and trust funds, golden handshakes, stock option plans, and other devices to distribute profits.

In theory, the control of prices should result in the control of profits, but the virtual impossibility of effective control of the hundreds of thousands of price-setting decisions that are made daily make this instrument of control less effective than the layman would imagine. For example, how do you control prices of imports and exports, of new products, or of products that are markedly changed in quality? How do you prevent enterprises that have been giving discounts to certain customers from reducing or ending these discounts?

Even if it is possible to control profits, it may be harmful to do so within the framework of the present Canadian economy. Profits are the motor that drives the capitalist system forward. Profits provide finance for the expansion of new growing firms and industries through retained earnings and an ability to borrow in the money market. Expected profits provide inducements for real investment, which maintains employment. Finally, profits provide a stimulus for efficiency. Fixing profits would mean that firms would be working on a cost-plus basis with a resulting loss of efficiency in firms that are able to reach easily the regulated level of profits.

---

[203] For a description of the Canadian program see, Government of Canada, *Attack on Inflation*, policy statement tabled in the House of Commons by Donald S. Macdonald, Minister of Finance, 14 October 1975, pp. 20-25. For a critique of the program see, Cy Gonick, *Inflation and Wage Controls* (Winnipeg: Canadian Dimension, 1976) and Canadian Labour Congress, *Labour's Manifesto for Canada* (Ottawa, 1976).

148

The moral of all this is that, so long as we maintain the capitalist "rules of the game," so long as we reject the idea of wide-ranging national economic planning, profits cannot easily be controlled.

But wage control without effective profit control means that workers will bear the burden of inflation either in the deterioration of their **real** or **relative** income position. This was precisely what happened as a result of the 1975-1978 AIB experience. Wages were controlled, profits were supposed to be controlled but were hardly touched, and workers' real wage increases fell below even the government's measure of the trend increase in national productivity.

While the AIB successfully controlled wage increases, most economists believe it had no effect on long-run inflation. D.A. Wilton, a well-known economist at the University of Waterloo, sums up this view:

> Since the raison d'être of the AIB was to "reduce inflationary expectations" and lower the long-run inflation rate, the AIB obviously failed to achieve its major objective. Even though the AIB may have won the battle on the wage front, it lost the war against inflation expectations.[204]

INCOME CONTROLS: THE 6 & 5 SOLUTION

The combination of a monetarist policy designed to restrict aggregate demand and the AIB, which restricted advances in real wages, both introduced in 1975, had disastrous effects on the Canadian economy. In September 1982, Statistics Canada reported:

> The recession in Canada, which has reduced production [GNP] by slightly over 6.0% since its onset in mid-1981, has been the steepest among the major industrialized nations, as households and business demand have declined at rates unprecedented in the post-war era.[205]

Confronted by a threatening deterioration in popular support, the federal Liberal government needed a policy that appeared to be dealing with depression-like levels of unemployment. Their solution, launched in the June 1982 budget, was a crusade to limit income and price increases to 6 and 5 per cent.

Influential elements in the corporate power structure that had urged the program on the government immediately joined the crusade.[206] And Ian Sinclair, Chairman of the Board of Canadian Pacific Enterprises, headed a government-sponsored committee to promote the program.

The June 1982 budget aimed to limit increases in all compensation payments (and payments from federal welfare programs) to 6 and 5 per cent during the

---

[204] D.A. Wilton, "The Case for Wage Price Controls," *op. cit.*, p. 66.
[205] Statistics Canada, *Statistics Canada Daily*, 22 September 1982, p. 2.
[206] Interview with Ian Sinclair on the program "The House," CBC Radio, 21 August 1982, available on tape from CBC.

two post-budget years. But why the numbers 6 and 5? The only attribute of these numbers, mentioned in the budget, is that they are percentage increases that are below the expected rate of inflation. The purpose of this choice is stated clearly in the budget. Money incomes will advance more slowly than the price level, and there will be a lower level of real production of all goods and services (real Gross National Product). Lower prices (including lower interest rates) then will emerge, for what is produced cannot be sold and already weak investment will be curtailed because of the absence of demand for goods and services. Lower wages and salaries, promoted by the 6 and 5 policy, eventually save the day as enterprises discover that they have both lower interest and labour costs per unit of product. They heed the Minister of Finance's plea "to lower price increases as costs go down and profit margins are restored. . . ."[207] Profits are restored because at lower prices more goods and services will be sold, thereby increasing employment. And private investment will expand as possibilities for profits improve.

The budget declares:

> This strategy will lead in the short run to a lowering of our real income. But it will soon slow the process that is eroding our pay cheques. It will check the rise of unemployment and it will establish a firm basis for resumption of real income growth throughout the economy.[208]

This is the identical dogma that contributed to the length and depth of the Great Depression. The economic theorists of **laissez-faire** capitalism argued that, if only free markets existed (and in particular labour markets without unions), wages would fall more than prices and full employment would be restored. This argument struck a sympathetic chord among the rich and powerful, who hated unions and did not understand that, while lower wages in one enterprise might increase profits or reduce losses in that enterprise, a general decrease in money wages in all enterprises was bound to result in lower demand for goods and services and therefore lower total employment and profits in the economy. The English economist John Maynard Keynes made this point perfectly clear **in 1936**. (See Chapter 4.)

The economic argument of the June 1982 budget and the **laissez-faire** economic theory of the depression differ on one point. The laissez-faire economists depended on free markets (pure competition) to bring down prices as labour costs fell in individual enterprises. As this is unlikely to be an effective mechanism in an economy dominated by domestic and foreign-controlled multi-national corporations functioning in monopolistic and oligopolistic industries, the budget asks for an act of faith by those Canadians whose money incomes are to be limited by the 6 and 5 program. They are to rely on the government to convince

---

[207] Canada, Hon. A.J. MacEachen, *The Budget*, 28 June 1982, p. 4.
[208] *Ibid.*

these powerful corporations and other price setters to control price increases voluntarily.

With respect to its own price-setting role, the budget declared that the government "is obligated to do all it can to ensure that prices established under federal jurisdiction are similarly restrained."[209] In fact, there is little evidence that either private- or public-sector prices were controlled by government. The depression-like conditions of slow economic growth and high unemployment that began in the summer of 1981 were enough to lower the rate of inflation throughout 1982 and 1983.

The Targets of the 6 & 5 Incomes Policy

The mandatory elements in the federal 6 and 5 program limited income increases to federal public-sector employees, retirees from federal government employment, and Old Age Security (OAS) and Family Allowance recipients and reduced disposable income (take-home pay) of those who pay personal income taxes.

While other recipients of wages and salaries were **urged** to limit their income demands and business was **urged** to lower prices, the government usurped the collective bargaining process in the federal public sector, denied these employees the right to strike, abrogated existing collective agreements, and arbitrarily fixed compensation increases at 6 per cent and 5 per cent, that is, below the expected rate of inflation.

The government did not allege that federal public-sector employees were better paid than comparable private-sector employees. Available evidence indicates that in 1979, 1980, and 1981, the wages and salaries of federal employees covered by collective agreements advanced more slowly than those of employees in the private sector.[210] Indeed, the June 1982 budget admits that federal public-sector employees "have been trying to catch up with rising prices, but their incomes have risen no more and often rather less than those of employees in other sectors."[211]

The government also repudiated promises it made to retired federal employees when they were working. These employees contributed a portion of their

---

[209] *Ibid*, p. 5.

[210] Base rate increases in major collective agreements without COLA clauses show federal employees advancing less than employees in All Industries in 1979, 1980, and 1981. See, Economic Council of Canada, *Nineteenth Annual Review 1982, Lean Times*, p. 11. With respect to wages and salaries for comparable jobs, a 1982 study observed, "Au niveau du gouvernement fédéral, il apparaît que les salaires sont sensiblement équivalents à ceux du secteur privé dans l'ensemble et tendent même à être inférieurs pour les emplois 'seniors' . . ." Pierre-Paul Proulx, "Rémunération dans les secteurs public et para public au Québec, éléments d'une nouvelle politique," *Relations Industrielles*, Vol. 37, No. 3, 1982, p. 489.

[211] *Op. cit., The Budget*, p. 5.

pay to a pension fund and accepted lower wages and salaries (deferred income) that became government payments to the pension fund. In return, the employees were promised, among other things, pensions that were protected against inflation. The June 1982 budget limited inflation protection of retired federal employees' pensions to 6 per cent in 1983 and 5 per cent in 1984.

The federal government's attack on union contracts, collective bargaining, and conditions of employment of public-sector employees was limited by provincial governments all across the country, with the notable exception of the New Democratic Party government of Manitoba.

Old Age Security (OAS) and Family Allowance payments were limited also by the 6 and 5 policy. These sources of income, which had been fully protected against inflation by indexation to the Consumer Price Index (CPI), now were protected only against 6 per cent inflation in 1983 and 5 per cent in 1984.

Finally, personal income tax payments to the government were expected to increase by placing 6 and 5 per cent limits on the inflation protection provided by the indexation of tax exemptions and tax brackets.

Solidarity and Sharing

The expected increase in government revenues from all these actions over the fiscal years 1982-1983 and 1983-1984 totals $2.4 billion.[212] The budget cynically describes this method of financing as

> . . . a concrete application of the principle of solidarity and sharing. Some Canadians are being asked to give up certain benefits to help the unemployed and troubled sectors of the economy.[213]

"Solidarity," "sharing," and "being asked" all imply voluntarism. None of these programs were voluntary. A significant number of those who were "volunteered" for real income reductions were in low-income categories. The 6 and 5 per cent limitation, which was applied to public-sector compensation, to pensions, and to family allowances, imposed a larger burden on groups with low incomes than on groups with high incomes. This is because there is less after-tax personal income tax loss to those with high incomes than to those with lower incomes.

In brief, the mandatory controls in the 6 and 5 program were designed to mainly hit incomes of low- and middle-income persons.

This incomes policy, whose goal was the reduction of aggregate demand, contributed to continued high rates of unemployment in Canada.

---

[212] The revenue estimates were as follows: the public-sector compensation restraint program — $800 million; limiting indexing of OAS, Family Allowance, and federal employees' pensions — $360 million; limiting the indexation of the personal income tax system — $1.3 billion, *ibid.*, p. 10.
[213] *Ibid.*

SUPPLY SIDE ECONOMICS: REAGANOMICS

Supply side economics provides an economic theory and associated economic policies that are supposed to deal simultaneously with economic stagnation and inflation (stagflation). Its basic idea is that, rather than restricting aggregate demand and production in order to lower inflation, it is better to promote the production of goods and services, that is, to increase supply and thereby to lower the tendency of prices to rise. There is the underlying assumption that competitive markets exist so that making supply increase relative to demand will lower the rate of price increases.

Soon after President Ronald Reagan first took office in the United States in 1980, he applied this theory by giving tax breaks to the rich on the grounds that the more the rich saved the more would be invested, thereby expanding aggregate demand, production, and employment. At the same time he cut back on social programs for the poor. The poor, deprived of income protection by the dismantling of social programs, were supposed to work longer and harder. Neither of these policies worked. The rich, who saw few opportunities for profitable investment in new machinery, plant, equipment, and housing, used their increased savings to launch a wave of corporate takeovers and for other forms of financial speculation that increased interest rates and contributed to the destabilization of financial institutions. Employment opportunities that already were inadequate for the poor shrank drastically, and massive unemployment in 1981 and 1982 put millions of additional Americans on unemployment insurance and welfare. Supply side economics failed. The massive unemployment it created contributed to the world-wide depression in 1981 and 1982, which did reduce inflation.

Economic growth and a reduction of unemployment rates to the 7 to 8 per cent range in 1983 and 1984 in the United States had nothing to do with supply side economics. Massive spending on war production and the accompanying increase in deficit spending provided a classic Keynesian stimulus to the United States economy.

THE SEARCH FOR A CANADIAN SOLUTION

No single "gimmick" can prevent periodic bouts of inflation. Canada has a small open economy, that is, it has a small economy relative to its main trading partners in international trade, and a significant amount of its total production and employment is related to its exports and imports. (These matters are dealt with in detail in the following chapter.) The price of Canada's imports cannot be controlled and it is not in the country's interest to keep the price of its exports below world market prices. It is particularly difficult to control the prices of agricultural and fish products, which are traded on competitive world markets. Interest rates are determined also to a large extent by an international market over which Canada has virtually no control. Furthermore, even the prices of domestically traded goods and services are notoriously difficult to control.

Attempts to control Canadian inflation with policies to reduce the growth of aggregate demand and increase unemployment have not succeeded in reducing inflation and have been tremendously costly in terms of lost production, human misery, and alienation of youth, women, and the populations of affected regions of the country.

Incomes policies similarly have not had any discernible effect on inflation, while they **have** restricted workers' incomes and thereby contributed to unemployment.

The most significant cost of income controls in Canada is the economic and political costs of the attack on collective bargaining and thereby on the labour movement. On questions of income, working conditions, and a broad range of social questions, unions are the primary representatives of employed Canadians and their families. Incomes policies in the present Canadian political context are an assault on one of the unions' vital functions — the ability to negotiate compensation agreements. They are therefore a direct assault on the institution itself.

Some economists have advocated an incomes policy as part of a **social contract** between the labour movement, business, and government, which would determine mutually agreed-upon compensation increases.[214] They cite the success of such co-operation in countries such as Austria, Sweden, and West Germany. However, these economists fail to recognize that the labour movements in these countries are able to negotiate such agreements because they have the bargaining strength that comes from their close ties with powerful social democratic parties in these countries and because they represent a large percentage of all employed workers.

As has been pointed out earlier in this chapter, inflation is caused by changes in or shocks to the economic system, which affect existing economic and political power relations. A change in power relations sets off an adjustment process, which when completed produces a new pattern of prices, income distribution, and employment. The primary concern about inflation is that the resulting redistribution of income will likely harm the poor, the retired, and others who have little or no bargaining power with respect to their incomes. These groups need special government programs to protect them against inflation. More comprehensive solutions to control the transmission mechanism of inflation are possible only within a framework of a coherent national economic policy that has as its central objectives full employment and a more equitable distribution of income. This can be accomplished by a government committed to democratic socialism. (See Chapter 12.)

---

[214] See, for example, Clarence Barber and John McCallum, *Controlling Inflation: Learning from Experience in Canada, Europe and Japan* (Ottawa: Canadian Institute for Economic Policy, 1982).

Appendix A
CALCULATING THE AVERAGE REAL WAGE RATE OF A GROUP OF WORKERS

The current Consumer Price Index (CPI) is constructed on the basis of 1981 prices, and the 1981 index is arbitrarily set equal to 100.0. The purchasing power or **real wage rate** can be calculated by determining how much money would have been necessary in 1981 to purchase the same amount of consumer goods and services that the current average wage rate of a group of workers can purchase. For example, if a group of workers received an average wage rate of $8 per hour in 1981 and an average wage rate of $10 per hour in 1982, the average **real wage rate**, or the purchasing power equivalent of the 1982 average wage rate in terms of the number of 1981 dollars that could buy the same amount of consumer goods and services as the 1982 average wage rate, of the group can be calculated as follows:

1981 CPI $= 100.0$
1982 CPI $= 110.8$
1981 average wage rate $\qquad = \$\ 8.00$ per hour
1982 average wage rate $\qquad = \$10.00$ per hour
1982 average real wage rate $\qquad = \$\ \ ?\ \ $ per hour

$$\frac{\text{1982 average wage rate}}{\text{1982 average real wage rate}} = \frac{\text{1982 CPI}}{\text{1981 CPI}}$$

OR

$$\frac{\$10.00 \text{ per hour}}{\text{1982 average real wage rate}} = \frac{110.8}{100.0}$$

Therefore, the

$$\text{1982 average real wage rate} = \frac{\$10.00 \text{ per hour} \times 100.0}{110.8} = \$9.03 \text{ per hour.}$$

In this example, even though the actual average wage rate of the group rose from $8 per hour in 1981 to $10 in 1982 or by 25 per cent, the purchasing power of the $10 in 1982 is equivalent to what the purchasing power of $9.03 was in 1981 because prices were lower in 1981. The percentage change in the average **real wage** rate of the group between 1981 and 1982 was

$$\frac{\$9.03 - \$8.00}{\$8.00} \times 100 = \frac{\$1.03}{\$8.00} \times 100 = 12.9\%.$$

The formula for calculating the average real wage rate of a group of employees for a given year (y) can be simplified to:

$$\text{Average real wage rate}_y = \frac{\text{Average wage rate}_y \times 100.0}{CPI_y}$$

Now let us carry the example one step further. If the actual average wage rate of the group rose from \$10 per hour in 1982 to \$11 per hour in 1983, the change in the group's average real wage rate could be calculated by computing the 1983 average real wage rate and comparing it to the 1982 average real wage rate that was calculated above. In 1983, the CPI was 117.2. Therefore, the

$$\text{Average real wage rate}_{1983} = \frac{\text{Average wage rate}_{1983} \times 100.0}{CPI_{1983}} =$$

$$\frac{\$11.00 \text{ per hour} \times 100.0}{117.2} = \$9.39 \text{ per hour}.$$

Therefore, the change in the average **real wage** rate for the group between 1982 and 1983 was

$$\frac{\$9.39 - \$9.03}{\$9.03} \times 100 = 4.0\%.$$

Appendix B
SPECULATION AND SPECULATIVE MARKETS

Speculation can take place in **futures markets**. A speculator who believes the price of a commodity will **rise** will make a contract to **purchase** the commodity **now** for delivery in the future. If the speculator's judgement is correct, when the time for delivery arrives prices will be higher and the speculator will sell the contract for delivery to someone who actually uses the commodity at a price higher than the original purchase price. The speculator has never seen the commodity, but has reaped a speculative profit. In the course of these events, the initial purchase of the commodity by the speculator contributes to the increase in price that the speculator believes will occur for other reasons (for example, a poor crop).

Speculators who believe the price of a commodity will fall will make a contract to **sell** the commodity **now** but for future delivery. If the speculator's judgement is correct, when the time for delivery arrives prices will be lower and the speculator can purchase a contract for immediate delivery of the commodity at a lower price than the speculator originally received. In the course of these events, the original sale of the commodity by the speculator contributes to the fall in the price that the speculator believes will occur for other reasons (for example, an exceptionally plentiful crop).

PART FOUR

INTERNATIONAL TRADE

CHAPTER 11

INTERNATIONAL TRADE, EXCHANGE RATES, AND COMMERCIAL POLICY

Many textbook discussions of economic theory and policy proceed on the assumption that the economy is self-contained or "closed." Such an assumption simplifies many discussions and is useful until the reader understands economic reasoning, concepts, and theory. However, the world economy is now highly integrated, and it is necessary to view most economies as being "open" in the sense that international trade has an impact on domestic output, employment, and income distribution. This is especially true for Canada where about half of the value of goods produced domestically is exported and a quarter of total Gross National Product is generated in international trade.

This chapter examines the national accounts associated with international economic transactions, the role and importance of exchange rates, world and Canadian trade developments, and the relationships between international trade and domestic economic policy.

THE CLOSED ECONOMY

Production and consumption give rise to a flow of income within a given country. If countries were self-sufficient, so that firms and government produced all that was necessary for investment and household consumption, the demand for output would consist of domestic consumption demand (C), domestic investment demand (I), and government demand (G). The Gross National

Expenditure (Yg), the measure of the economy's output (and income) during a given year, would be expressed as

$$Y_g \equiv C + I + G.^{215}$$

No modern nation has this kind of isolated economic system. However, when economists want to simplify discussion about an activity where foreign trade is unimportant, they will assume that there is a "closed" economy.

THE OPEN ECONOMY

Even if they could be, nations seldom want to be completely self-sufficient. Households and enterprises in one country wish to purchase goods and services produced by enterprises in other countries. Enterprises located in one country will produce goods and services, which they sell to household and enterprises in other countries. The search for the most productive use of assets also produces the movement of capital between nations. These activities also produces the movement of capital between nations. These activities taken together produce net exports (En) equal to exports minus imports so that

$$Y_g \equiv C + I + G + En.$$

NET EXPORTS AND THE NATIONAL INCOME ACCOUNTS

International trade in **goods and services** is recorded in the **balance of payments** section of the national income accounts in an entry called the **current account balance**. The current account balance reflects the difference between Canadian **exports** and **imports** of goods and services.

Exports and imports of **goods** are called **visible trade**, while exports and imports of **services** such as transport,[216] insurance, and the use of financial and physical assets are called trade in **invisible items**. Interest and dividend payments for the use of foreign-owned assets are the largest invisible items in Canadian imports.

The place of the **current account** in Canada's balance of payments is illustrated in *Table 1-11*. In 1982, the current account balance was +$3,017 million, that is, receipts from foreigners exceeded payments to foreigners for goods and services traded by this amount.

---

[215] See Chapter 6 for a discussion of the measurement of national output and income.

[216] Because Canada does not have presently an offshore maritime fleet, payments for the transportation of goods are an important invisible import item.

TABLE 1-11

Canadian Balance of International Payments, 1982
(Millions of dollars)

Merchandise Trade	
Exports	84,577
Imports	− 66,239
Trade balance	+ 18,338
Service balance	− 16,763
Net transfers	+ 1,442
Current account balance	+ 3,017
Long-term capital flows	
Net direct investment	− 1,625
Portfolio transactions	
New issues of Canadian securities	+ 16,190
Retirement of Canadian securities	− 3,750
Other long-term transactions	− 1,725
Total long-term capital flows	+ 9,090
Short-term capital flows	− 8,758
Total net capital flows	+ 332
Net errors and omissions	− 4,044
Net official monetary movements	− 695

Source: Statistics Canada, *System of National Accounts, Quarterly Estimates of the Canadian Balance of International Payments, Third Quarter 1983*, Table 16, pp. 58 and 60 (Catalogue No. 67-001, quarterly).

When exports of goods and services exceed imports of goods and services, that is, when receipts exceed payments on current account, there is a **surplus** on current account. When imports exceed exports so that payments exceed receipts on current account, there is a **deficit** on current account.

The 1982 surplus on current account was an unusual event, which was caused by a nearly $10,000 million fall in the import of goods between 1981 and 1982, while exports of goods remained about the same during this period. The appearance of the surplus reflected the severe economic downturn of 1982. Canada has run surpluses on its current account only three times between 1960 and 1982. Except for 1960 and 1975, Canada exported more goods than it imported, but payments for services typically exceed receipts from services sufficiently to produce a deficit on current account. In 1982, $10,628 million was paid in the form of interest and dividends to foreigners owning assets in Canada.[217] This accounted for 32.7 per cent of all Canadian service payments to foreigners.

In addition to receipts and payments for goods and services on current account, there is a movement of funds between countries associated with the lending and borrowing of money as well as the purchase and sale of property rights. These movements are recorded in the balance of payments sections of the national income accounts as **capital flows**. Capital in this context means finance or claims on property rather than stocks of machinery, plant, and equipment.

Capital outflow or **foreign lending** consists of items such as loans to foreigners, the purchase of foreign securities by Canadians, and funds sent to foreign branches of Canadian companies by their headquarters. **Capital inflow** or **foreign borrowing** consists of the same kind of transactions, but in the opposite direction.

The place of the capital account in the balance of payments is illustrated in *Table 1-11*. In 1982, **net capital flows** in the capital account added $332 million to the balance of payments. This addition consisted of a net inflow of $9,090 million capital in long-term forms (direct investment in machinery, plant, and equipment and purchase of securities) and a net outflow of $8,758 million of short-term capital. Short-term capital flow is sensitive to changes in interest rates and sometimes is referred to as "hot money" because this money tends to move across national borders relatively easily. The implications of these movements for economic policy are discussed later in this chapter.

THE BALANCE OF PAYMENTS

A country's **balance of payments** is the result of all the transactions involving receipts and payments across its boundaries during a year. It reflects the combined effect of the current account balance, capital flows, and the adjustments in national lending and borrowing associated with these transactions.

A positive balance of payments on **current account** is shown in *Table 1-11*, that is, in 1982 Canadians received $3,017 million more in payments for goods and services sold abroad than they paid for goods and services purchased from abroad. In the same year there was a net capital flow of $332 million into Canada as a result of long- and short-term capital movements. (See *Table 1-11*.) However, the figure of − $4,044 million for **net errors and omissions**, which represents an outflow of funds, "which is thought to reflect primarily unrecorded financial transactions,"[218] meant that the net result of these movements was that Canadians had to meet obligations to foreigners equal to − $695 million (+ $3,017 mil-

---

[217] Canada, Department of Finance, *Economic Review April 1983*, Reference Table 71, p. 207 (Catalogue No. F1-21/1983E).
[218] *Ibid.*, p. 57.

lion + \$332 million − \$4,044 million). These obligations were met by the movement of assets in an internationally acceptable form of money (for example, gold or United States dollars). Thus, the − \$695 million entry in net official monetary assets balances the international trade account. (See *Table 1-11*.)

In general, when there is a net outflow on capital account **less than** the current account **surplus**, or a net inflow on capital account **greater than** the current account **deficit**, a country is said to have a **favourable** balance of payments. When there is a net inflow on capital account **less than** the current account **deficit**, a country is said to have **unfavourable** balance of payments.

A favourable or unfavourable balance of payments for a nation means an increase or decrease in its holdings of international reserves.[219] Movements of international reserves among nations are watched closely in financial markets and influence domestic economic policy. This influence will be discussed later in this chapter.

FOREIGN INVESTMENT

Foreign investment enters Canada in two forms:

1. direct investment in the ownership of Canadian property, resources, and industries; and

2. portfolio investment consisting mostly of the purchase of provincial, municipal, and corporate bonds plus the purchase of federal securities when the federal government occasionally borrows in foreign markets.

Between 1976 and 1982, total foreign investment in these long-term forms has been positive and at times substantial. However, **direct investment** on an annual basis has been either small or negative during this period. Nevertheless, foreign ownership and control of Canadian industry has continued to increase because these companies have reinvested a portion of their Canadian profits and accumulated depreciation allowances in Canadian industry.

Foreign investment is not necessarily in the best interest of the Canadian economy. Substantial payments of dividends and interest to foreign owners of Canadian assets have contributed to large Canadian deficits on current account. And contrary to popular opinion, it has been argued that foreign direct investments make a negligible contribution to economic growth and a favourable

---

[219] The composition of Canada's international reserves on May 31, 1984, was as follows: U.S. dollars \$1,665.3 million; other foreign currencies \$428.6 million; gold \$735.2 million; special drawing rights \$99.1 million; reserve position in International Monetary Fund \$742.5 million. Total reserves were \$3,670.8 million. Source: Canada, Department of Finance, *Release*, Tuesday, 5 June 1984.

164

balance of payments because of the lack of dynamism of foreign-controlled firms.[220]

There is also concern that Canadian subsidiaries of foreign corporations are reaping unfair tax advantages to the detriment of Canadian taxpayers and workers. One recent study reports:

> The corporate income taxes paid in Canada by Canadian subsidiaries of foreign corporations (CSFCs) greatly concern Canada's tax authorities (or at least they should). It is well known that CSFCs dominate the markets for profitable high-technology growth products and that the transfer prices they pay for goods and services purchased from their parents or from other affiliates abroad can be manipulated to avoid the corporate income tax in Canada.

> When the price charged to a CSFC for a product or service is increased, the parent's consolidated pre-tax profit is unchanged, but the taxable profit in Canada is reduced. Insofar as the profits are transferred to tax havens or to countries with lower tax rates, the consolidated after-tax profit is increased by reducing the tax paid in Canada.

> The avoidance of the corporate income tax by CSFCs has two undesirable consequences. First, the tax burden on Canadians is increased correspondingly: they are required to pay a disproportionate share of the cost of the public services which help make Canada an attractive market for the high-technology products of the CSFC. Secondly, Canadian firms that hope to compete with the CSFC are put at a competitive disadvantage, since they cannot avoid the income tax. Furthermore, insofar as CSFCs are used to merchandise products manufactured abroad, the employment opportunities for Canadians in production, research and development, and other areas of business are reduced correspondingly.[221]

INTERNATIONAL TRADE AND EXCHANGE RATES

The exchange rate between the currencies of any two countries is the **price** of one currency in terms of the other. The price of the currencies of eight different countries on March 2, 1984, is shown in *Table 2-11.*

---

[220] This argument is made in, H. Lukin Robinson, *Canada's Crippled Dollar: An Analysis of International Trade and Our Troubled Balance of Payments* (Ottawa: Canadian Institute for Economic Policy, 1980), pp. 98-102.

[221] Myron J. Gordon, *The Taxation of Canadian Subsidiaries of Foreign Corporations* (Ottawa: Canadian Institute for Economic Policy, 1984), p. 5.

TABLE 2-11

The Price of Selected Currencies in Canadian Dollars and the Amount of Foreign Currencies That Could be Purchased with One Canadian Dollar, March 2, 1984

Country	Currency	Price in Canadian Dollars	The Amount of Foreign Currencies That Could Be Purchased with One Canadian Dollar
West Germany	Mark	0.5103	1.96
Spain	Peseta	0.00902	110.87
United States	Dollar	1.2338	0.81
France	Franc	0.1696	5.90
Greece	Drachma	0.01474	67.84
Italy	Lira	0.000855	1169.59
Japan	Yen	0.005166	193.57
England	Pound	1.8254	0.55

Source: *Le Devoir*, 3 mars 1984, p. 10 (Banque Nationale du Canada).

Thus, Canadians going to England who wanted to purchase pounds on March 2, 1984, would have had to pay 1.8254 Canadian dollars (plus a bank service charge) for each pound purchased, while an English person coming to Canada who wanted to purchase Canadian dollars would have had to pay 0.55 pounds (plus a bank service charge) for each dollar purchased.

Exchange rates exist because the currency of one country is not a legal means of payment for expenditures in another country. A Canadian who wishes to purchase English goods and services or to invest in English assets must do so with English pounds. Similarily, a foreigner who desires Canadian goods, services, or investment must acquire Canadian dollars.

For example, a Canadian **importer** of goods from England requires English pounds in order to purchase from English enterprises. The importer will exchange Canadian dollars for pounds and will be a **demander of pounds** and a **supplier of Canadian dollars** on the **foreign exchange market**. Likewise, a Japanese **importer** of Canadian goods is a **demander** of Canadian dollars and a **supplier** of yen on the foreign exchange market.

At any moment in time, given the prices of goods and services of each country and given the attractiveness of foreign investment, there is a supply and demand for the currency of each country that **tends** to establish the exchange rate or price of each currency in terms of others.

When the forces of supply and demand for currencies on international money markets are allowed to determine exchange rates, there are said to be **free** or **floating exchange rates**.

Since the 1930's most trading countries have preferred **fixed exchange rates** that are adjusted infrequently to take account of major changes in the supply and demand for particular currencies. In general, the preference for fixed exchange rates reflects the fact that trade can proceed more smoothly when purchasers and sellers of foreign currencies can be sure that the value of these currencies will not be changing continuously. However, fixed exchange rates may work against the domestic interests of some countries and to the unfair advantage of others during particular periods. Further, when there are unsettled conditions in international money markets, speculative buying and selling of currencies makes fixed exchange rates impossible. Thus, since 1972 almost all exchange rates have been floating and the value of the Canadian dollar in relation to other currencies is still floating. However, the government of Canada intercedes in foreign exchange markets when it believes changes in the relative value of the Canadian dollar are either too large or too rapid.If the government wants to increase the value of the Canadian dollar, it will increase the **demand for Canadian dollars** and increase the **supply of foreign currencies** by buying Canadian dollars on international financial markets with its reserves of foreign currencies. Other things remaining equal, this will tend to increase the price (value) of the Canadian dollar. Similarly, selling Canadian dollars and buying foreign reserve currencies will tend to lower the price (value) of the Canadian dollar. Other governments also attempt to regulate movements in the relative values of their currency. Under these conditions exchange rates are said to be determined by a "dirty float."

GOLD, U.S. DOLLARS, AND FIXED EXCHANGE RATES

Gold — and to a lesser degree silver — has been a universally accepted medium of exchange between countries in international trade and a means of settling international debts.

In 1934, the United States, then emerging as the dominant world economic power, fixed the price of gold by offering to buy and sell unlimited amounts of gold at a price of $35 U.S. per ounce. Under these conditions gold **and** the U.S. dollar became the media for settling debts in international trade (the pound sterling maintained a minor role), and the value of other currencies could be fixed in terms of U.S. dollars.

For example, if the British Exchequer bought and sold an ounce of gold for £12.5 British and the Canadian Department of Finance bought and sold gold at $34.80 Canadian per ounce, this would mean that

£12.50 British = $35.00 United States = $34.80 Canadian.

Then one pound would have a fixed parity exchange rate of

$$\frac{\$35.00 \text{ U.S.}}{£12.50 \text{ Br.}} = \$2.80 \text{ U.S. per pound,}$$

and one Canadian dollar would have a fixed parity exchange rate of

$$\frac{\$35.00 \text{ U.S.}}{\$34.80 \text{ Cdn.}} = \$1.006 \text{ U.S. per dollar Canadian.}$$

In 1972, as a result of deficits in its balance of payments and the consequent loss of gold reserves, the United States ceased selling and buying gold at a fixed price, and the market price of gold almost doubled during the following year.

Between 1972 and January of 1980, the price of gold increased erratically and spectacularly. By January 1980 its price had reached $800 U.S. an ounce. Deterioration of the value of U.S. dollars, world-wide inflation, political instability, and the threat of war all provoked liquid wealth holders to convert national currencies into gold holdings, which were believed to be a safer store of value than paper money as well as a hedge against inflation. The rapid rise in gold prices was compounded by widespread speculation throughout the world that gold prices would continue to rise. However, by mid-1984 the price of gold had returned to prices in the range between $300 and $400 U.S. an ounce.

DEPRECIATION, APPRECIATION, AND DEVALUATION

The Canadian dollar is **depreciating** relative to another currency when the price of the Canadian dollar is going down in foreign exchange markets relative to that currency. For example, if the value of the Canadian dollar is depreciating relative to the U.S. dollar, fewer U.S. dollars would be needed to purchase a Canadian dollar than previously.

The Canadian dollar is **appreciating** relative to the U.S. dollar when more U.S. dollars are needed to purchase a Canadian dollar than previously.

In a free exchange market, currencies continually depreciate and appreciate. In a fixed exchange market, currencies appreciate and depreciate infrequently and often only under agreed-upon conditions. **Devaluation** of a currency in a fixed exchange market is a term usually reserved for a change in the value of the currency relative to the price of gold. All currencies would be devalued if there were proportionately higher prices for gold without currency appreciations or depreciations. Gold-producing countries and countries with large gold reserves would gain from such an event.

Devaluation of a country's currency so that it **depreciates** relative to other currencies under fixed exchange rate arrangements tend to **increase** its **exports** of goods and services and to **decrease** its **imports** of goods and services. Depreciation of a currency under floating exchange rate arrangements has the same effects.

This occurs because the depreciation of a country's currency makes it cheaper to buy in foreign exchange markets and therefore results in lower prices to those who convert their foreign currency in order to purchase a country's domestic products. For example, if the Canadian dollar depreciates 10 per cent relative to the U.S. dollar, a product that costs a U.S. buyer $10 U.S. to purchase would now cost 10 per cent less or $9 U.S. This decrease in real cost to U.S. importers should increase the purchase of Canadian goods and services and therefore employment in Canadian industry.[222]

At the same time, the depreciation of the Canadian dollar will make U.S. dollars more expensive to Canadians and thereby raise the price of U.S. imports.

While depreciation may increase employment and income in export industries, it may not increase the nation's standard of living. Whether it does or not depends on the relation between the net gains in income from added employment and the loss in purchasing power resulting from the higher prices of imported products.

A country will try to depreciate its currency or will find that its currency is depreciating when it is having persistent **balance of payments** problems, that is, when the value of its exports chronically tends to be lower than the value of its imports. For awhile a country may make up the difference between exports and imports by using its official international reserves to pay its bills to foreign creditors.[223] However, if imports continue to exceed exports, these reserves will be depleted, and the currency will be depreciated either by devaluation under a fixed exchange rate regime or by market forces if exchange rates are floating freely in international money markets.

ECONOMIC INTEGRATION AND WORLD TRADE

International trade and international economic integration have increased markedly since the Second World War. Large-scale direct foreign investment by multinational firms throughout the world has contributed to a more integrated world economy. Third world nations who were traditionally mainly exports of raw materials and agricultural products now are entering world trade competition as producers of semi-processed and fully-processed manufactured products. In some cases, this increased trade activity is the result of state-directed planning;

---

[222] This assumes that the U.S. does not "retaliate" by a similar devaluation or by raising tariffs on Canadian goods.

[223] Canada's official international reserves are made up of gold, foreign exchange (a large portion of which is U.S. dollars), and special drawing rights (SDRs) and reserves at the International Monetary Fund. For a detailed discussion of the role of international reserves see, R.G. Lipsey, D.D. Puris, G.R. Sparks, and P.O. Steiner, *Economics*, 4th edition (New York: Harper and Row, 1982), Chapter 36.

in others, it is a by-product of the policies of multinational firms seeking to maximize profits by producing in low-wage areas, using modern plants with advanced technology.[224] Eastern European countries also are participating actively in world trade. "The annual growth rate of exports from Eastern Bloc countries soared from 9.6 per cent during the period 1960-65 to 47.2 per cent in 1974."[225]

CANADIAN FOREIGN TRADE

Canada's exports of goods and services account for a significant proportion of Canadian employment and income. In 1982, exports were valued at $81.8 billion and accounted for about a quarter of the nation's domestic production.

Canadian commodity exports in 1982 are shown in *Table 3-11*. This table reveals that 57 per cent of exports were made up of farm and fish products, forest products, energy materials, and other metals, minerals, and products. These exports are in large measure produced in capital intensive industries that on average use less labour per dollar value of output than would be found in the manufacture of consumer and industrial goods.

TABLE 3-11
Canadian Commodity Exports, 1982

	Exports	
Commodity	Millions of Dollars	Percentage of Total Domestic Exports
Farm and fish products	10,482	12.8
Forest products	11,961	14.6
Energy materials	12,673	15.5
Other metals, minerals, and products	11,472	14.0
Chemicals and fertilizers	4,102	5.0
Motor vehicles and parts	17,051	20.8
Other manufactured goods	14,088	17.2
Total domestic exports	81,829	100.0
Exports of foreign products	2,706	
Total exports	84,535	

Source: *Bank of Canada Review*, January 1984, Table 74, pp. S138-S140.

---

[224] The classic study of the movement of production and jobs across international boundaries is, F. Frobel, J. Heinrichs, O. Kreye, *The New International Divisions of Labour* (Cambridge: Cambridge University Press, 1980).

[225] Canadian Institute for Economic Policy, *Out of Joint with the Times* (Ottawa: 1979), p. 13.

By far the most important customer for Canadian exports is the United States. Canada's principal trading areas are currently the United States, Japan, and the United Kingdom. In 1982, the United States received 68.2 per cent of Canadian exports, while Japan and the United Kingdom were a distant second and third in export importance with 5.6 and 3.3 per cent respectively. (See *Table 4-11*.)

TABLE 4-11

Exports to Principal Trading Areas (Excluding Re-Exports), 1982

Country	Dollar Value (billions)	Percentage of Total Canadian Exports
United States	55.8	68.2
Japan	4.6	5.6
United Kingdom	2.7	3.3
Total Canadian Exports	81.8	

Source: Statistics Canada, *Summary of External Trade*, December 1983, Table X-1, p. 32 (Catalogue No. 65-001, monthly).

While the United States was Canada's biggest export market in 1982, it also is interesting to note the **rates of growth** of Canada's exports to various areas of the world. These rates of growth for the five-year period 1977-1982 are shown in *Table 5-11*.

TABLE 5-11

Canada's Exports by Area, 1982, and Percentage Change, 1977-1982

	1982 $ million	1982 vs 1977 % change
North America	55,480	+87%
Western Europe	8,530	+60%
Asia	8,060	+115%
Eastern Europe	2,570	+301%
Middle East	1,820	+169%
South America	1,510	+32%
Central America	1,500	+92%
Africa	1,150	+144%
Oceania	840	+73%
Total	81,460	+87%

Source: Data from Statistics Canada and Chase Econometrics presented in *The Financial Post*, 26 February 1983, p. 16.

Canadian imports are for the most part highly processed and fully manufactured goods. Industrial materials, construction materials, motor vehicles and parts, other transportation equipment and parts, machinery and equipment, and other consumer goods account for 82.4 per cent of total imports. (See *Table 6-11.*)

TABLE 6-11

Canadian Imports by End-Use, 1982

Commodity	Imports Millions of Dollars	Percentage of Total Imports
Energy materials	6,684	9.8
Industrial materials	13,934	20.5
Construction materials	1,236	1.8
Motor vehicles and parts	15,696	23.1
Other transportation equipment and parts	2,008	3.0
Machinery and equipment	15,383	22.6
Food	4,244	6.3
Other consumer goods	7,719	11.4
Special items	1,022	1.5
Total imports	67,926	100.0

Source: *Bank of Canada Review*, January 1984, Table 75, pp. S141 and S142.

The United States is Canada's most important source of imports. In 1982, it supplied 70.5 per cent of total imports, while Japan, the second most important source, supplied only 5.2 per cent of total imports.[226]

CANADIAN COMMERCIAL POLICY

The government can regulate international trade by means of tariff agreements with other countries that affect the prices at which Canadian exports can be sold and Canadian imports can be purchased. International trade also can be regulated by **non-tariff barriers** that limit the quantities of exports and imports of particular goods.

[226] Statistics Canada, *Summary of External Trade*, December 1983, Table M-1, p. 18 (Catalogue No. 65-001, monthly).

172

There is perennial controversy among economists and those concerned with international trade about the merits of **free trade** and **protectionism**, that is, whether a country should have high or low tariffs ("free" implying no tariffs). **If political complications are put aside**, the economic issues are relatively simple.

Those who advocate protectionism argue that when domestic industry is suffering from foreign competition, a duty (tariff) on imports raising the price of these foreign goods will lead to increased demand for domestic products and thus increase employment and profits at home, at least in the short run.

Those who advocate free trade argue that artificial barriers to trade lead to inefficiency of production. The fact that an industry needs to be protected in one country is evidence that it can be conducted more efficiently elsewhere. Protective tariff policies sacrifice the advantage of division of labour between nations, cause economic resources to be used less productively than they might, and leave all parties worse off than they could be.

In fact, there is nothing incompatible in these two abstract arguments. The free trade argument is that tariffs reduce efficiency (average output per worker), and the protectionist argument is that they increase employment in the domestic economy (usually at the expense of unemployment in other countries). The relative importance of the two arguments depends upon the seriousness of unemployment in a given country. Typically, periods of high unemployment provoke nations to protectionism of one kind or another.

The argument becomes more complicated once real cases are examined. At any moment of time, there is an international structure of tariffs. If one country seeks to export its unemployment by raising tariffs, other countries will respond in order to protect their own employment position. And while raising tariffs on imports may protect existing employment or even raise employment in certain industries, if these tariffs persist there may be tendencies for these industries to become relatively inefficient because of the tariff protection against foreign competition. With depression-like levels of unemployment in most industrial economies and a rapid and dramatic restructuring of the world economy, demands for protectionism of one kind or another became commonplace in most advanced industrial countries at the beginning of the 1980's.

The stock market crash in 1929 marked the beginning of the Great Depression with its accompanying high unemployment throughout the developed capitalist world. One reaction to this unemployment in the 1930's was protectionism and therefore an increase in barriers to international trade. Canada participated in this, while at the same time joining in the creation of preferential tariff arrangements among Commonwealth countries.

The *Seventh Annual Review* of the Economic Council of Canada describes Canadian commercial policy in this period:

> In the past, Canadian commercial policy focused strongly on two
> themes: (a) negotiation of reduced tariff and other barriers to our

exports to foreign countries, particularly for resource-based products in which it was considered that Canada has a "natural advantage," and (b) the maintenance of protection for a considerable range of manufactured products, mainly on the premise that protection was required if the country was to maintain various lines of industrial activity and employment. The highest tariffs have generally been imposed on final products, and higher tariffs have been set for partly manufactured goods than for raw materials used in manufacturing. This tariff structure tends to keep raw material costs relatively low. It does, however, permit processing and manufacturing activities to be conducted at costs that are high relative to production costs in other countries with large internal markets or tariff-free access to large external markets.[227]

After the Second World War, with world economic activity expanding, restrictive tariffs began to lower. In 1947, Canada joined with other nations in negotiating the General Agreement on Tariffs and Trade (GATT).

Under the GATT agreement countries meet periodically to negotiate mutually advantageous cuts in tariffs. Significant progress was made in reducing tariffs in 1967 during the Kennedy Round of negotiations.[228] However, in subsequent years the reduced tariffs were replaced to a considerable extent by **non-tariff barriers** to international trade. These barriers are defined as anything other than tariffs that prevents the free flow of international trade. They include production and export subsidies, quotas on imports, standards purporting to maintain the quality of imports, difficult administrative procedures, minimum allowable import prices, and special forms of variable indirect taxation.

In 1979, the Tokyo Round of GATT negotiations, which began in 1975, were concluded. Efforts were made to produce rules of conduct regarding the use of non-tariff barriers, and many specific tariff reductions were negotiated. But there was no general reduction in tariffs as had been agreed to in the 1967 Kennedy Round, and experts are not clear about the ultimate effects of the agreements that were reached.[229]

The trend toward free trade that began in the 1940's ran out of steam in the 1970's. High unemployment in North America, Britain, and some Western European countries is part of the explanation. The inability of the United States to reduce large deficits in both its balance of trade and balance of payments also has produced strong pressures for a return to protectionism in that country. In addition, the organization of the European Economic Community (EEC) has

[227] Economic Council of Canada, *Seventh Annual Review, Patterns of Growth* (Ottawa: Queen's Printer, 1970), p. 80.
[228] This round of GATT negotiations is named after President John F. Kennedy of the United States who set up the negotiations and obtained permission from the U.S. Congress to negotiate reductions of up to 50 per cent in U.S. tariffs.
[229] See, *International Monetary Fund (IMF) Survey*,7 May 1979, pp. 133-137.

become essentially a protectionist device as far as outside nations are concerned.[230] It has organized a common market within which countries enter into preferential agreements among themselves, all of which discriminate against the exports of outsiders. Elsewhere, countries in the Eastern Bloc, South East Asia, South America, and Asia Minor have banded together to form world trading blocs aimed at increasing internal self-sufficiency.[231]

Given these conditions, some have argued that it would be in Canada's interest to set up a free trade area with the United States. Those who support this proposal claim that a single open North American market would allow efficient Canadian firms to grow and thrive, while inefficient firms would disappear. They believe in the long run all Canadians would be better off.[232]

Those who oppose this proposal believe that the giant U.S. multinationals would absorb even more of Canadian industry and resources than they presently control and that this control ultimately would result in higher unemployment, slower economic growth, and a satellite political status for Canada.[233]

The severe world-wide recession that began in the summer of 1981 — and was slowly moderating as this chapter was being written — caused mass unemployment and threatened the existence of a number of North American industries, among them the critical automobile and steel industries. Under these circumstances corporations attacked wage rates, working conditions, and social programs under the slogan of making the domestic economy internationally competitive. At the same time, these corporations and a number of unions pressured both the United States and Canadian governments to negotiate or impose quotas on the importation of certain goods to their respective countries. In 1983 and 1984, bilateral negotiations with Japan produced quotas on the importation of Japanese cars in both the United States and Canada. In 1984, the Americans considered establishing quotas on steel imports. Consideration is being given still, but for the present Canada's steel industry is not affected.

In the debate between free trade and protectionist policies in international trade, it is assumed that there is competition among producers in different countries so that the free movement of resources and production between countries will result in maximum efficiency and thereby in benefits to consumers in the form of lower prices and higher employment for all. However, the dominance of multinational corporations in the international economy produces a far different result. In response to this reality the Canadian division of the United

---

[230] In 1978, the EEC had a larger Gross National Product and conducted more world trade than the U.S.A.

[231] These blocs are: the Council for Mutual Economic Assistance (COMECON) for countries in the Eastern Bloc, including the Soviet Union; the Association of South East Asian Nations (ASEAN); the Andean Pact Commission, which includes six South American countries; and the free trade zone between Iran, Pakistan, and Turkey agreed to in the 1976 Treaty of Ismir.

[232] See, for example, Economic Council of Canada, *Looking Outward: A New Trade Strategy for Canada* (Ottawa: Information Canada, 1975).

[233] See, for example, Canadian Institute for Economic Policy, *Out of Joint With the Times, op. cit.*

Automobile, Aerospace and Agricultural Implement Workers' of America International Union (UAW) is advocating a **Canadian content** policy to deal with the activities of the multinationals in the international economy.

Robert White, UAW Director for Canada, described the proposal for Canadian content in production this way:

> The basic idea of "Canadian content" is that any corporation selling in the Canadian market must make a commitment to providing proportional jobs in Canada. This proposal is an alternative to the dominant policy of letting the marketplace and the multinational corporations decide where plants and jobs should be located. But this issue goes far beyond developments in the auto industry. If working people accept the current rules — the rules which force us to play the corporations' game of trying to become internationally competitive — all workers and their families will be adversely affected. . . .[234]

The main thrust of the UAW's position is that "the alternative to leaving our international economic relations to the market and the multinationals is to move towards planned trade and greater self-sufficiency."[235] Such an approach requires moving towards a planned economy.

INTEREST RATES, UNEMPLOYMENT, AND THE BALANCE OF PAYMENTS

Changes in the level of domestic interest rates can affect significantly aggregate demand and therefore employment and unemployment. Increased interest rates will make loans for business and government investment, housing, and consumption spending more expensive and therefore tend to reduce aggregate demand. (See Chapter 7 for a review of this subject.) However, Canadian Ministers of Finance under both Liberal and Progressive Conservative governments have not hesitated to change Canadian interest rates whenever American interest rates changed. This policy became a major source of debate in Canada as already high interest rates caused by the energy crisis and its associated inflation were driven even higher by the United States Federal Reserve Bank policy of monetarism and high interest rates.

The Bank of Canada, supported by both Liberal and Conservative governments, pushed up the Canadian interest rates so as to maintain their relation with American rates. The rationale for this policy was that, should U.S. interest

---

[234] In a discussion book prepared by the UAW in Canada, *The International Competition Game* (North York: Public Relations Department, UAW, 1984), Introduction.
[235] *Ibid.*, p. 6.

rates rise too far above Canadian rates, corporations and financial institutions holding funds in fairly liquid short-term securities[236] (for example, 90-day Treasury notes) would transfer these funds to the U.S. These transfers would cause the Canadian balance of payments to move further into deficit, thereby provoking a depreciation of the Canadian dollar on the international exchange market. While a fall in the value of the dollar might improve exports (a desirable outcome), the increased cost to Canadians of American imports would increase the rate of inflation (an undesirable outcome). Thus, the Governor of the Bank of Canada, Gerald Bouey, increased Canadian interest rates and undoubtedly increased Canadian unemployment in what he conceived was part of a war against inflation.

Those who opposed the high interest policy, including the New Democratic Party and the Canadian Labour Congress, argued that lower interest rates would not provoke a massive flight of liquid assets because of the ever present risk to those who move their money into foreign currencies that an appreciation of the Canadian dollar may result in losses to those who want to return their money to Canada. They also maintained that selective controls of the movement of liquid assets are possible if this is necessary to maintain lower Canadian interest rates. Finally, they argued that the flight for lower interest rates was part of a full employment policy, which would lead to a solution of Canada's balance of payments problems.

---

[236] These funds are often referred to as "hot money." See pages 161 and 162 in this chapter.

PART FIVE

THE WAY AHEAD

CHAPTER 12

NATIONAL ECONOMIC PLANNING
AND DEMOCRATIC SOCIALISM

P
ersistent, widespread, and growing unemployment became a fundamental economic problem in Canada during the latter half of the 1970's.
By the end of the decade the national unemployment rate hovered
around 8 per cent as real economic growth was insufficient to create
enough employment to absorb the growing labour force and also replace jobs lost because of technological change. High unemployment was accompanied by a marked fall in the use of machinery, plant, and equipment so
that idle capacity existed side by side with idle workers.[237] Inflation, coupled
with the institution of the *Anti-Inflation Act*[238] and its accompanying Anti-Inflation
Board (AIB), kept the growth of labour income below the trend rate of growth of
national productivity and contributed to slow economic growth and a redistribution of national income away from wages and salaries and towards profits and
other forms of non-labour income.

In 1981, Canada and the rest of the world entered an economic downturn
unequalled since the Great Depression. Canadian Real Gross National Product
decreased by 4.8 per cent between 1981 and 1982 and was still below 1981 levels
in 1983. As a result the national unemployment rate increased from 7.5 per cent
to 11.9 per cent between 1981 and 1983.

---

[237] The Department of Industry, Trade and Commerce, Economic Analysis Branch, reported that
capacity utilization rates for manufacturing fell from about 92 per cent in the first half of the 1970's
to about 85 per cent in the second half.

[238] Bill C-73, the *Anti-Inflation Act*, was passed by the House of Commons on December 3, 1975.
Prime Minister Trudeau described the Act and its accompanying regulations as a "massive intervention in the decision-making power of . . . economic groups."

Inflation and interest rates decreased markedly in response to inadequate demand on a world scale, but in Canada the **real** rate of interest, the difference between the rate of interest and the rate of inflation, rose as inflation decreased more than interest rates in the 1981-1983 period. These high real rates of interest, combined with **attempts** by the federal government to reduce deficits in successive budgets in 1981 and 1982, exacerbated Canada's economic difficulties.

The continued growth of corporate power in Canada and the problems associated with managing an economy whose key manufacturing and natural resource sectors are dominated by American interests also contributed to the difficulties in developing adequate policies to deal with poor economic performance. Part of this problem has been the absence of policies to establish Canada's place in the newly emerging highly integrated world economy, an economy in which Third World and socialist countries are both important producers and potential consumers of consumer and capital goods and services.

Where does a solution for both Canada's long- and short-term economic problem lie?

Canada is endowed with both renewable and non-renewable natural resources. The energy shortages that bedevil other industrialized countries pose few short-run problems and any long-run advantages. Canada has a highly educated and skilled labour force and the physical plant, transportation, communication, and public service infrastructure necessary to support economic growth. Finally, in a world characterized by unstable political and social relations, Canada is a model of social stability where adjustments in political relations, such as those being debated with respect to the relative importance of federal and provincial powers and the role of Quebec in Canada, still seem possible without undue turbulence.

What then are the solutions to our problems of slow economic growth, unemployment, and maldistribution of income and wealth?

Two fundamental economic and political philosophies are at issue. The first, supported by the Liberal and Progressive Conservative parties, believes that private enterprise can be relied on to solve Canada's economic problems. The second, supported by the New Democratic Party and political parties to its left, believes that one form or another of national economic planning and democratic socialism is needed.

CAN WE RELY ON THE PRIVATE SECTOR TO PROVIDE FULL EMPLOYMENT?

While John Maynard Keynes urged vigorous short-run government intervention to launch a recovery from the Great Depression, he was less sure that such policies provided a permanent solution to the instability of modern capitalism.

He believed that ultimately it would be necessary to have a general social control over investment. He wrote:

> I expect to see the State, which is in a position to calculate the marginal efficiency of capital-goods on long views and on the basis of the general social advantage, taking an ever greater responsibility for directly organizing investment. . . .[239]

Today, with national and international political and economic uncertainty, individual enterprises — even rather large enterprises — require government assurances, co-operation, and support to carry out significant investments. In some sectors of Canadian industry, joint public-private ventures are required. In other sectors, there may be no private Canadian or foreign firm willing to invest either individually or in a joint venture. Here, publicly-owned or Crown corporations may be the sole source of investment.

The private firms that can "manage" in the current situation are the giant multinationals. But these firms are not concerned primarily with Canadian employment nor are they concerned with the health and growth of the Canadian economy. Indeed, the political pressures on these firms, which are mainly based in the United States, cause them to reduce operations in Canada whenever unemployment becomes an American domestic problem.

In this general atmosphere, which will be with us for a long time to come, federal policies such as fast write-offs on capital equipment, corporate tax breaks, subsidies, and other aid to the private sector will not create the kind of investment and modernization needed to revitalize economic activity and to lower unemployment.

The mainspring of government economic policy in the 1970's and the early 1980's has been to promote the flow of funds into private corporate treasuries on the presumption that higher profits lead to investment and therefore employment, as well as to more productive and therefore more competitive Canadian industries. But high profits and the accumulation of corporate funds do not lead to the building of new plant machinery and equipment in Canada when there is idle domestic capacity and uncertainty about future demand for products and therefore long-run profitability.

NATIONAL ECONOMIC PLANNING

A Canadian full employment policy required national economic planning. National economic planning must take account of immediate cyclical (deficient demand) unemployment through the application of fiscal and monetary policy, but it also takes responsibility for the evolution of the structure and control of the economy. This latter commitment would result in projects in those sectors

---

[239] John Maynard Keynes, *The General Theory of Employment, Interest and Money, op. cit.*, p. 164.

182

of the economy and in those regions of the country that require economic development to meet concrete production and social needs.

As existing capacity is used more fully, efficiency will rise and unit costs of production will fall. As employment and output expand, private firms will see the possibility of future profits and will themselves expand output, partly in existing facilities and partly through increased investment in new plant and equipment. The unequivocal commitment to full employment will give confidence to progressive firms in the private sector in the future and thereby will improve the investment climate. The expectation of a future flow of returns on investment, not one-shot tax breaks and subsidies, can lay the groundwork for solid economic growth.

Similarly, Canadians who are assured of steady employment and growing purchasing power will increase their consumption. This is a real remedy for inadequate consumption demand — a solution far more effective than a cabinet minister urging Canadians to spend more and save less of their income.

Finally, it is in the context of guaranteed employment and expanding output that sensible labour market policies can be developed. Training and mobility programs designed to adapt the Canadian labour force to new technology and new markets can succeed only under conditions where needs are clear and employment follows preparation.

Government intervention in the economy to guarantee economic growth and full employment can take many forms. Crown corporations and joint private-public ventures with individual firms or in consortiums are all within the Canadian tradition and experience.

NATURAL RESOURCES AND ENERGY

In the natural resource and energy fields, a primary requirement for economic growth is that Canadians receive the benefits (rents) from these valuable resources. Foreign ownership and control of these sectors by multinational firms must be reduced and finally ended. Government intervention in these sectors, in whatever form, must guarantee that production control and stockpiling take account of employment requirements and that processing of natural resources produced in Canada take place in Canada whenever possible.

The 1980 National Energy Program (NEP) instituted by the Trudeau Liberal government provides a prime example of the motivations, rationalizations, and issues that have and will continue to surround government intervention in this sector.[240]

---

[240] See, Energy, Mines and Resources Canada, *The National Energy Program, 1980.*

The NEP is viewed as having been "primarily an exercise in political power intended to restructure relations between the federal government and Alberta and between the federal government and the oil and gas industry."[241] Its stated objectives, however, were Canadianization of the petroleum industry, security of energy supply for Canada through self-sufficiency in energy by 1990, and a fairer distribution of the income derived from the ownership and control of this natural resource.

The federal government through the NEP asserted its control over the natural gas and petroleum industries and succeeded in raising the share of revenues going to the federal government from these industries from about 7 per cent to 16 per cent in 1983.[242] At the same time, the operations of Petro-Canada as well as a number of privately-owned Canadian firms expanded markedly in the industry.[243] In 1983, Canada exported more oil than it imported, and **overall** self-sufficiency in energy now seems possible even though eastern Canada will continue to be dependent on imported oil in the foreseeable future.

It also is evident that the government of Alberta has not considered the NEP as fair, and foreign-owned firms in the petroleum industry continue to condemn the program as being unfair and discriminatory. That the NEP discriminates against foreign-owned and controlled firms in the industry is not under dispute. This was one of the program's intentions. However, periodic polls of Canadian attitudes towards Petro-Canada and on the issue of Canadian control of energy resources indicate strong public support for the intervention of the federal government in this field.

This is not to say that the future of the NEP is assured. Some of its provisions, like those that subsidize the costs of the search for oil rather than the costs of finding oil, have been criticized widely and are likely to be changed. A more fundamental attack on Canadian government ownership and control of this vital energy resource continues to be supported by American oil interests and Canadian conservatives. These attacks will make energy policy a live political issue for some time to come.

THE MANUFACTURING SECTOR

The relative decrease in manufacturing production and investment as a share of total production and investment has contributed to weak employment growth and persistent balance of payment problems.

---

[241] G. Bruce Doern and Glen Toner, "National Energy Program's mixed record of success, failure," *The Citizen*, Ottawa, 26 June 1984, p. 9.

[242] *Ibid*.

[243] The most important privately-owned Canadian firms in the industry are Dome Canada, Nova-Husky, Pan Canadian, Norcen, Home Oil, Canterra, and Bow Valley. Dome Petroleum, the largest of these firms, has been kept out of bankruptcy by a series of reorganizations and government loan guarantees needed to cover a multi-billion dollar debt load.

Two interrelated factors have contributed to the lack of dynamism of Canadian manufacturing in the recent past: the absence of effective industrial planning by government and the fact that over 60 per cent of Canadian manufacturing is foreign-owned or controlled. The weakness of the manufacturing sector has contributed to the movement of production and jobs out of Canada and into low-wage areas in which unions are extremely weak or non-existent.

The Labour Report to the Co-ordinating Committee for the Twenty-three Industry Sector Task Forces, submitted by the Research and Legislation Department of the Canadian Labour Congress in July 1978, provides an excellent summary of the problems related to these two factors. It points out that Canadian manufacturing development has been impeded by the failure to take advantage of the potential for processing raw materials, the lack of proper transportation planning, inadequate research and development in Canada, and the absence of manpower planning. *The Labour Report. . . .* also provides particular insights into lagging average productivity in Canadian manufacturing relative to U.S. manufacturing.[244]

i) Plant size in Canadian manufacturing industries, relative to industries in the United States, is an important factor contributing to productivity differences between the two countries. . . . [A]mong major industrial countries, Canada ranks low in terms of plant size — only slightly more than half the level of the United States. There is a clear relationship between plant size, wages and productivity. In 1974, for example, 61.8 per cent of all manufacturing establishments in Canada were small firms (those employing less than 20 employees) and they employed only 7 per cent of manufacturing production workers. These small firms produced only 5 per cent of total manufacturing value added. The lower productivity of small firms was reflected in earnings. The average earnings of production workers in small firms were 15 per cent below the average for manufacturing and a whopping 29 per cent less than those in firms employing over 500.

ii) Distinct from the question of plant size is the question of length of production run. Even where plant size is comparable by international standards, Canadian costs are higher because plants are involved in multi-product activities rather than concentrated in one product. One source of higher costs is machinery "downtime" as alterations are required to switch from one product to another.

iii) The relatively low and declining levels of research and development in Canada, and especially in the manufacturing sector, have contributed to the productivity differences between Canada and the

---

[244] It is important to note that in a number of industries, such as the basic steel industry, productivity in Canada exceeds that in the U.S.

U.S. . . . Canada has not only lagged behind in research and development by international standards but . . . Canada over time has placed a lower priority in this area. The most recent statistics indicate that research and development, as a percentage of Gross National Product, has fallen below one per cent. Especially discouraging, however, are the research and development trends in the manufacturing sector. As a percentage of the value of output, research and development expenditures in manufacturing declined from 0.80 per cent in 1965 to 0.58 per cent in 1975. These problems are compounded by the fact that most of the research and development has been concentrated in the adaptation and the imitation of foreign production processes and technologies, rather than in product, marketing and technology innovation.

iv) Skilled labour shortages have in some instances contributed to the productivity differences between Canadian and U.S. manufacturing industries. This is a problem even in a depressed economy like the current one. Indeed, even if conditions were generally favourable to an economic expansion, skilled labour shortages would be a serious "bottle-neck" to taking advantages of such conditions.

v) The foreign ownership of much of the Canadian manufacturing sector has been responsible for some of the above productivity related problems. In the case of the scale of plant and the product rationalization problems, the unwillingness or inability of foreign-owned firms to compete with their head offices and break into new foreign markets makes it difficult to deal with these problems. Moreover, foreign ownership tends to limit the amount of research and development in Canada, since most of it is performed in the home country.[245]

The above litany of problems that must be dealt with in the vital manufacturing sector calls for government **intervention and co-ordination** at three levels. Exports and imports must be regulated properly by tariff and non-tariff barriers to foreign trade. Private investment in manufacturing should be promoted and regulated where this is deemed necessary and useful. Finally, direct government participation in production may be desirable where private investment is not forthcoming and/or when private control is undesirable. The following comments can be made about the direction of intervention and co-ordination at each of these three levels of economic activity.

The regulation of tariff and non-tariff barriers to foreign trade always must be linked to a conscious employment and industrial development policy. When it

---

[245] Canadian Labour Congress, Research and Legislation Department, *The Labour Report to the Co-ordinating Committee for the Twenty-three Industry Sector Task Forces* (Ottawa: 1978), pp. 30 and 31.

becomes necessary to reduce tariff and non-tariff protection to an industry that provides a significant amount of employment in particular regions of the country, government planning should provide for the growth of alternative industries in these regions as tariff protection is removed.

Private investment in manufacturing can be influenced by the nature of public investment in infrastructure, that is, in highways, rail and air transport facilities, land development, energy sources, communications, and social amenities. Foreign investment can be controlled better and steps can be taken to guarantee greater efforts by foreign-owned subsidiaries in the export field even when such exports compete with the products of the parent corporation. Canadian subsidiaries of foreign corporations (CSFCs) dominate the markets for profitable technologically advanced products. As has been pointed out in the previous chapter, these subsidiaries manipulate the transfer prices they pay for goods and services purchased from their parent firms or from other affiliates abroad to avoid the Canadian corporate income tax. Canadian firms that compete or hope to compete with the CSFCs are at a competitive disadvantage, since they cannot avoid the income tax. And to the degree that CSFCs are used to sell products manufactured in other countries, employment opportunities for Canadians are reduced. The implementation of proposals to plug this tax loophole would strengthen Canadian manufacturing industries.[246]

A more direct role for government in industrial planning and investment can take place. *The Labour Report to the Co-ordinating Committee for the Twenty-three Industry Sector Task Forces* presents the following suggestions:

i) legislation to set up some type of **investment fund** that will plan or co-ordinate **major** private and public investments. This fund could be used to even out the timing and the regional pattern of investment. It could also be used to make the necessary investments to increase productivity in the manufacturing sector and diversify the manufacturing sector. The investment fund could be financed from pension funds and from a certain percentage of general government revenues. Another possible source of funds could be corporate profits. For example, a certain percentage of corporate profits, during an expansionary period, could be "locked in" to the investment fund to be used by the corporation during periods of lower economic activity, in regions of lower manufacturing investment, and/or in activities that would increase productivity in the manufacturing sector or diversify the manufacturing sector. We should add that large corporations from all sectors of the economy (and not just manufacturing) would participate in this investment fund.

---

[246] A discussion of this problem and of possible solutions to it can be found in Myron J. Gordon, *The Taxation of Canadian Subsidiaries of Foreign Corporations* (Ottawa: Canadian Institute for Economic Policy, May 1984).

This arrangement would have the benefit of promoting a greater degree of processing of our natural resources by the corporations in the resource sector;

ii) the use of existing **Crown corporations**, and/or the establishment of new ones (if they are needed in the manufacturing sector) to carry out necessary investment decisions when and where private industry is unwilling to invest. Such public institutions are well within Canadian tradition and experience. However, these public enterprises should not be limited to the take-over of faltering private enterprises and/or other high cost and high risk activities. They should also enter into lucrative activities as well. There will be cases where private corporations will not invest because the private rate of return will be lower than what could be earned in alternative investments. However, public enterprises can operate not on the basis of this private rate of return but on the basis of the social rate of return, which would include such revenues as the savings from reduced unemployment insurance payments and the increased tax benefits from greater employment and growth. Special emphasis should also be placed on resource sector Crown corporations, such as Petro-Can, to ensure that they enter into processing activities to a much greater extent than in the past; and,

iii) the use of joint **public-private ventures** as an instrument to influence the planning of investment decisions. Again, such ventures are well within Canadian experience and tradition. They similarly benefit from the fact that they can operate on the basis of social costs.[247]

THE SHORTER WORKWEEK

Economic growth and higher productivity (increased output per hour worked in the economy) have allowed the standard of living of Canadians to rise. The higher standard of living has taken the form of higher **real** income per person combined with shorter hours of work. Society has chosen to take some of the benefits of higher productivity in more leisure time instead of in the consumption of those goods and services that would have been produced if hours of work had not been reduced.

Unions have played a key role in reducing hours of work. In the early 1870's, unions in southern Ontario launched the Nine-Hour Movement, which campaigned for a nine-hour workday for ten hours' pay. In those days the normal

[247] Canadian Labour Congress, Research and Legislation Department, *The Labour Report to the Co-ordinating Committee for the Twenty-three Industry Sector Task Forces, op. cit.*, pp. 52 and 53.

workweek for most workers in manufacturing industries was between 59 and 60 hours.[248]

By the 1940's the normal workweek in Canadian manufacturing industries was 40 hours and by the 1970's most white-collar and government employees were working a 37.5-hour week. In 1973, 30 per cent of all union members were working less than a 40-hour normal workweek. By the end of 1982 that figure increased to 46 per cent — mainly because of the increase in public-sector union members, whose normal hours of work per week tend to be below those of industrial workers.[249]

Total working hours **per year** of regularly-employed workers also has decreased as a result of the increase in the hours paid for time not worked in the form of vacations, holidays, sick leave, and maternity, paternity, and educational leave. For example, in 1947 the average employed Canadian worker received 2.2 weeks in paid vacation. By 1982 this figure rose to 4.3 weeks. During the same period, the number of paid holidays (including statutory holidays) increased from 4.2 to 11.4.[250] These improvements in paid time-off provisions have largely been the result of collective bargaining.

In all these cases, workers have received a share of the gains made possible by increased productivity in the form of shorter hours.

It is in periods of high unemployment when union demands and political pressures to reduce unemployment combine to produce reductions in working hours.[251] Economic stagnation in the world economy that became evident in 1975 has been reflected in campaigns to reduce working hours with no reduction in pay in most industrial countries.

Unions in West Germany, the Netherlands, Britain, and France have been fighting actively for a 35-hour week. France cut the standard workweek to 39 hours in 1982 and added a fifth week of paid vacation for all workers. In 1984, two hundred thousand West German metal and engineering workers went on strike, demanding a 35-hour week with no reduction in pay. The object of the demand was a reduction in unemployment among industrial workers. After a 7-week strike that paralyzed most of European automobile production, the strike was settled with the unions achieving a 38.5-hour workweek with no reduction in pay. Dutch unions also concluded agreements that will result in 36- to 37-hour

---

[248] From the Report of the Commissioners appointed to enquire into the working of the mills and factories of the Dominion and the labour employed therein. Canada, Sessional Papers, XV, V. 9, No. 42, pp. 9, 10, and 14; cited in Michael S. Cross, ed., *The Workingman in the Nineteenth Century* (Toronto: Oxford University Press, 1974), p. 74.

[249] See, Labour Canada, *Wage Rates, Salaries and Hours of Labour*, October 1982, Table B.

[250] For detailed information on paid holidays and vacations see, Labour Canada, *Working Conditions in Canadian Industry, 1982* (Catalogue No. L2-15/1982, annual).

[251] This phenomenon is discussed in Lise Poulin-Simon, *Le loisir industriel et le chômage au Canada: Une histoire économique* (Montreal: Doctoral dissertation, Department of Economics, McGill University, 1977).

workweeks becoming increasingly common, beginning in 1985. In 1984, Belgians were working a standard 38-hour week.[252]

The May 1984 convention of the Canadian Labour Congress overwhelmingly supported a resolution calling for a 32-hour workweek for 40 hours' pay. The motivation for the resolution as reflected in discussions from the floor of the convention was to combat the persistent unemployment associated with inadequate economic growth and job losses accompanying technological change.

The actual pace in the reduction of hours of work will be determined in part by the success of individual unions in negotiating shorter working hours and in part by the political process, which will affect labour standards legislation in the federal and provincial jurisdictions.

THE REDISTRIBUTION OF INCOME AND WEALTH

Direct intervention by government in economic planning and production implies that there will be a redistribution of income and wealth from private to public control. How can such redistribution occur?

The emergence of the modern capitalist system in which ownership of enterprises by shareholders has separated most owners from control and opened the way for the emergence of a broad class of rentiers who benefit from technological progress, capital accumulation, and the work and business skills of others was discussed in Chapter 9. In principle, there is no reason why governments also cannot acquire ownership without control where management by private enterprise is considered preferable. Where public control is deemed necessary, this is also possible. Governments have the ability to tax and to borrow funds for these purposes.

Progressive taxation is another means available to redistribute income. However, as was pointed out in Chapter 9, the seemingly progressive income tax structure is circumvented easily by the rich who slip through tax loopholes with the aid of high-priced lawyers. Business executives milk the profits of corporations with exorbitant salaries and fringe benefits, including expense accounts. All of these, in principle, could be limited.

Large individual and family fortunes amassed during feudalism and during the rise of capitalism have produced great inequalities of wealth. This now **inherited** inequality for the most part is self-perpetuating. Those who have money find it easy to make money and those without it, except for rare exceptions, at best just get by.

---

[252] James Bagnall, "Shorter Workweek Tempts Labour Leaders," *The Financial Post*, 2 June 1984, p. 4.

Joan Robinson pointed out:

> Concentrations of private property could be wiped out in a genera-
> tion by confiscatory death duties (leaving a reasonable life interest to
> widows and orphans, and buttressed by equally heavy taxation on
> gifts). The titles to property could be handed over in the form in
> which it exists, to be held like any other endowment of a trust, and
> the income from it devoted to public purposes. This would not mere-
> ly check the growth of rentier income, as nationalization with com-
> pensation does, but take a large bite out of it.[253]

Perhaps the most important form the redistribution of income should take is
an increase in the **social wage**. **Universal** programs of support for child care,
education, hospital, medical and dental care, and public pensions can provide
instruments for eliminating poverty throughout the country. A civilized society
— a socialist society — must also give high priority to the support, training, and
development of those who are disadvantaged. In this category would be included the physically, emotionally, and mentally handicapped.

With regard to private wages (and salaries), extreme differences between those
on the top and the bottom of wage and salary structures must be questioned and
narrowed when considerations of fairness and equity demand such changes.

It is argued that attempts by government to reduce the unequal distribution of
income and wealth will result in a flight of trained persons (human capital) and
wealth from Canada. This is certainly a serious consideration, but it often is
exaggerated. The United States is a haven for trained persons seeking higher
incomes after taxes, but there are many negative aspects to life in America. It
may also be the case that emigrants are replaced readily by equally competent
immigrants.[254] The rich can also seek tax-protected safe havens for their wealth,
but such havens are less and less available. A sensible policy to provide a more
equal distribution of income and wealth must consider these factors.

POLITICS AND ECONOMICS

The thesis of this chapter has been that there is little choice for Canada if it is
to solve the now persistent problems of slow growth, unemployment, and an
unjustified distribution of income. Laissez-faire capitalism with its reliance on
the private sector will work no longer. One form or another of national planning
is needed. But if national economic planning is to be done our standards of
judgement in the political arena must change considerably. Effective government requires political leadership by a government that is both responsive to the

---

[253] Joan Robinson, *Economics: An Awkward Corner, op. cit.*, p. 69.
[254] An example of this is the immigration of Commonwealth and Third World trained medical
doctors. See, Lee Soderstrom, *The Canadian Health System* (London: Croom Helm, 1978), p. 95.

economic and social goals of a diverse population **and** technologically able to manage a complex economy. There is a need for effective government following a policy of democratic socialism.

On the technological side, the means to finance a policy of national planning and more vigorous intervention by government in production is not at issue. The fundamental issue is whether a majority of Canadians can be convinced to follow this path despite the fact that the ruling establishment will defend its special interests in every way possible. It is here that practical politics comes to centre stage.

INDEX

The index entries, compiled by Enid Clement, are filed word by word. The "n" after a page reference indicates that the information is found in a footnote.